T0292952

BREAKTHROUGH

BREAKTHROUGH

The Promise of Frontier Technologies
for Sustainable Development

Homi Kharas, John W. McArthur, and Izumi Ohno
Editors

BROOKINGS INSTITUTION PRESS
Washington, D.C.

Copyright © 2022
THE BROOKINGS INSTITUTION
1775 Massachusetts Avenue, N.W.
Washington, D.C. 20036
www.brookings.edu

All rights reserved. No part of this publication may be reproduced or transmitted in any form or by any means without permission in writing from the Brookings Institution Press.

The Brookings Institution is a private nonprofit organization devoted to research, education, and publication on important issues of domestic and foreign policy. Its principal purpose is to bring the highest quality independent research and analysis to bear on current and emerging policy problems. Interpretations or conclusions in Brookings publications should be understood to be solely those of the authors.

Library of Congress Control Number: 2021950364

ISBN 9780815739654 (pbk)
ISBN 9780815739661 (ebook)

9 8 7 6 5 4 3 2 1

Typeset in Adobe Garamond

Composition by Elliott Beard

CONTENTS

ACKNOWLEDGMENTS

The editors thank Selen Özdoğan, Meagan Dooley, Shrijana Khanal, and Odera Onyechi for invaluable research assistance and project coordination efforts in support of this volume. Alex Awiti, Amar Bhattacharya, Thomas J. Bollyky, Han Sheng Chia, Shenggen Fan, Jeff Freeman, Elissa Golberg, Bharath Jairaj, Addisu Lashitew, Uma Lele, Thomas Lovejoy, Anit Mukherjee, Megan Roberts, Edoson Eyji Sano, Parmesh Shah, Sonal Shah, Paul Winters, and Masaru Yarime all contributed vital insights and suggestions through their peer reviews of individual draft chapters. The editors also thank Shimpei Taguchi and Jitsuya Ishiguro for their role in fostering the partnership between the Brookings Institution and the JICA Ogata Sadako Research Institute for Peace and Development that has made this book possible. They further thank Olga Gardner Galvin for excellent copyediting and the entire team at the Brookings Institution Press, especially Bill Finan, Elliott Beard, and Cecilia González, for their patience and dedication to producing this volume.

ONE

Breakthroughs
Why We Need Them for
Sustainable Development

Homi Kharas, John W. McArthur, and Izumi Ohno

Imagine a world in which a daily home coronavirus test is as common and easy as brushing your teeth. A world in which, while on a lunch break, you can look at your phone to check on the real-time wanderings of a family of giraffes in the African savannah. Sitting on a bench outside your office, you take a refreshingly clean and deep breath, proud that your city's cloud computing system has enabled a stark decline in local particulate emissions, curtailing the asthma that affected you so much as a child. You dip into your digital wallet to send money to the mother giraffe's own virtual bank account, excited because you know the resources will support local conservation efforts targeted directly at the mother's preferences, as revealed through the local artificial intelligence (AI)–backed animal tracking systems.

For dinner, you order a delicious plant-based hamburger, one of many varieties that took over the fast-food market once traditional beef became too expensive—due partly to the cattle farmers who kept illegally expanding into tropical forests until eye-in-the-sky technology made the costs of doing so prohibitive. The burger ingredients happen to include rice grown by an enterprising farmer in Borno, the northeastern-most state in Nigeria. She recently started using low-cost solar panels to power her farm's irrigation pumps, paired with digitally verified high-yield seeds—ending a long battle against counterfeits—and some fertilizer--replacing microbes she used to increase the organic nutrients in her soil. All of this helped her annual crop output jump tenfold over the past few years. The huge productivity boost enabled her to start exporting to global markets through

1

a new online agribusiness aggregator platform that provides all the services and technical assistance she needs to reach customers anywhere in the world.

Unbeknown to you as you chomp on your juicy burger, the rice farmer is only still in business thanks to the United Nations' AI-based disaster preparedness system. The previous year, the UN had worked with Agrotrack, Nigeria's trusted local multi-stakeholder data connector, to send the farmer an emergency text message, giving her a seventy-two-hour warning of the flood coming to her village. This allowed her to safeguard her farm equipment. Thanks to the national digital ID platform and integrated financial system, the farmer's family received an anticipatory digital cash transfer to buy emergency supplies prior to the flood. Borno's local safety net program had been set up in record time thanks to its open-source software and a design-for-scale approach.

This scenario may seem far-fetched but, technology-wise, it is not far off. In fact, all the relevant technologies either already exist or are likely to come to fruition very soon. If their cost is cheap enough and their design is good enough, each has the possibility for widespread global adoption. That is the view of the extraordinary range of authors contributing to this volume focused on breakthrough technologies relevant to the Sustainable Development Goals (SDGs)—the world's economic, social, and environmental objectives adopted by all countries in 2015, aiming at a 2030 horizon.

Why focus on technology amid a time of so much global economic, social, and environmental strain? Many readers might think, with good reason, that the world's foremost problems hinge on better policies and politics rather than science and technology. This would only be partly correct. There is no question that, in most societies, there is ample space for improving policies and politics. But there is also no question that, in most societies, better technology needs to play a crucial role in smoothing the path toward better sustainable development outcomes.

In a previous volume, focused on the SDG mantra of "Leave No One Behind,"[1] we outlined the world's overall trends relating to human deprivation. The overview of that book described the results of a careful country-by-country assessment of trends. It warned that the gap between business-as-usual trajectories and SDG achievement added up to roughly 44 million lives at stake by 2030, nearly 500 million people at risk of being left in extreme poverty in the same year, around 570 million people left without access to electricity, and nearly 2 billion people left behind on basic issues like access to sanitation. Meanwhile, in Sub-Saharan Africa, the region with the most extensive extreme poverty, agricultural

---

1. Kharas, McArthur, Ohno.

yields still lag far behind other regions,[2] despite framing a critical path to long-term poverty reduction.[3, 4] These are all issues on which gradualist approaches to progress simply will not achieve the SDG objectives. Breakthroughs are needed, in scientific underpinnings, in development of new products, and in supporting institutional systems.

More recently, COVID-19 has already contributed to at least 5 million premature deaths since early 2020, if not multiples more.[5] The pandemic has curtailed or reversed SDG progress in many parts of the world. It has placed additional strain on the basic tenets of international cooperation, which were already under widespread duress. By one estimate, the pandemic pushed an extra 100 million people into extreme poverty, wiping out all the gains since 2015, although hopefully some of the affected households will recover rapidly.[6] It has exacerbated inequalities within countries, as the most skilled and wealthy people benefited from soaring equity markets. It has heightened disparities between countries, as a handful of advanced economies quickly deployed economic stimuli and then vaccines at a breathtaking pace, while lower-income countries wait at the back of the line for their chance to do the same.

On the environmental side, recent evidence has also underscored the need for global breakthroughs. Despite a sharp drop-off in greenhouse gas emissions during the initial economic shutdowns, the International Energy Agency reports that global carbon dioxide emissions bounced back by December 2020 to be 2 percent higher than during the same month in 2019.[7] An August 2021 scientific report of the Intergovernmental Panel on Climate Change underscored the high current likelihood of at least a 1.5-degree Celsius increase in average global temperatures over the next two decades, accompanied by widespread increases in extreme weather events.[8] Absent imminent widespread transformations in the world's energy systems, many societies will be grappling with sharply intensified climate-related burdens in the pursuit of sustainable development.

Notwithstanding all the bad news, science and technology have offered some of the brightest sources of hope throughout the pandemic. Most prominently, multiple vaccines have been developed at unprecedented speeds, including highly efficacious versions deploying recent scientific breakthroughs in the use of messenger RNA (mRNA). The first approved vaccines were rolled out at the end of

2. Jayne and Sanchez.
3. Christiaensen and Martin.
4. McArthur and McCord.
5. *The Economist*; Anand and others.
6. Kharas and Dooley.
7. IEA (2021).
8. IPCC.

2020, and within nine months, more than 3 billion people around the world received at least one dose—far short of adequate for the modern world's needs, but extraordinarily rapid by any historical standard.

In other sectors, many economies have taken advantage of new digital payments technologies to provide rapid and hyper-targeted emergency support for people affected by the pandemic. The Bahamas, for example, introduced the world's first Central Bank virtual currency to improve access to finance across hundreds of islands. Sri Lanka overcame two decades of coordination challenges to introduce an electronic platform for its twice-weekly wholesale tea auction at the Ceylon Chamber of Commerce.[9] In Togo, the government leveraged its pioneering digital payments platform to partner with mobile providers, external nonprofits, and academics on AI-based algorithms that identify people most likely to need immediate support. The result was rapid-response social protection for citizens who would have previously only been identified through much more expensive, labor-intensive, and time-demanding survey methods.

New thresholds have been met in the energy industry, too. As of mid-2021, the cost of wind and solar energy generation has decreased enough for it to be the lowest new source of power for two-thirds of the global population.[10] For health, energy, agriculture, and many other technologies, the underlying forces of scientific and technological progress are offering unprecedented opportunities for change, if the world can align its economic and policy systems to take advantage of them. In December 2020, blogger Noah Smith quipped that "cheap taxis and fancy smoothies are out. Big Science is in."[11] In early 2021, *MIT Technology Review* went so far as to ask, "Are you ready to be a techno-optimist again?"[12]

Technology—the Bigger Picture

It is worth taking a moment to reflect on the broader role of technology in overall societal progress. Economists tend to track the evolution of societal technology through the indicator of "total factor productivity." In accounting terms, this is the residual contribution to aggregate economic output once all the inputs such as workers' labor, machines, and other forms of physical capital have been taken into account. Macroeconomic data suggest that the rate of total factor productivity growth in the world has declined since 1972, despite the many advances since that time, but the pandemic may reverse this trend.

9. Dorst.
10. Eckhouse.
11. Smith.
12. Rotman.

Consider major technology transitions in years past, like the shift from mainframes to personal computers, and now to the cloud and AI.[13] Some analysts predict new innovations over the coming decade could be even more consequential. Others are skeptical about the geographic coverage of new innovations, noting the complexities of encouraging technological uptake in lower-income countries—or technological diffusion, in economics jargon. For example, it is now more than 140 years since Thomas Edison lit the first light bulb in Menlo Park, New Jersey. Yet, as of 2019, there were still 770 million people in developing countries lacking access to modern electricity.[14] With this track record, will new breakthrough technologies be primarily for the world's wealthier consumers? Or is it conceivable that the poorest individuals on our planet, those who are a top priority for the SDGs, could share in the benefits by 2030 as well?

Some analysts argue that traditional metrics can underestimate the widespread impacts of technology. For example, it is widely understood that consumer satisfaction does not always track gross domestic product (GDP), so deriving the impact of technological innovation from its effect on GDP—which is itself notoriously imprecise in capturing measures of quality or new products—could be highly misleading. Research by Erik Brynjolfsson and colleagues suggests that technology has actually led to far more rapid growth in consumer welfare via the addition of new goods (like Facebook) and free goods (like WhatsApp long-distance phone calls or smartphone cameras) than is captured by measured GDP growth.[15]

More recent research draws attention to the varying rates of progress across different types of technology. A notable 2021 study by Anuraag Singh and colleagues examines multi-decade rates of improvement across 1,757 technology domains within the United States.[16] They estimate that more than two-thirds of the domains are improving by less than 15 percent per year, with the slowest rates registered for relatively simple mechanisms like automatic vehicle washing and handheld tools for cutting, scraping, and drilling. At the other end of the spectrum, slightly more than 10 percent of technology domains are improving by more than 36 percent per year, with a handful of domains related to software, the internet, and enterprise network management improving the fastest, sometimes by more than 200 percent per year.

Within the broader context of global sustainable development, governments recognized the multi-dimensional challenge of measuring progress when they

13. Gordon (2014).
14. IEA (2020).
15. Brynjolfsson and others.
16. Singh, Triulzi, and Magee.

agreed to seventeen SDGs in 2015. Sustainable development cannot be collapsed into a single metric. Nor has any country yet succeeded in fostering adequate progress across the interconnected economic, social, and environmental challenges of sustainable development to declare overall societal success.[17] Issues of equity, agency, natural resource protection, and well-being must all be taken into account. The contribution of technology to the SDGs, then, must go beyond its direct contribution to growth or any specific SDG outcomes and incorporate the indirect effects it will have on the 5 Ps of the SDGs—People, Planet, Prosperity, Peace, and Partnerships.

Crucially, the uptake of technology depends on both the market demand for new products and, usually, a decline in price. Many of the technologies described in this book follow Wright's Law: a steady drop in price linked to the cumulative production of a given product. Put forward by an aeronautical engineer, T. P. Wright, in 1936 to estimate the decline in cost for airplanes,[18] Wright's Law has since been found to apply to many, if not most, new technologies. Its importance derives from two considerations: existing technologies have an in-built cost advantage because they already have years of accumulated production under their belt; but new technologies that appear to be far too expensive to be of use when first introduced can see very rapid price declines in a short period of time. As an example, consider the case of photos: 85 billion photos were taken in 2000 compared to 25 billion in 1980. But by 2021, that number has leapt ahead—an estimated 1.4 trillion photos will be taken. This is the power of readily available technology coupled with low (or zero) prices.

This leads to another powerful insight, known as Amara's Law, which states that people tend to overestimate what can be achieved in a year but underestimate what can be achieved in a decade. This is due to the potential exponential nature of progress, which can lead to nonlinear change in the adoption of a specific technology and unprecedented opportunities in complementary technologies. Consider, for example, the introduction of the iPhone in 2007. Its "app store" established a new framework for mobile technology that allowed huge numbers of people from around the world to develop countless apps, for a seemingly infinite array of purposes, spanning everything from communications to entertainment, astronomy, horticulture, physical fitness, mental health, and even digital vaccine passports.

In the most profound cases, the systematic diffusion of new technologies can amount to a matter of life and death. Antiretroviral therapy (ART) for HIV/AIDS treatment frames a poignant example of this over recent decades, deeply

17. Kharas and McArthur.
18. Wright.

interwoven with the successes of the Millennium Development Goals (MDGs), the anti-poverty predecessors to the SDGs. It was only in 1996 that ART's break-through results in translating HIV/AIDS from a death sentence to a treatable disease were presented publicly.[19] But as of the early 2000s, when the vast major-ity of people infected by the virus lived in low-income Sub-Saharan African countries, the technology was not accessible due to its price and a lack of global systems to deliver medication to those most in need.

Over the subsequent two decades, a combination of new donor-funded insti-tutions like the Global Fund to Fight AIDS, Tuberculosis, and Malaria and the U.S. Presidential Emergency Program for AIDS Relief combined with pioneer-ing local leaders and pooled purchasing agreements to drive costs down. The result, coupled with evolving health protocols developed through evidence-based academic debates in top health journals, plus a fastidious international policy focus on tracking service delivery targets through scaled-up health systems in lower-income geographies, is more than 27 million people now receiving life-saving ART, as shown in figure 1-1. Today, the vast majority of people receiving treatment live in low- and middle-income countries. A mix of science, products, and business and delivery systems combined to generate the global breakthrough.

A separately complex array of factors is presently playing out in global energy

Figure 1-1. Antiretroviral Therapy Coverage, 2000–2020

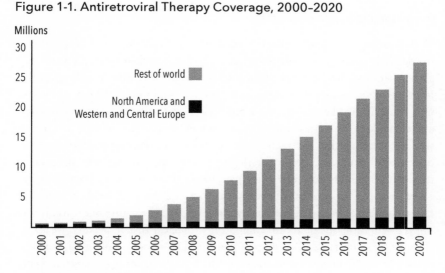

Source: UNAIDS 2021 estimates

19. Forsythe and others.

markets that will drive much of the world's path on climate change. Unlike the ART example above, emissions-reducing energy sources like solar and wind power are competing against existing sources like coal and other fossil fuels, which are typically brought to market through expensive infrastructure systems built to last for decades. To "win" the competition against older technologies, new energy technologies ultimately need to be cheaper per unit of energy produced and consumed, in order for incentives to align around widespread adoption. Until recently, the low-carbon technologies have not been adequately low-cost, and the rate of progress in reducing cost has not been fast enough to displace high-carbon technologies.

A blend of policy subsidies, market incentives, and expanded productive capacity helped drop the price of photovoltaic solar energy by roughly 90 percent between 2010 and 2020, as shown in figure 1-2. According to Bloomberg, solar power now offers the world's lowest levelized cost of energy.[20] In parallel, energy storage has long been an ambition for capturing any breakthroughs in renewable generation, so the 89 percent decline in lithium-ion battery costs over the same period marks a powerful complementary development. The concurrent pricing breakthroughs offer great potential for economies that can mobilize adequate capital to take advantage, which shifts attention toward government spending and systemic policy incentives.

A Remarkable Range of Insights

With these broader trends in mind, and against the backdrop of COVID-19 and the deepest, widest peacetime recession in history, we asked a dozen remarkable authors from science, business, civil society, and policy worlds to reflect on the impact that technology could have on the human condition in the next ten years. Our challenge to the authors was simple: given the current state of technology and technological progress within your domain of expertise, what is a vision of success? What are the key ingredients needed for a nonlinear breakthrough to be achieved? And what are the priority actions for implementation? Our experts tackled these questions under three parameters. First, we asked them to focus on what could reasonably happen by the SDG deadline of 2030. This meant that technologies had to be reasonably mature, given the nature of diffusion and impact—no futuristic quantum computing or nuclear fusion. Second, we asked them to focus on issues directly pertinent to SDG-relevant outcomes, whether economic, social, or environmental—not the future of gaming or entertainment. Third, we asked authors to focus on technologies that will affect outcomes at

20. Eckhouse.

Figure 1-2. Global Levelized Cost of Energy Benchmarks, 2009-2021

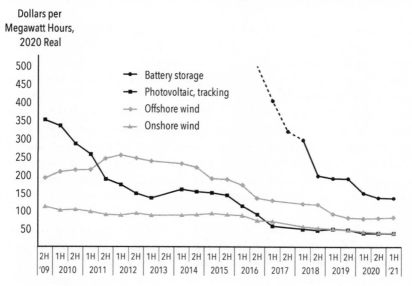

Dollars per
Megawatt Hours,
2020 Real

Legend:
- Battery storage
- Photovoltaic, tracking
- Offshore wind
- Onshore wind

Source: BloombergNEF (2021)

The global benchmark is a country-weighted average using the latest annual capacity additions. The storage levelized cost of energy (LCOE) is reflective of a utility-scale Li-ion battery storage system with four-hour duration running at a daily cycle and includes charging costs assumed to be 60 percent of the wholesale average power price. All LCOEs calculations are unsubsidized. In 2H 2017, BNEF did not publish any update. The dashed line with the circle markers reflects derived LCOEs based on historic batter pack prices, while the continuous line reflects collected project data from 2018. For hydrogen-fired power and coal- and gas-fired power with carbon capture and storage (CCS), the global LCOE benchmark is a simple country average including China, Europe, the U.S., Japan, and India.

a substantial scale, such as hundreds of millions of people or substantial geographic coverage—no private space travel or flying cars.

Each of our experts responded with stories that reflect big dreams and ambitions for what the future may bring. These are not projections or forecasts as to what will happen—merely reasoned and reasonable conjectures about what *could* happen. The topics covered are not exhaustive. There are dozens if not hundreds of other technologies that could have been included. We do not claim that the topics that have been chosen are *the* most important breakthroughs—unlike, say, the inspiring annual top ten breakthrough technologies compiled by the *MIT Technology Review*.[21] Our intent is to provide a glimpse into the possibilities for the future of sustainable development.

21. *MIT Technology Review.*

A Pragmatic Approach

People are often classified as techno-optimists or techno-pessimists.[22] Like any pendulum of public debate, most of the time is spent at the ends of each swing, with one or the other group being in the ascendancy. We prefer to describe ourselves and our chapter authors as techno-realists—aware of both the essential role of technological advance and mindful of the many risks that new solutions can bring. Admittedly, we did ask all of the authors to consider risks, but we did not seek here to harp on them. This volume aims to draw attention to ways in which nonlinearities in technology can drive progress. As a blanket caveat, we can only underscore the frequency with which positive technological breakthroughs are accompanied by unexpected downsides. These always require careful monitoring and response, especially from policymakers who are mandated with protecting public well-being.

In this book, our pragmatic approach to technology is segmented into three parts, focused on (1) underlying scientific advances, (2) the evolution of applications, and (3) supportive systems. When all three are progressing at the same time, technologies see huge advances in their potential to drive progress at scale.

Scientific Advance

Consider first the question of whether the rate of scientific progress, what the economist Tyler Cowen terms the "science of science," is accelerating.[23] Cowen and coauthor Ben Southwood summarize their findings by noting that the growth rate of high-quality patents is slowing, that crop yields are no longer rising as rapidly as before, that Moore's Law is decelerating, and that life expectancy is flattening. True, the number of scientists and the resources devoted to research and development are growing, but those are inputs into the scientific process rather than outcomes. Nicholas Bloom and others have estimated that research productivity—the contribution of research to economic growth per unit of research input—has declined by more than 5 percent per year in the United States over the last ninety years—implying that research today is only 1 percent as productive as it was ninety years ago.[24]

Most metrics of scientific progress consider whether existing production of goods and services is being done in a faster, cheaper, or more efficient way. It is

22. Among the most renowned pessimists are the economists Robert Gordon and Tyler Cowen, and venture capitalist Peter Thiel. Among the most renowned optimists are economists Erik Brynjolffson and Joel Mokyr, and the billionaire entrepreneur Elon Musk.

23. Cowen and Southwood.

24. Bloom and others.

far harder to measure and understand the contributions of science to new products or different quality products. William Nordhaus examines related questions for a single product, the price of light.[25] He finds that the true price of light has been falling far faster than what is shown by traditional price indices, so that the "volume" of quality-adjusted light consumed is much higher than officially measured. This is important for understanding how much scientific progress in light (most recently, the advent of LED bulbs) has contributed to real consumer welfare.

Another feature of Nordhaus's work is of relevance to this book. In his long historical study, dating back to 1800 (with some conjectures for pre-Neolithic times), Nordhaus shows that technological advances are not linear but display step functions. In his example, the price of light was stagnant for twenty years between 1970 and 1990, before collapsing to one-fifth of its level in 1992 with the introduction of compact fluorescent bulbs.

It is these step changes that the first four chapters in this book seek to capture.

The introduction of the mRNA vaccines to combat COVID-19 is one of the major successes of our times. The biomedical advances that made it possible are very recent. The early detection of the virus was made possible through genome sequencing; Fred Sanger sequenced the first virus in 1977, but the speed of sequencing and reduction in costs only took giant steps forward in 2007, when a new technique combining gene chip technology with modern gene sequencing machines replaced the relatively more cumbersome, expensive, and slower polymerase chain reaction technology.[26] Pardis Sabeti, one of our contributors, rapidly generated and made public genetic sequence data on the Ebola virus in the middle of the major 2014 outbreak in West Africa, a seminal contribution that helped inform medical and policy responses. Several years later, similar technologies enabled the SARS-CoV-2 virus to be sequenced by Chinese researchers just ten days after a rapid response team was dispatched by the China Center for Disease Control to Wuhan. Today, new technology already is advancing to produce monoclonal antibodies to defend against potential future epidemics.

In chapter 2 of this volume, Yolanda Botto-Lodovico and Pardis Sabeti suggest that we should celebrate the new medical technologies for their life-saving potential. But they are even more ambitious in their vision about the impact of biological advances. When combined with new information systems that permit real-time viral surveillance, they envisage a world where the ravages of epidemics and pandemics can be dramatically reduced. The impact would be extraordinary. The costs of COVID-19 are still being tallied, but the economic losses

25. Nordhaus.
26. Shendure and others.

alone amount to US$10 trillion dollars, according to the Global Preparedness Monitoring Board.[27] What is more, the rapid spread of infectious disease is not a rarity; SARS, Ebola, MERS, Zika, and Nipah outbreaks preceded COVID--19 in this century. If pandemic preparedness can be built so as to mitigate the impact of future infectious disease, the benefits to the world, and to the poorest populations, could be highly significant. Botto-Lodovico and Sabeti show how this could be done through global cooperation to use the many advances of biomedical science and information technology. Pandemic preparedness everywhere would be a major breakthrough in global sustainable development.

In chapter 3, Zachary Bogue focuses on how new food and agricultural technologies can contribute to sustainability and planetary health. He describes the world as moving from the petroleum century to the microbe century. The Haber--Bosch process, sometimes dubbed the most important invention of the twentieth century,[28] poses a wicked problem. It creates synthetic nitrogen fertilizers that have allowed billions of people to live prosperous lives, but its production requires large amounts of energy, typically from fossil fuels, which is disastrous for climate change. Fertilizer's distribution contributes to nitrification and dead zones in oceans and lakes, which is disastrous for biodiversity. Simply put, it is an unsustainable technology that must be replaced. Bogue gives examples of companies already using microbial manufacturing to deliver nitrogen to plants and to make new kinds of environmentally friendly pesticides. He offers other examples of how science is reducing carbon emissions associated with farming: adding kelp to animal feed can reduce methane emissions by up to 99 percent; leather can be replaced with fabrics made from mycelium, found in mushrooms. Use of these technologies can permit sustainable, healthy nutrition for billions of people without recourse to the nitrogen fertilizers of Haber-Bosch.

A third example of a step-change scientific advance is the extraordinary fall in the price of solar power. As Vijay Modi shows in chapter 4, utility scale solar power has become nearly free, with some contracts as low as 1.5 cents per kilowatt hour (kWh). This is only one-tenth the price that the International Energy Agency forecasted for 2020 back in 2010,[29] and it can be compared to typical household solar systems often being implemented in much of Africa at costs of around 100 cents per kWh, when storage also needs to be included. The age of unlimited cheap power could be descending on us. Modi's chapter describes how such technologies can now be leveraged to benefit smallholder farmers. He points out that most of the cost of solar home systems today is actually for battery storage

27. Global Preparedness Monitoring Board.
28. Kuijpers.
29. IEA (2010).

and for metering, rather than for the electric power itself. Modi shows how these costs can be reduced dramatically if consumers shift their power demand to the daytime, when solar is readily available, instead of to evening hours. Almost-free power, at least at midday, could revolutionize the lives of millions of smallholder farmers who currently lack access to national electric grids, and to the lives of the women and girls in their households who are forced to collect fuel-wood and inhale particulates from dirty, open-fire combustion.

Ecosystem science is also expanding. In chapter 5, Jonathan Ledgard proposes "interspecies money" as a way of revolutionizing how conservation is practiced. He points out that the 2020s will be the most consequential decade for nonhuman life in recorded history. Furthermore, because the richest areas of biodiversity are in the tropics, poor people—the 1.6 billion living in fragile ecosystems—will be the principal beneficiary of new forms of conservation. Cheap sensors, mobile phones, and acoustic signals could provide input data from which AI could identify the best and cheapest ways of preserving life-forms of all kinds in what he calls an Internet of Life (as opposed to the Internet of Things). The benefits would be substantial. To take just one example, African elephants are estimated to provide $1.75 million per animal, or $700 billion for the whole continent.

Ledgard's vision goes beyond advocating for the funding of charismatic animals. He envisages a whole new financial ecology that is built around an understanding of the needs and preferences of nonhumans revealed by their behavior. Just as cash transfers are becoming an instrument of choice for reducing human poverty, Ledgard proposes a Financial Trust that will be devoted to programs that support the survival and prosperity of a range of nonhumans. The science of what is necessary to stem mass extinctions exists and is rapidly improving. It has to be implemented effectively.

Applications Development

Frontier technologies can only realize their potential if they solve practical problems on the ground. Not all technologies are equally relevant in all geographies. For example, an agricultural technology that helps one type of crop grow in one part of the world might be irrelevant in another part of the world with a different agro-ecology. Moreover, as several of the following chapters note, technology adoption is highly dependent on economic, regulatory, and social factors. Liberia has provided a positive example of this during the COVID-19 pandemic. Despite the country's very low average income levels, strong political leadership was able to mobilize trusted health workers—already embedded in communities—to help contain virus transmission through a range of public health tools that used the new technologies. In Senegal, farmer groups already collaborating for marketing and sourcing of seeds and other agricultural inputs have become collective owner-operators of shared solar power systems, which have proven to be a key approach to scaling up solar power with ample storage. The broader lesson is that applications need to account for local context, and preferably be developed locally, if new technology is to have a scaled-up impact.

In adapting to a local context, new technologies also often need to have kinks taken out. An instantaneous smash hit is far less common than a cycle of good idea and innovation, followed by a temporary period of disillusionment when there can be setbacks and failures (remember Tesla's exploding batteries), then a steady rollout of improvements and applications, and finally a maturation and slowdown of diffusion as the market gets saturated. This basic framing was introduced by Everett Rogers as far back as 1962, in his book *Diffusion of Innovation*.[30]

Within this cycle, the period when impact is greatest is during the improvements and applications phase. This is particularly the case for applications of so-called general-purpose technologies, which affect many industries. Economist Robert Gordon, in his monumental work *The Rise and Fall of American Growth*, documents a twenty-year time lag between Edison's electric light bulb and the mass uptake in American cities after 1900.[31] The waiting period for the twenty-first-century technology of digital platforms and AI, dubbed the Fourth Industrial Revolution by World Economic Forum Chairman Klaus Schwab, is still ongoing. One big question is if and when it will reach the stage of widespread improvements and applications.

Several of our chapter authors feel this stage is imminent. In chapter 6, Tarek Ghani and Grant Gordon describe AI's potential to anticipate, respond to, and recover from crises. Research into the long-run determinants of economic growth systematically shows that countries that have the fewest episodes of slow growth, and the shallowest recessions, have the fastest long-run growth.[32] In other words, avoiding crises is the best recipe for achieving long-run prosperity. Ghani and Gordon suggest that machine learning applications will permit analysts to assess the risks of new and ongoing crises, especially the risk of natural disasters, which cost the world US$210 billion in 2020, of which about half was in developing countries.[33] Better and earlier prediction can then lead to better targeting and service delivery mechanisms. These, in turn, would permit new insights into how resources, including financial resources, can be pre-positioned so as to be

30. Rogers.
31. Gordon (2016).
32. Commission on Growth and Development.
33. Munich Re.

accessible as quickly as possible. Humanitarian workers have known for a long time that rapid response is critical for mitigating the impact of natural disasters.[34]

In similar vein, in chapter 7, Lesly Goh looks at the potential for transforming smallholder agriculture. Long regarded as technologically backward, with few innovations, at least compared to manufacturing or services, agriculture could be on the cusp of a new productivity revolution. The driver is not just new seeds and technologies—although these are on the horizon, too—but new digital platforms connecting smallholder farmers with customers in a far more direct fashion than the slow chain of passing through numerous middlemen. Goh's maxim is "think big, act fast, start small." She documents the huge gains in farm productivity that can arise from higher price transparency, better matching of supply and demand, better farmer access to finance, and data collection and analytics to improve agronomic decisions such as fertilizing, watering, and harvesting. She discusses the new business models already being adopted to harness AI's potential and offers some recommendations as to how public-private partnerships can jump-start these smallholder innovation ecosystems in developing countries.

Quick response is also needed for combating tropical deforestation. In chapter 8, Hiroaki Okonogi, Eiji Yamada, and Takahiro Morita look at this across contexts of the Amazon and Congo Basins and in Southeast Asia. They propose scaling up new technologies to improve our "Eyes on the Planet." Based on extensive field experience, they show that the loopholes through which unscrupulous actors continue to cut trees can be closed by vigorous implementation of new technologies. Cloud cover, which prevents optical satellites from identifying areas of deforestation, can be penetrated by new radar satellites using radio waves, and these are becoming more sophisticated and able to detect illegal deforestation in a more granular way. Knowing where the forest is being cut, however, is only one step in the process of slowing down illegal operations. The next steps are to alter incentives and accountabilities of large companies by combining imagery with better forest governance and providing data to local stakeholders to use as their own surveillance tool in enforcing their rights.

The emphasis on how people respond to applications is taken up in chapter 9 by Tomoyuki Naito on "smart cities." Naito argues that smart cities have evolved from demonstration showcases of new technologies, especially in transport and environmental areas, to data-driven societies where sensors and cameras collect large amounts of data that is analyzed by AI to come up with solutions to human problems. The smart city commercial industry is already worth some US$80 billion and is doubling in size every three years. The gains could be very substantial, not least because, as UN secretary-general Antonio Guterres has remarked, "the

34. Knoll.

only place where we really have a clear picture about what the people really want is when we work at the local level and municipal level."[35] A breakthrough on smart cities is now possible if we are able to combine visionary technology with good governance and citizen-level collaborations and partnerships.

Systems Change

Technological change does not only come in the form of products. A great deal occurs through small, incremental improvements in processes. Incremental change is good when improving efficiency in a steady way, but sometimes change has to be wholesale, discarding current practice and creating a new system. This kind of systems change, sometimes known as radical change, calls for a total redesign.

Themes of systemwide alignment—and realignment—appear throughout this volume: technologies, policies, regulatory treatment, infrastructure, and partnerships among governments, NGOs, and private companies. The focus is less on the technology itself, or even on how it is applied, and more on how it can be embedded into new ecosystems and platforms that, in turn, learn how to learn and adapt.

For any market economy, money forms one of the most fundamental building block systems, having probably emerged around five thousand years ago. Paper money, issued with the monopoly right of the state, was introduced about a thousand years ago. But as Tomicah Tilleman writes in chapter 10, "cash is so insecure that responsible regulators would likely never approve it for use today if it were proposed as a new medium of exchange." His vision is that a new digital payment architecture is on the horizon, one that will permit fast, inexpensive, secure, and inclusive payments for all. He documents enormous efficiency benefits from reducing waste, fraud, and abuse in public finance, and additional indirect benefits from the expansion of economic activity that results whenever transaction costs go down. His big concern is with the control or governance of such a new system, with objections to centralized structures operated by governments or where financial information is owned and controlled by large tech firms. But new open-source platforms can mitigate such risks and make digital payments into a new type of a global public good.

How do we get big changes like this? The ideas of social entrepreneurship, mainstreaming social purpose into business activity, are now well accepted, and a large ecosystem of social entrepreneurs is helping implement these ideas throughout the world. Bright Simons wants to take this to the next level, in

---

35. Guterres.

chapter 11. Rather than having an army of social entrepreneurs, who often serve as intermediaries between key nodes in an economic network, he calls for an army of systems entrepreneurs who can help reshape the relations between nodes in the same networks. These people would start from the premise that many of the obstacles to using new technologies come from points where social interactions are important. When systems need to be changed, and individual behavior needs to change, outcomes can move in many different directions. In the new "transmediation" techniques he identifies, relationships among different players can be recast with the help of sophisticated digital algorithms but with agility to respond to changing circumstances. Using the powerful example of Agrotrack, Simons showcases a new way of designing solutions, a new way of breaking down interconnected barriers, and a new way of using technology innovation systems.

Getting the design principles right is also the theme of Ann Mei Chang's concluding chapter in this volume. The biggest breakthrough, in her words, would be "a new approach to innovation, not yet another new technology." It is encouraging that there is a growing consensus on what such a new approach could be. The Whistler principles to accelerate innovation for development impact are a starting point that stress the real needs of real people, an understanding of the problem at hand, before any attempt to come up with a solution. As an example, the simple technology of community radio has provided life-saving information in Ethiopia's COVID-19 response. Building in feedback loops and designing for scale at the outset are other design principles for systemwide impact. The real breakthrough, however, will come when more effort is put into open-source platforms with common infrastructure and tools. Rather than developing end-to-end solutions from scratch, a design ecosystem, on which myriad new problem-solvers can build, is needed. This new approach is already underway, giving confidence to the potential for new breakthroughs in addressing the SDGs, even if we cannot predict where these will come from right now.

Imagining the Future

The contributors to this volume have identified technologies with the potential to achieve huge scale and huge impact over the coming decade. Without such technological breakthroughs, there is no chance of achieving the SDGs. For example, even before COVID-19, the pace of extreme poverty reduction had slowed rapidly because economic growth—the most effective technology system for poverty reduction—had faltered in some of the poorest countries. The pandemic has only heightened the range of uncertainty for outcomes in 2030.

Breakthroughs represent the step changes that kick off new cycles of positive change. Initially, the pace of change and impact might be slow, so emergent trends can be hard to spot. There are often many false leads and overhyped narratives of promising technologies that fail to live up to their billing. It takes an expert in the field to sort out what could really make a difference. That is exactly what the contributors to this volume have done, across their respective fields of expertise.

A focus on technology prompts awareness of how different the world could soon be. According to our experts, the world in 2030 could:

- Anticipate and mitigate health pandemics originating in any country

- Make fertilizers and pesticides from microbes, not petroleum, and grow leather from mushrooms

- Have solar power that is too cheap even to meter, at least at some times of the day

- Provide money in trust for nonhumans, as a way of driving the direction of nature conservancy

- Create tools to transform (and predict need for) the response to natural and man-made crises

- Link millions of smallholder farmers directly with technology platforms and market information

- Monitor deforestation in real time to allow rapid pursuit of criminals

- Move "smart cities" from slogan to reality, underpinned by ethical data governance

- Have safe, universal access to financial services and save trillions of dollars annually by eliminating fees

- Scale social entrepreneurs into systems entrepreneurs, transforming entire social systems

- Incentivize smart risks in funding technological breakthroughs

Altogether this frames an inspiring vision rather than a prediction. The process of technological change can be difficult. There are often winners and losers, and people will fight hard to avoid a sense of loss. From a business perspective, change for the SDGs must confront vested interests and retain competitive markets. From a societal perspective, acceptable new technologies must empower people, reduce inequality, and protect privacy, while building trust in government, science, and other institutions.

A final note of caution is important, too. Most of the technologies considered in this volume rely heavily on large-scale data processing, inevitably raising the issue of how data can be governed in an ethical way. For example, the use of AI for crisis prevention and mitigation can reduce suffering and damage, but it relies on imperfect algorithms. Moreover, machine learning processes might be trained by low-quality data. As a result, "precision social service delivery" may fail in delivering on its underlying intentions and might lack democratic checks on its generated outcomes. High levels of detail might be inconsistent with data privacy. Issues of bias, quality, feedback, and consent all need to be addressed to foster confidence in results-based learning. It is crucial for citizens to be engaged on how their data is managed and used.

Humility is essential, too. Technology does not solve problems on its own. It must advance, align, and succeed with its community and society of users. New technologies need to be accompanied by clear-headed debates about why they are needed, how they work, and who will ultimately benefit. Sometimes the answers will be hard to pin down. Somethings they will be highly context-specific.

A belief in technology's power to fuel SDG progress does not benefit from any underestimate of the challenge. Each step forward in advancing science, developing applications, and building systems will require many forms of human ingenuity, resourcing, and persistence. When a critical mass of key ingredients comes together, the overall odds of a breakthrough become much higher. There is no guarantee of progress. But imagining the opportunity forms a first step toward achieving a world of sustainable development for all.

References

Anand, Abhishek and others. 2021. "Three New Estimates of India's All-Cause Excess Mortality during the COVID-19 Pandemic." Center for Global Development Working Paper 589. www.cgdev.org/publication/three-new-estimates-indias-all -cause-excess-mortality-during-covid-19-pandemic.

Bloom, Nicholas and others. 2020. "Are Ideas Getting Harder to Find?" *American Economic Review*, v. 110, no. 4.

BloombergNEF. 2021. "BNEF Executive Factbook: Power, Transport, Buildings and Industry, Commodities, Food and Agriculture, Capital," John Moore and Nat Bullard, eds., March 2.

Brynjolfsson, Erik and others. 2019. "GDP-B: Accounting for the Value of New and Free Goods in the Digital Economy." NBER Working Paper 25695.

Christiaensen, Luc, and Will Martin. 2018. "Agriculture, Structural Transformation and Poverty Reduction: Eight New Insights." World Development 109, special issue. www.sciencedirect.com/science/article/pii/S0305750X1830175X.

Commission on Growth and Development. 2008. "The Growth Report: Strategies for Sustained Growth and Inclusive Development." Washington, D.C.: World Bank.

Cowen, Tyler, and Ben Southwood. 2019. "Is the Rate of Scientific Progress Slowing

Down?" https://docs.google.com/document/d/1cEBsj18Y4NnVx5Qdu43cKEHMaV
BODTTyfHBa8GIRSec/edit.

Dorst, Steven. 2021. "Digital Dollars for Online Tea." *Finance and Development*, v. 2021, no. 1.

Eckhouse, Brian. 2020. "Solar and Wind Cheapest Sources of Power in Most of the World." Bloomberg, April 28. www.bloomberg.com/news/articles/2020-04-28/solar-and-wind-cheapest-sources-of-power-in-most-of-the-world.

The Economist. 2021. "Why Official COVID-19 Deaths Do Not Capture the Pandemic's True Toll." September 20. www.economist.com/the-economist-explains/2021/09/20/why-official-covid-19-deaths-do-not-capture-the-pandemics-true-toll

Forsythe, Steven and others. 2019. "Twenty Years of Antiretroviral Therapy for People Living with HIV: Global Costs, Health Achievements, Economic Benefits." *Health Affairs* v. 38, no. 7.

Global Preparedness Monitoring Board. 2020. "A World in Disorder." GPMB 2020 Annual Report.

Gordon, Robert J. 2014. "The Turtle's Progress." https://voxeu.org/article/turtle-s-progress-secular-stagnation-meets-headwinds.

———. 2016. *The Rise and Fall of American Growth.* Princeton University Press.

Guterres, Antonio. 2019. "Guterres: 'Cities Are Where the Climate Battle Will Largely Be Won or Lost.'" UNFCC, October 11. https://unfccc.int/news/guterres-cities-are-where-the-climate-battle-will-largely-be-won-or-lost.

Intergovernmental Panel on Climate Change (IPCC). 2021. "Climate Change 2021: The Physical Science Basis. Contribution of Working Group I to the Sixth Assessment Report of the Intergovernmental Panel on Climate Change." Edited by Masson-Delmotte, Valerie and others. Cambridge University Press. www.ipcc.ch/assessment-report/ar6/.

International Energy Agency (IEA). 2010. "Technology Roadmap: Solar Photovoltaic Energy." Paris.

———. 2020. "SDG7: Data and Projections." www.iea.org/reports/sdg7-data-and-projections/access-to-electricity. Paris.

———. 2021. "Global Energy Review 2021." www.iea.org/reports/global-energy-review-2021.

Jayne, Thomas S., and Pedro A. Sanchez. 2021. "Agricultural Productivity Must Improve in Sub-Saharan Africa." *Science*, v. 372, no. 6546.

Joint United Nationals Program on HIV/AIDS (UNAIDS). 2021. "HIV 2021 Estimates—Antiretroviral Therapy." Geneva: UNAIDS.

Kharas, Homi, and Meagan Dooley. 2021. "Extreme Poverty in the Time of COVID-19." Brookings Global Economy and Development Policy Brief. www.brookings.edu/research/extreme-poverty-in-the-time-of-covid-19/.

Kharas, Homi, and John W. McArthur. 2021. "Rethinking Development: Broadening the Goals and Altering the Approach." In Douarin, Elodie, and Oleh Havrylyshyn (eds.), *The Palgrave Handbook of Comparative Economics.* London: Palgrave Macmillan.

Kharas, Homi, John W. McArthur, and Izumi Ohno (eds.) 2020. *Leave No One Behind.* Brookings Institution Press.

Knoll, Catherine. 2016. "Why Rapid Response Is So Important for Disaster Relief Recovery." *Mahaffey Blog*, June 8. www.mahaffeyusa.com/blog/why-rapid-response-is-so-important-for-disaster-relief-recovery-emergency-shelter.

Kuijpers, Maikel. 2020. "The Most Important Invention of the Twentieth Century." *Correspondent*, October.

McArthur, John W., and Gordon C. McCord. 2017. "Fertilizing Growth: Agricultural Inputs and Their Effects in Economic Development." *Journal of Development Economics*, v. 127, no. C.

MIT Technology Review. 2021. "Ten Breakthrough Technologies 2021."

Moore, Jon, and Nathaniel Bullard. 2021. *BloombergNEF Executive Factbook*.

Munich Re. 2021. "Record Hurricane Season and Major Wildfires—The Nature Disaster Figures for 2020." www.munichre.com/en/company/media-relations/media -information-and-corporate-news/media-information/2021/2020-natural-disasters -balance.html#1351999949.

Nordhaus, William D. 1998. "Do Real Output and Real Wage Measures Capture Reality? The Price of Light Suggests Not." Cowles Foundation Paper No. 957. https: //lucept.files.wordpress.com/2014/11/william-nordhaus-the-cost-of-light.pdf.

Rogers, Everett. 1962. *Diffusion of Innovation*. New York: Free Press.

Rotman, David. 2021. "Are You Ready to Be a Techno-Optimist Again?" *MIT Technology Review*.

Shendure, Jay and others. 2017. "DNA Sequencing at 40: Past, Present, and Future." *Nature*, v. 550.

Singh, Anuraag, Giorgio A. Triulzi, and Christopher L. Magee. 2021. "Technological Improvement Rate Predictions for All Technologies: Use of Patent Data and an Extended Domain Description." *Research Policy* v. 50, no. 9.

Smith, Noah. 2020. "Techno-Optimism for the 2020s." https://noahpinion.substack .com/p/techno-optimism-for-the-2020s.

Wright, Theodore P. 1936. "Factors Affecting the Cost of Airplanes." *Journal of the Aeronautical Sciences*, v. 3.

TWO

Breakthrough Technologies for Pandemic Preparedness

Yolanda Botti-Lodovico and Pardis Sabeti

n March of 2020, COVID-19 was officially declared a global pandemic, rapidly exposing gaps in public health systems worldwide and intensifying the inequalities that disproportionately affect marginalized communities everywhere. Scientists and public health experts warned for years of an imminent, deadly, and rapidly spreading virus, identifying potential geographical hotspots for its origin and devising plans to catch and contain it.[1] Previous outbreaks, such as SARS in 2002, Ebola in 2014, and Zika in 2016, continuously reminded us of the need to shore up our global pandemic preparedness infrastructure. But as recently as 2019, not one country had built a strong enough national pandemic preparedness system to stave off or contain a potential epidemic, according to the Global Health Security Index.[2]

Today, the world is on the cusp of a new era. Thanks to modern advances in biomedicine and information science, we have the capacity to build a systematic approach for detecting and tracking outbreaks of common and fatal infectious

1. McKay and Dvorak.
2. Prevent Epidemics.

The authors are grateful to the Sentinel team in Nigeria, Sierra Leone, Senegal, Liberia, and the United States, whose work and vision have inspired this piece, including Dr. Christian Happi and the entire African Centre of Excellence for Genomics of Infectious Diseases, and partners of the Broad Institute of MIT and Harvard, including Dr. Bronwyn MacInnis and Dr. Matthew Stremlau. We are especially grateful for the support from Flu Lab and a cohort of generous donors through TED's Audacious Project, including the ELMA Foundation, MacKenzie Scott, the Skoll Foundation, and Open Philanthropy.

diseases, and preventing novel ones from emerging. To make this vision a reality and achieve global pandemic preparedness, two main pillars of progress are key (see table 2-1). The first pillar is advances in biomedical and genomic technologies that can detect virtually any pathogen; produce simple, point-of-care diagnostics that can be deployed anywhere in the world; and enable rapid development of countermeasures such as vaccines and therapies. The second pillar incorporates powerful new information systems and data collection tools that allow real-time viral surveillance, data sharing, and integration of health systems, on both a regional and global level. These tools also open a critical pathway for public health officials to interface with communities, respond to needs, and provide real-time information on the trajectory of the virus.

This chapter explores breakthrough technologies that comprise each pillar, in the context of the existing recommendations for global governance and coordination of pandemic preparedness, including those provided by the Independent Panel for Pandemic Preparedness and Response (IPPPR), as well as the G20 High Level Independent Panel on Financing the Global Commons for Pandemic Preparedness and Response. Given that most of the technologies we describe are

Table 2-1. Pillars for a Breakthrough in Pandemic Preparedness

Pillar 1	Biomedical and Genomic Advancements	Detection Tools (for example, PCR and antibody tests; LAMP; CRISPR-based SHERLOCK, DETECTR, and HOLMES; and synthetic biology-based INSPECTR)
		Countermeasures (for example, monoclonal antibodies and vaccines, including mRNA vaccines and ongoing R&D for universal flu vaccine)
Pillar 2	Information Technologies	Public Health Response Tools (for example, CommCare; DHIS2)
		Citizen Data Capture Tools (for example, Flu Near You; Outbreaks Near Me)
		Proximity Sensing Tools (for example, GAEN API by Apple and Google; NOVID)
		Forecasting Networks (for example, Infectious Diseases Modeling Team at the National Institute for Public Health and Environment in the Netherlands; Scientific Advisory Group for Emergencies in the United Kingdom)

already available in most advanced economies and to varying degrees in low- and middle-income countries (LMICs), this chapter also elucidates the foundational elements that allow them to translate effectively to pandemic preparedness in advanced economies and LMICs alike. First, a centralized and well-coordinated public health infrastructure, with policies that promote inter- and intra-agency collaboration, are critical, but too often lacking in LMICs and advanced economies. Second, equity and community empowerment must underline the rollout of both pillars. Third, adequate and sustainable financing are key, which may be lacking in LMICs or ineffectively distributed and prioritized in wealthier economies.

Global Coordination for Pandemic Preparedness

A vastly improved global approach is within reach. By 2030, every country should enjoy the fundamental building blocks of pandemic preparedness, including the capacity to sequence emergent threats, the expertise and resources to rapidly build diagnostics, treatments, and vaccines, and the infrastructure to both surveil viral spread locally and share data in real time. Because viruses are so fast-moving, penetrating, and volatile, no country can be left behind if we are to successfully preempt another global pandemic. Pandemic preparedness and response require the full participation of every nation and must be undertaken with the precision and speed of military alliances such as NATO, the diplomatic tact of the World Health Organization (WHO), and the inclusive nature of the United Nations General Assembly.[3] To achieve this vision, governance and coordination are key. Among the many recommendations outlined by the IPPPR and G-20 High Level Independent Panel, there emerges a common theme: strengthening global leadership and coordination at every level for pandemic preparedness—from building and improving surveillance systems to developing "pre-negotiated" platforms for production and distribution of tests and medical countermeasures—with financing as a key facilitator.[4]

Even before the next outbreak or pandemic strikes, immediate action to advance the recommendations of both panels are critical for a number of reasons. Most evidently, infectious disease has generated more personal and economic devastation than any war in modern history. Every year, the impacts of annual infections eclipse those of all major wars, but traditional defense budgets, including that of the United States, contribute very little to combating the bioterror threat posed by infectious pathogens. The cost of crisis response, once a major

3. Osterholm and Olshaker.
4. Independent Panel for Pandemic Preparedness and Response.

outbreak hits, far exceeds that of building resilient health systems for pandemic preparedness. In 2016, the Commission on a Global Health Risk Framework for the Future explained why an additional US$4.5 billion dedicated to pandemic preparedness each year would considerably improve global resilience against infectious disease.[5] By comparison, the 2014–16 Ebola outbreak in West Africa cost an estimated US$53 billion in economic losses and 11,300 deaths.[6] One year into the COVID-19 pandemic, estimated economic losses thus far have reached several trillions of dollars and deaths have surpassed 4 million, with extensive morbidity beyond.[7,8]

Furthermore, the tools needed to stop a viral outbreak are broadly applicable to any virus and routine care. Pandemic preparedness is not separate from, but rather core to, a healthcare system capable of fighting malaria, TB, neglected tropical diseases (NTDs), and the common cold. Anywhere in the world, the tools needed to stop our families, neighbors, and coworkers from falling ill are the same tools needed to stop an outbreak. Both pandemic preparedness and general healthcare work hand in hand to improve health and wellness worldwide.

Finally, our universal vulnerability to infectious pathogens, made evident by COVID-19, means that everyone has an important role to play in outbreak prevention. Because of the exponential spread of viruses, one person can launch a pandemic, but one person can also stop it from spreading. To avoid future devastation, the global community must unite now in empowering every actor in the system to fully engage in their own health. This means eliminating global disparities in access to detection tools, countermeasures, and information technologies, connecting local health systems and providers with national, regional, and global health systems, and building newfound community trust in science and medicine.

Pillar 1: Biomedical Advances in Detection and Countermeasure Technologies

Biomedicine has undergone a recent revolution that transformed our ability to identify and characterize a virus—that is, detection—as well as our ability to treat and prevent it—that is, countermeasures. One of the key technologies that underlies this revolution is genome sequencing, which allows us to detect and characterize novel threats and informs the design of targeted diagnostics, treatments, and vaccines.

5. Commission on a Global Health Risk Framework for the Future and National Academy of Medicine, Secretariat.

6. Miles.

7. Cutler and Summers.

8. World Health Organization, 2020c.

Detection Technologies

When a virus first enters a human population, containment hinges on rapid and accurate detection. Once it is detected and characterized, a distributed and reliable diagnosis is the foundation of pandemic preparedness and response. This is partly because many infectious diseases present with overlapping symptoms, so precise, an early diagnosis is necessary to prescribe appropriate clinical or public health measures. It is also because some infectious diseases spread through asymptomatic or presymptomatic carriers, like COVID-19, of which 20 percent of transmission comes from cases that are asymptomatic and 30–40 percent from those who are presymptomatic, meaning that those infected may spread the virus without knowing. Thus, widespread early detection efforts are critical to containment.[9, 10] Moreover, early detection can reverse the course of a disease by signaling the need for lifesaving treatment, like in the case of Lassa fever, where early treatment has reduced case fatality from 55 percent to 5 percent.[11]

The first major breakthrough in our ability to detect viruses is genome sequencing, which allows us to identify and characterize the genome of viruses circulating in clinical and environmental samples and to gain continual insights into their genetic diversity, evolution, and transmission. For example, within a month of COVID-19 entering the human population, genome sequencing allowed Chinese scientists to identify and characterize SARS-CoV-2—the causative agent. Since then, there have been over 3.4 million genome submissions and counting, as of September 2021, to GISAID, the publicly accessible global database, which have helped uncover patterns of transmission (for example, super-spreader events, increases in virus transmissibility) and identify variants of concern.[12]

Traditionally, scientists have relied on two kinds of diagnostics—polymerase chain reaction (PCR) and antibody tests. A classic molecular diagnostic, PCR works by extracting genetic material (DNA, RNA) from a sample, which is then copied several times over to confirm or negate the presence of a virus. It is sensitive and specific, suitable for clinical testing, and readily adaptable to new infectious pathogens.[13] Alternatively, antibody tests can detect either the virus or antibodies to a virus. This group includes antigen capture tests, often used as point-of-care tests, which use antibodies that bind to viral proteins and other elements to signal if they are present in a patient's body.[14] Another type of antibody test, classic serology tests, determine if a patient is currently mounting

9. Buitrago-Garcia and others.
10. Citroner.
11. McCormick and others.
12. GISAID.
13. Botti-Lodovico and others.
14. Centers for Disease Control and Prevention.

Table 2-2. Major Barriers to Implementation

Pillar 1	Deployability	Some detection tools such as PCR require sophisticated and bulky machinery, limiting deployability in low-resource settings. Cold chain requirements add additional obstacles to COVID-19 vaccine delivery.
	Time to Develop	Antibody tests and vaccines can take months or years to develop. As the virus evolves, tests, treatments, and vaccines must adapt along with it. Regulatory approval processes can be slow and cumbersome.
	Cost/Access	Clinical grade PCR tests for COVID-19 can cost from US$25 to thousands of dollars, and even in advanced economies, too few laboratories have the capacity to build and validate their own PCR tests.
Pillar 2	Connectivity and Digital Divide	Frontline healthcare workers and health departments across the globe often still rely on pen, paper, e-mail, and/or bespoke electronic medical systems to record, share, and communicate data, due to limited internet access or lack of ability to update systems.
	Voluntary Buy-In	Lack of trust and understanding within communities around the role of information technologies, as well as their use and rights to privacy, can thwart buy-in, making citizen reporting less effective and sometimes even misleading.
	Interoperability	The existing range of information technologies often do not communicate with each other in a seamless fashion. There is still no global public database for reporting and storing COVID-related patient data.
	Data Modeling Capacity	Data-modeling capacity needs improvement in regions across the globe, particularly in LMICs, and scientists need a centralized infrastructure to regularly coordinate and share information with policymakers.

an immune response or previously had an infection that left memory antibodies. Both classes face barriers to implementation (see table 2-2). PCR requires sophisticated machinery, thereby limiting its deployability; and antibody tests—like the U.S. FDA-approved antigen test for COVID-19—require bespoke development, which often takes several months.[15]

New technologies are emerging that have enabled increased diagnostic development and operability in lower-resource settings worldwide. Thanks to genomic advancements and new discoveries around isothermal amplification, CRISPR, and synthetic biology, scientists have developed a range of new, ultrasensitive, low-cost, rapidly programmable, and widely deployable point-of-care diagnostics. Isothermal amplification technologies such as LAMP (Loop-Mediated Isothermal Amplification) operate similarly to PCR, but at a single lower temperature, so that they can be performed with minimal equipment. As a test, LAMP was found to be highly specific, scalable, and cost-effective, and can produce results within an hour (compared to the four to eight hours required by PCR methods).[16, 17] CRISPR, which consists of a guide protein and nuclease originally discovered in nature as a bacteria's immune system to viruses, has been paired with isothermal amplification to enable the development of even more sensitive, fast, and portable diagnostic tests, such as SHERLOCK, DETECTR, and HOLMES.[18, 19] The synthetic biology-based INSPECTR—a molecular diagnostics platform—has also enabled accurate and specific viral detection on a portable and affordable lateral flow test strip.[20] Meanwhile, efforts to accelerate the development of antibody tests have been underway to prepare for new and emerging threats, and could provide a viable option for household testing kits by 2030.[21]

Countermeasures

Prior to the genomic advancements described above, the development of medical countermeasures was slower, more experimental, and less precise. Traditionally, therapies were often discovered in nature and had to undergo a long evaluation process to understand effects on patients. Classic vaccines required a complex process of inactivation of the antigen or viral protein—that is, the

---

15. Hahn and Shuren.
16. Dao Thi and others.
17. Kashir and Yaqinuddin.
18. Chen and others.
19. Li and others.
20. Wyss Institute.
21. Baraniuk.

part of the virus that induces production of antibodies—to trigger a natural immune response, and development generally took up to a decade before safe public deployment was possible.[22] Today, with the unprecedented ability to target pathogens based on their genome, countermeasure development has been faster, more innovative, and more specific than ever before. Examples of treatment and vaccines made possible by genomic advancements include monoclonal antibodies, messenger RNA (mRNA) vaccines, and universal vaccines to target all types of flu and coronavirus.

Monoclonal antibodies underlie treatments for HIV, Zika, Ebola, MERS--COV, RSV, influenza, and COVID-19.[23] Scientists can manufacture monoclonal antibodies to imitate the effects of naturally produced antibodies that arise as a result of viral infection. In the context of COVID-19, administering monoclonal antibodies has been found to reduce hospitalization rates, especially if given to patients early in the onset of illness.[24] Today, microbiology experts have proposed efforts to begin producing monoclonal antibodies that can defend humans against one hundred of the most probable future epidemics, allowing faster disease response and mitigation.[25]

In parallel, scientists have developed a host of novel vaccines based on genomics, such as DNA and RNA vaccines. Particularly relevant today, the mRNA vaccine is one example of a DNA/RNA vaccine that has revolutionized our ability to prevent transmission of SARS-CoV-2. The injected mRNA gives the host immune system directions to produce and present SARS-CoV-2's spike protein, and thus generate antibodies against the virus.[26] These vaccines are safe for humans, because mRNA is compact and specifically processed for expression, making it easy to deliver and less likely to affect the host genome when injected.

Scientists are also working to develop a universal influenza vaccine, and may eventually venture toward developing a universal coronavirus vaccine to prepare against new variants of each.[27] Such vaccines would provide wider immunity by targeting the stem of the virus, a part that varies less between different strains. One candidate vaccine for influenza, H1ssF_3928, is currently undergoing evaluation at the National Institute of Allergy and Infectious Diseases (NIAID).[28]

22. Hubaud.
23. U.S. Food & Drug Administration.
24. Edwards.
25. Weintraub.
26. Empinado.
27. Weintraub.
28. National Institutes of Health.

Pillar 2: Information Technologies

In 2015, the WHO Ebola Interim Assessment Panel announced a broad need for "innovations in data collection . . . including geospatial mapping, mHealth communications, and platforms for self-monitoring and reporting."[29] More than five years later, there is still no global public database for reporting and storing COVID-related patient data, according to a *Lancet* report from May 2020.[30] Due to limited internet connectivity and the ongoing digital divide, frontline healthcare workers and health departments across the globe depend on e-mail, paper, and/or bespoke electronic medical systems to record, share, and communicate data.[31] Data modeling capacity, another critical piece to outbreak preparedness, needs improvement in several LMICs, particularly in Africa, while scientists in even advanced economies sometimes lack a centralized infrastructure to coordinate and share this information with policymakers in a seamless and rapid manner.[32,33]

Pillar 2 is critical because the most successful COVID-19 containment stories came out of regions that prioritized a combined test-and-trace approach. This approach not only elevates hypothesis-driven testing (that is, symptomatic cases and their contacts), but also regularly *informs* public health experts on the movements, behaviors, and needs of communities amid an outbreak, as well as the likely evolution and trajectory of the virus. Three categories of breakthrough information technologies, in addition to data-driven forecasting networks, can together help facilitate outbreak containment.

First, a range of professional public health tools, already embedded in communities, are empowering responses worldwide. Recently enhanced for COVID-19 response, these tools help public health workers accelerate surveillance efforts, and analyze and share data in real time. CommCare and District Health Information Software (DHIS2) are two examples. CommCare is an open-source, data collection platform operationalized for mobile data gathering and reporting in eighty countries.[34] It enables public health workers to access data from an individual's phone, connect with the contacts of a patient, and request individual symptom reports by WhatsApp or SMS. These reports are then passed on to the relevant healthcare providers and public health departments to inform necessary measures for containment. DHIS2 is another integrated, centralized system that enables data

29. Colubri and others.
30. Cosgriff and others.
31. Sabeti and Salahi.
32. Travaly and Mare.
33. Rivers and George.
34. Dimagi.

management, analysis, logistics management, and mapping of health services for communities in a given nation or region. It can function offline and is currently operating in seventy-three LMICs, facilitating data-driven public health measures and connecting stakeholders at every level of the healthcare system.[35]

Second, a range of integrated tools for capturing citizen data and empowering communities have been developed, many operating through smartphone-based mobile applications. Examples include Flu Near You, available in the United States and Canada, and Outbreaks Near Me, available in Mexico, Canada, and the United States. Both rely on crowdsourcing data from individuals who elect to report their symptoms and health status online. That information is then used to produce real-time visualizations of citizen data, which can help epidemiologists and health officials better understand COVID-19 transmission in target areas and alert individuals when a case has been confirmed in their geographical area.[36]

Third, proximity-sensing technologies are another option for enabling more accurate contact tracing and surveillance. Some of these technologies use Bluetooth for proximity sensing, such as Google Apple Exposure Notification (GAEN) application programming interface (API), which enables governments and the public health community to send smartphone alerts to individuals if they have been exposed to an infected individual.[37] Another proximity-sensing tool, NOVID, created by Carnegie Mellon University, combines Bluetooth with ultrasonic technology, to determine with an even higher degree of accuracy the level of contact one has made with an infected individual.[38] As mobile phone use continues to increase, with 67 percent of the entire world population owning a mobile phone (and 65 percent owning a smartphone) in 2019, all of these applications are proving more relevant today.[39]

Finally, forecasting networks are another breakthrough tool that combines epidemiological surveillance with predictive modeling and coordinated data analysis around a range of factors, including host and agent mobility, healthcare institutional capacity, virus transmissibility, and population density.[40] They systematically forecast the potential number of cases that could arise in a certain location over time, determine and assess various interventions, and identify areas of high need. Existing models include the Infectious Diseases Modelling Team at the National Institute for Public Health and the Environment in the Netherlands, and the Scientific Advisory Group for Emergencies in the United Kingdom.[41]

35. DHIS2.
36. Jacobs.
37. Landi.
38. Payne.
39. Budd and others.
40. Wick.
41. Rivers and George.

Case Studies: Low-Income vs. Advanced Economy

This section explores how two countries at very different stages of economic development—Liberia and South Korea—applied the essential pillars of pandemic preparedness and, to varying degrees, the breakthrough technologies discussed. As a low- and high-income economy, respectively, they each provide a model for how similarly positioned nations might build pandemic preparedness, with the help of the global community to fill resource and capacity gaps where needed.

Liberia

In a review of national responses to COVID-19 from early 2021, Tom Frieden, former director of the U.S. CDC, designated Liberia as the "best at learning from recent epidemics," noting only one COVID-19 death out of every 55,040 Liberians, compared to one death out of every 990 Americans over the same time period.[42] Despite having one of the most resource-poor health systems in the world, Liberia had already instituted many of the public health policies needed to facilitate an effective COVID-19 response. Their approach was centralized and unified, marked by strong and effective leadership. With a great deal of political will driven by memories of the Ebola outbreak of 2014–16, national leadership rapidly set out to build the "coronavirus task force," a committee that focused on reviving the core foundation that powered their previous outbreak response.[43, 44] This involved an aggressive strategy of rapid testing, contact tracing, and imposed quarantine where needed.[45]

With the necessary infrastructure and human capacity in place, scientists began rapidly implementing PCR tests,[46] while the government obtained additional tests from the WHO to fill gaps in local laboratory capacity.[47] Contact tracing and data gathering was coordinated under the Active Case Finders and Awareness Team, but due to a lack of broad connectivity and local preferences, the Liberian approach was dependent on "door-to-door" interaction and community-based prevention techniques, designated as "active case finding."[48] In concert with trusted community health workers, contact tracers were able to deliver information on the virus, build trust, and respond to community

42. Frieden.
43. Maxmen.
44. Wallace.
45. Frieden.
46. World Health Organization. 2021b.
47. Maxmen.
48. Winny.

concerns—something that many advanced economies failed to do. Their COVID task force also shared data and met periodically to enable adaptations in their approach, based on evolving needs.[49]

As in many LMICs, Liberia has faced challenges with the higher tech components of pandemic response, including the near real-time data gathering and contact tracing capabilities achieved through information technologies and widespread connectivity. Like many other nations, they have also experienced shortages of tests.[50] The World Bank and others provided assistance earlier on in the pandemic, including a grant worth US$3.75 million, as well as a concessional International Development Association (IDA) credit of US$3.75 million to build capacity in local laboratories, facilitate coordination and collaboration, and support the Liberian government's outbreak response measures.[51] Ultimately, more financial and infrastructural assistance is needed both now and in the long term for Liberia to overcome COVID-19 and achieve long-term pandemic preparedness. Yet their comparative success and focus on community needs provide a hopeful model for LMICs and advanced economies alike on how a well-coordinated, prepared, and aggressive approach to infectious pathogens can transform outbreak response.

South Korea

In the same review cited above, Frieden designated South Korea as "best at testing," noting only one COVID-19 death out of every 63,290 Koreans. Early on in the outbreak, Korean leadership established an aggressive and highly coordinated testing strategy, allowing the nation to deploy double the number of tests per capita in the initial weeks after the pandemic began, compared to other nations.[52] Their speed in response can be largely attributed to the outbreak response infrastructure they developed during the MERS outbreak in 2015, as well as their preexisting genomic capacity, strong leadership from the Korea Disease Control and Prevention Agency, and a revamped emergency process that sped up the approval time for diagnostics from a year to a week or under.[53]

The information technology and data integration pillar has been driven by the extraordinary levels of connectivity in South Korea, as well as a preexisting "legal and cultural framework" that facilitates highly accurate contact tracing

49. Maxmen.
50. Ibid.
51. World Bank.
52. Frieden.
53. Campbell and Lee.

and epidemiological surveillance.[54] According to a recent Brookings post by Justin Fendos, more than 96 percent of Koreans enjoy daily access to the internet, while approximately 95 percent have a smartphone.[55] To better target testing and contact tracing, Korea's post-MERS amendment of the Infectious Disease Control and Prevention Act enabled health authorities in times of outbreak to access the same information on citizens that police can access for law enforcement purposes. On average, citizens are largely amenable to the regulated use of their personal data to keep themselves and their families safe, including information gathered from mobile devices and location logs, surveillance footage in public spaces, and electronic transactions. Citizens also receive alerts when they may have come into contact with an infected individual, which empowers them to seek testing if necessary.

While South Korea has had challenges containing the virus, their aggressive detect-and-connect strategy has enabled them to evade a strict lockdown since the start of the pandemic, without the devastating consequences of rampant viral spread.[56] Thanks to a strong preexisting public health infrastructure, mass community buy-in, and the resources needed to broadly finance these efforts, technological progress proved invaluable to the pandemic response in South Korea. Further, the trust citizens had in their government and public health system proved to be a critical factor in empowering communities to fully engage in pandemic response.

Priorities for Implementation

Thanks to advances in genomics and information technology, scientists have developed tests, vaccines, and tools at record speed amid COVID-19, proving that the world can prepare for the next pandemic if incentives are aligned. Success stories in contexts as different as Liberia and South Korea provide insight regarding a path forward. A combination of public health infrastructure, a commitment to equity and community empowerment, and scaled-up investments will be key priorities for ensuring a necessary breakthrough in the uptake and success of these technological advancements within all countries (see table 2-3).

54. Ibid.
55. Fendos.
56. Campbell and Lee.

Table 2-3. Foundational Elements for Implementation

Public Health Infrastructure	Three characteristics determine the level of pandemic preparedness and quality of pandemic response: (1) a centralized and unified health infrastructure; (2) constant data sharing across institutions and regions, with interoperability between systems and tools for data-sharing; (3) a prioritization framework based on need and equity.
Equity and Community Empowerment	More global coordination is needed to make diagnostics, vaccines, and therapies broadly and equitably accessible. Production must be expanded globally, patent protections for vaccines amended, manufacturing recipes shared, and a standardized global framework for equitable distribution developed. Voluntary buy-in will require building community trust and empowering citizens to use information technologies in an informed, secure manner.
Financing	Financing pandemic preparedness requires rapidly scaled up domestic and international investments across countries of all income levels in order to support public health infrastructure, community empowerment, and equitable access to fast-changing technologies. One prominent estimate indicates that LMICs need to add roughly 1 percent of GDP to their domestic public spending on health and international financing needs to increase by at least US$15 billion annually, in order to avoid potential costs at least three hundred times as large.

Public Health Infrastructure

Even the wealthiest economies struggle with inadequate public health infrastructure. During the COVID-19 pandemic, problems have ranged from a lack of distributed response capacity to poor coordination and prioritization of funding, lack of equity and transparency in how resources are distributed, bureaucratic delays in disbursement, and obscurity around the needs of various stakeholders. At the outset of COVID-19, most countries lacked the appropriate health infrastructure needed to respond to the pandemic, but certain countries responded more effectively due to the crisis-centered policies and systems they built and leveraged. Whether in an LMIC or advanced economy, three main characteristics determined the initial quality of their COVID-19 response—defined as an ability to implement rapid and widespread testing, accurate contact tracing, and other government-imposed safety measures early in the pandemic.

First, a centralized and unified national health infrastructure is critical to successful outbreak response. Regular communication and coordination between public health agencies must become a definitive component of health systems globally. By reenvisioning public health as equally critical to national defense, federal entities and leaders will be more likely to provide steady support to local health departments in times of quiet and crisis. Bureaucratic processes must also be updated to better respond to emergency needs, and nations must pave a clear regulatory pathway toward supporting rapid approval of diagnostic tools, therapies, vaccines, and data technologies.[57] On a local level, academic labs, hospitals, and healthcare workers need more training and support to set up rapid and wide-scale test-and-trace campaigns, whereas communities must have their basic needs met as they engage in government-imposed safety policies, such as social distancing and imposed quarantine.

Second, constant data sharing plays a major role in any health system, and particularly pandemic response. When COVID-19 arrived, largely neglected public health agencies, local health departments, and providers across the globe were unprepared to update and sync their data systems, hindering their capacity to rapidly access, share, evaluate, and communicate information broadly.[58] In advance of the next major outbreak, data systems must be updated and standardized across regions, and public health workers and departments must be trained in their use.

Tech leaders, health officials, and political leaders must also unite in creating an interoperable ecosystem to enable different applications to not only communicate seamlessly but also integrate into one secure data repository where information can be gathered and analyzed. Similar to e-mail or SMS, users could then select the media they prefer and easily connect with others, while providing accessible information to public health leaders. For data privacy purposes, standardized guidelines around the use of any and all data must be implemented through a legally binding national, regional, or global framework. To protect individuals' privacy and prevent malicious actors from accessing sensitive citizen information from information technologies, the data repository should only be accessible to trusted healthcare agencies and decisionmakers. Individuals would then have to provide their consent before their data can be analyzed or shared, and information would be destroyed once there is no longer any use for it.

Third, a good prioritization strategy or framework is something that any public health infrastructure must perfect and continually adapt based on evolving public health needs. This becomes more feasible with ongoing data sharing, but

57. Botti-Lodovico and others.
58. Lipsitch and Grad.

also revolves around some universal principles. For example, any public crisis calls on leaders to prioritize and allocate scarce resources based on equity and need. Services to at-risk or underprivileged communities must be prioritized, as they are most often disproportionately affected by any health crisis. This may include pop-up testing centers, treatments and early vaccination, sanitation supplies, socioeconomic resources to facilitate quarantine, and so on. To successfully contain outbreaks, clinical and hypothesis-based testing needs (that is, of symptomatic patients and their contacts) must also be prioritized before significantly shifting resources to asymptomatic testing.[59] Finally, the enhanced visibility required for effective prioritization can only be achieved through ongoing coordination with local health departments and providers that directly serve communities, as well as constant data sharing to both evaluate and update the existing response strategy.

On Equity and Empowerment

All of the tools discussed above must be applied in an equitable and ethical manner, emphasizing citizen rights and empowerment. On the diagnostics front, collaborative initiatives like FIND (Foundation for Innovative New Diagnostics) have been leading efforts globally to support the development and distribution of cutting-edge diagnostic tools to LMICs. Ongoing efforts to produce more affordable rapid tests intended for surveillance could provide US$1 tests for consumption on the global market, or US$5 tests, like the FDA-approved Abbott antigen test.[60, 61] However, more collaboration is needed to expand these benefits to vulnerable populations worldwide, and facilitate broad participation by more laboratories and scientists in the development efforts.

Equity is an important consideration for countermeasures, too. Even amid a pandemic, the COVAX initiative, which manages the equitable delivery of COVID-19 vaccines, has no equal counterpart when it comes to therapies. As of November 2020, LMICs had deployed less than 2 percent of the global supply of monoclonal antibodies,[62] which are likely to become increasingly important in infectious disease mitigation over time. As new therapies are explored and optimized, the global community must work to enhance delivery of therapies to underserved communities everywhere.

Alternatively, on the vaccine front, Gavi and the Coalition for Epidemic

59. Botti-Lodovico and others.
60. Harvard T. H. Chan School of Public Health.
61. American Society of Hematology.
62. Paun.

Preparedness (CEPI)—a global collaboration convened to both facilitate vaccine development and promote equitable distribution[63]—have made considerable progress in delivering life-saving vaccines to underserved communities. Despite their efforts, however, disparities persist. For example, 20 million children across the globe lacked access to other life-saving vaccines in 2018, and competing priorities posed by COVID-19 have slowed routine vaccine delivery today.[64, 65] Once the COVID-19 vaccines were approved, wealthy countries bought out approximately 96 percent of the existing vaccine doses for COVID-19 from Pfizer-BioNTech and 100 percent of Moderna's vaccine, as well as over half of the most effective options altogether.[66,67] For many LMICs, cold chain requirements continue to thwart COVID-19 vaccine transport and delivery. As scientists build new breakthrough vaccines, research and development efforts over the next decade must also aim to enable safe delivery to remote regions everywhere.

Both now and after COVID-19 passes, the world will require a great deal of global coordination to make vaccines and therapies broadly and equitably accessible. The most critical step to achieve this is by expanding production and developing a standardized global framework for equitable distribution. The IPPPR recommends a "pre-negotiated platform" to both develop diagnostics and medical countermeasures such as vaccines and therapeutics, and ensure their quick and equitable distribution as "essential global common goods."[68] Others have urged wealthy governments such as the United States, Switzerland, and the United Kingdom to not only work to dismantle vaccine monopolies, but also cease efforts to obstruct proposals by emerging economies to amend patent protections and enable expanded manufacturing rights everywhere.[69] Vaccines, like diagnostics and treatments, are a global public good, for which monopolies are counterproductive amid a global pandemic. Pharmaceutical companies, which are getting significant governmental support, should therefore be required to not only publicly share manufacturing recipes and transfer technological know-how to manufacturers worldwide, but also work with those manufacturers to ensure vaccines are available at affordable prices for everyone.[70]

Beyond access, voluntary buy-in throughout LMICs and advanced economies alike will require increased community trust and broad empowerment.

63. Coalition for Epidemic Preparedness Innovations.
64. World Health Organization. 2019.
65. World Health Organization. 2020b.
66. Meredith.
67. Rigby.
68. Independent Panel for Pandemic Preparedness and Response.
69. Green.
70. The People's Vaccine Alliance.

Both are critical elements to the healthy functioning of any public infrastructure and particularly in outbreak prevention, as individuals play a role in stopping viral spread. Building trust and empowering individuals are duties tasked to community healthcare workers in many LMICs, but often left unfulfilled in advanced economies, where significant effort is needed to develop a real and lasting presence.

To this end, public health experts and leaders everywhere must build lasting partnerships with community health workers, local NGOs and nonprofits, tribal leaders, religious advisors, women's and minority groups, and other trusted stakeholders. These partnerships, if rooted in humility, will help build rapport with communities, identify their needs, and alleviate existing concerns over medical interventions and data privacy. International health organizations and biotechnology leaders will need to work with local and regional organizations to implement culturally and linguistically relevant information campaigns in underserved regions around the importance and safety of diagnostics, vaccines, and treatments, as well as information technologies for contact tracing and citizen reporting.

Finally, connectivity remains a hurdle to broad use of information technologies across the globe. In response, tech giant SpaceX is already planning to send 4,425 satellites to orbit in space, with the hopes of providing high-speed internet for "residential, commercial, institutional, government, and professional users worldwide."[71] As internet access expands, however, any use of information technologies should be encouraged rather than forced. Citizens should receive basic training on both their use and data privacy rights, so they are empowered to participate in outbreak response anywhere in the world.

Scaled-up Financing

The priorities described above will only be possible through a major scale-up of investments. The challenge of adequate and sustainable financing is as relevant in advanced economies as in lower-income settings. In the United States, for example, pandemic preparedness and public health were gutted by the Trump administration before COVID-19 hit. Funding cuts led the Centers for Disease Control and Prevention (CDC) to reduce their program budget for disease outbreak containment across the globe by 80 percent in 2018. Similarly, the administration collapsed the National Security Council's (NSC) "global health security" unit, stripped the U.S. Complex Crises Fund of US$30 million, and cut US$15 billion from U.S. public health spending even prior to the pandemic.[72]

71. Gibbs.
72. Sheth and Heeb.

For LMICs, initiatives like the Access to COVID-19 Tools Accelerator (ACT)—a collaboration between governments, industry, scientists, philanthropists, global health organizations, and civil society—are working to support rapid development of COVID-19 diagnostics, therapies, and vaccines, and promoting equitable access to these tools.[73] This has included commitments such as one from the Bill & Melinda Gates Foundation, in collaboration with diagnostics manufacturers such as SD Biosensor and Abbott, to pave a path toward the production of new rapid antigen diagnostic tests that cost US$5 and under.[74] However, costs of PCR tests for COVID-19 can still range from US$25 to thousands of dollars, and supply-side constraints to meeting global demand for testing and other countermeasures are persistent.[75, 76] A broader challenge is that, as of mid--2021, the ACT-Accelerator still faced a funding gap of more than US$16 billion for 2021 alone, and IMF economists have identified an incremental US$13 billion in funding needs beyond that.[77, 78] The world is not allocating adequate funding to pandemic mitigation or avoidance.

In early 2021, the G20 High Level Independent Panel convened a cross--section of global economic leaders to provide a systematic assessment of the financing required to prevent and contain future pandemics.[79] The group recommended that LMICs will need to add about 1 percent of their own GDP to public spending on health over five years, and that, as an absolute minimum, the cross-border financing will need to increase by US$15 billion per year. This is on top of complementary investments required to address issues like antimicrobial resistance, which itself requires roughly US$9 billion per year. The panel recommends an augmented global governance system involving a Global Health Threats Board, a Global Health Threats Council, and a Global Health Threats Fund, with the WHO at the center of the ecosystem. Crucially, the G20 advisory body stresses the extraordinary value of urgent action. Scaled-up investment efforts would help governments avoid budgetary costs at least three hundred times greater in future pandemics.

73. World Health Organization (n.d.).
74. World Health Organization. 2020a.
75. Markos.
76. Luthi.
77. World Health Organization. 2021a.
78. Agarwal and Gopinath.
79. G20 High Level Independent Panel on Financing the Global Commons for Pandemic Preparedness and Response.

A Call to Action

Outbreaks expose and intensify the underlying cracks in society. Issues like inequity, injustice, poverty, and food insecurity not only rise to the forefront during an outbreak or pandemic, but also worsen due to the strain on national infrastructure. The world cannot combat any sustainable development challenge without devising a plan to catch and contain infectious disease wherever it arises. COVID-19 serves as another reminder of this reality, urging nations to both invest in equitable and efficient healthcare infrastructure and empower communities to truly engage in pandemic preparedness and response.

Global pandemics highlight a truth that the public health community has known for years. No one country, region, or sector can stand on its own when it comes to fighting infectious disease. The pillars and principles proposed here are not a one-point, individual solution, but rather an integrated and collaborative approach of combining equitable and quality healthcare systems with breakthrough technologies. Together these can detect, connect, and empower communities to stop outbreaks and achieve pandemic preparedness across the globe.

References

Agarwal, Ruchir, and Gita Gopinath. 2021. "A Proposal to End the COVID-19 Pandemic." IMF Staff Discussion Note 2021/004, May 19.

Baraniuk, Chris. 2020. "COVID-19 Antibody Tests: A Briefing," *BMJ*, no. 369, m2284.

Botti-Lodovico, Yolanda, Eric Rosenberg, and Pardis C. Sabeti. 2021. "Testing in a Pandemic—Improving Access, Coordination, and Prioritization," *New England Journal of Medicine*, vol. 384, no. 3.

Budd, Jobie, Benjamin S. Miller, Erin M. Manning, Vasileios Lampos, Mengdie Zhuang, Michael Edelstein, Geraint Rees, and others. 2020. "Digital Technologies in the Public Health Response to COVID-19," *Nature Medicine*, vol. 26, no. 8.

Buitrago-Garcia, Diana, Dianne Egli-Gany, Michel J. Counotte, Stefanie Hossmann, Hira Imeri, Aziz Mert Ipekci, Georgia Salanti, and Nicola Low. 2020. "Occurrence and Transmission Potential of Asymptomatic and Presymptomatic SARS-CoV-2 Infections: A Living Systematic Review and Meta-Analysis," *PLOS Medicine*, vol. 17, no. 9.

Campbell, Matthew, and Heesu Lee. 2020. "COVID Pandemic: How South Korea Contained the Coronavirus without Lockdowns." *Bloomberg*, December 10.

Centers for Disease Control and Prevention. 2020. "Interim Guidance for Rapid Antigen Testing for SARS-CoV-2." www.cdc.gov/coronavirus/2019-ncov/lab/resources/antigen-tests-guidelines.html.

Chen, Janice S., Enbo Ma, Lucas B. Harrington, Maria Da Costa, Xinran Tian, Joel M. Palefsky, and Jennifer A. Doudna. 2018. "CRISPR-Cas12a Target Binding

Unleashes Indiscriminate Single-Stranded DNase Activity," *Science*, vol. 360, no. 6387.

Citroner, George. 2020. "20 Percent of Coronavirus Infections Are Asymptomatic but Still Contagious." Healthline Media. www.healthline.com/health-news/20-percent -of-people-with-covid-19-are-asymptomatic-but-can-spread-the-disease.

Colubri, Andres, Tom Silver, Terrence Fradet, Kalliroi Retzepi, Ben Fry, and Pardis Sabeti. 2016. "Transforming Clinical Data into Actionable Prognosis Models: Machine-Learning Framework and Field-Deployable App to Predict Outcome of Ebola Patients," *PLOS Neglected Tropical Diseases*, vol. 10, no. 3.

Dimagi. "CommCare by Dimagi," n.d. www.dimagi.com/commcare/.

Commission on a Global Health Risk Framework for the Future, and National Academy of Medicine, Secretariat. 2016. *The Case for Investing in Pandemic Preparedness*. National Academies Press (U.S.).

Cosgriff, Christopher V., Daniel K. Ebner, and Leo Anthony Celi. 2020. "Data Sharing in the Era of COVID-19," *Lancet. Digital Health*, vol. 2, no. 5.

Prevent Epidemics. 2020. "Country Preparedness and COVID-19." https:// preventepidemics.org/covid19/science/insights/country-preparedness-and-covid-19/.

Cutler, David M., and Lawrence H. Summers. 2020. "The COVID-19 Pandemic and the $16 Trillion Virus," *JAMA: The Journal of the American Medical Association*, vol. 324, no. 15.

Dao Thi, Viet Loan, Konrad Herbst, Kathleen Boerner, Matthias Meurer, Lukas PM Kremer, Daniel Kirrmaier, Andrew Freistaedter, and others. 2020. "A Colorimetric RT-LAMP Assay and LAMP-Sequencing for Detecting SARS-CoV-2 RNA in Clinical Samples." *Science Translational Medicine*. https://doi.org/10.1126/ scitranslmed.abc7075.

Edwards, Erika. 2021. "Monoclonal Antibodies Could Ease Record COVID Hospitalizations. Why Are They Going Unused?" NBC News, January 15.

Empinado, Hyacinth. 2020. "mRNA Vaccines Face Their First Test with COVID-19. How Do They Work?" www.statnews.com/2020/10/26/mrna-vaccines-face-their -first-test-in-the-fight-against-covid-19-how-do-they-work/.

American Society of Hematology. 2020. "FDA Authorizes Low-Cost Rapid-Response Antigen Test for COVID-19." www.ashclinicalnews.org/online-exclusives/fda -authorizes-low-cost-rapid-response-antigen-test-covid-19/.

Fendos, Justin. 2020. "How Surveillance Technology Powered South Korea's COVID-19 Response." Brookings. www.brookings.edu/techstream/how-surveillance -technology-powered-south-koreas-covid-19-response/.

Frieden, Tom. 2021. "Which Countries Have Responded Best to COVID-19?" *Wall Street Journal* (Eastern edition), January 1.

G20 High Level Independent Panel on Financing the Global Commons for Pandemic Preparedness and Response. 2021. "A Global Deal for Our Pandemic Age." https:// recommendations.theindependentpanel.org/main-report/.

Gibbs, Samuel. 2016. "Elon Musk Wants to Cover the World with Internet from Space," *Guardian*, November 17.

GISAID. "GISAID—Initiative," n.d. www.gisaid.org/.

Green, Andrew. 2021. "In Brief: Rich Countries Block Waiver on COVID-19 Vaccine IP." Devex.www.devex.com/news/in-brief-rich-countries-block-waiver-on-covid-19 -vaccine-ip-99077.

Hahn, Stephen M., and Jeffrey E. Shuren. 2020. "Coronavirus (COVID-19) Update: FDA Authorizes First Antigen Test to Help in the Rapid Detection of the Virus that Causes COVID-19 in Patients." www.fda.gov/news-events/press-announcements/coronavirus-covid-19-update-fda-authorizes-first-antigen-test-help-rapid-detection-virus-causes.

Harvard T. H. Chan School of Public Health. 2020. "Frequent, Rapid Testing Could Turn National COVID-19 Tide within Weeks." www.hsph.harvard.edu/news/press-releases/frequent-rapid-testing-could-turn-national-covid-19-tide-within-weeks/.

Hubaud, Alexis. 2015. "RNA Vaccines: A Novel Technology to Prevent and Treat Disease—Science in the News." http://sitn.hms.harvard.edu/flash/2015/rna-vaccines-a-novel-technology-to-prevent-and-treat-disease/.

Independent Panel for Pandemic Preparedness and Response. 2021. "COVID-19: Make It the Last Pandemic." https://recommendations.theindependentpanel.org/main-report/.

Wyss Institute. "INSPECTR™: Direct-to-Consumer Molecular Diagnostic," n.d. https://wyss.harvard.edu/technology/inspectr-a-direct-to-consumer-molecular-diagnostic/.

Jacobs, Andrew. 2020. "App Shows Promise in Tracking New Coronavirus Cases, Study Finds," *New York Times*, May 11.

Kashir, Junaid, and Ahmed Yaqinuddin. 2020. "Loop Mediated Isothermal Amplification (LAMP) Assays as a Rapid Diagnostic for COVID-19," *Medical Hypotheses*, vol. 141.

Landi, Heather. 2020. "Apple and Google Launch Contact Tracing API for COVID-19 Exposure." www.fiercehealthcare.com/tech/apple-and-google-launch-covid-19-exposure-notification-api.

Lipsitch, Marc, and Yonatan Grad. 2020. "How to Fix Public Health Weaknesses before the Next Pandemic Hits," *Washington Post*, September 24.

Li, Shi-Yuan, Qiu-Xiang Cheng, Jing-Man Wang, Xiao-Yan Li, Zi-Long Zhang, Song Gao, Rui-Bing Cao, Guo-Ping Zhao, and Jin Wang. 2018. "CRISPR-Cas12a-Assisted Nucleic Acid Detection," *Cell Discovery*, vol. 4.

Luthi, Susannah. 2020. "The $7,000 COVID Test: Why States Are Stepping in to Shield Consumers," *Politico*, June 8.

Markos, Mary. 2020. "A Local Research Institute Is Testing College Students for COVID-19. Here's What It's Finding." NBC10 Boston, September 3.

Maxmen, Amy. 2020. "Ebola Prepared These Countries for Coronavirus—but Now Even They Are Floundering," *Nature*, vol. 583, no. 7818.

McCormick, J. B., I. J. King, P. A. Webb, C. L. Scribner, R. B. Craven, K. M. Johnson, L. H. Elliott, and R. Belmont-Williams. 1986. "Lassa Fever. Effective Therapy with Ribavirin," *New England Journal of Medicine*, vol. 314, no. 1.

McKay, Betsy, and Phred Dvorak. 2020. "A Deadly Coronavirus Was Inevitable. Why Was No One Ready?" *Wall Street Journal*, August 13.

Meredith, Sam. 2020. "Poor Countries Set to Miss Out on COVID Vaccines as Wealthier Nations Hoard Doses, Campaigners Warn." CNBC, December 9.

Miles, Tom. 2018. "West Africa's Ebola Outbreak Cost $53 Billion—Study," *Reuters*, October 24.

National Academies of Sciences, Engineering, and Medicine, Institute of Medicine, and Board on Global Health. 2016. *Global Health Risk Framework: Pandemic Financing: Workshop Summary*. National Academies Press.

National Institutes of Health. 2019. "NIH Begins First-in-Human Trial of a Universal Influenza Vaccine Candidate." www.nih.gov/news-events/news-releases/nih-begins -first-human-trial-universal-influenza-vaccine-candidate.

Osterholm, Michael T., and Mark Olshaker. 2020. "Chronicle of a Pandemic Foretold." *Foreign Affairs*, July/August.

Paun, Carmen. 2020. "Closing the COVID Treatment Gap," *Politico*, November 25.

Payne, Emily. 2020. "NOVID Is the Most Accurate App for Contact Tracing." www .cmu.edu/news/stories/archives/2020/june/novid-update.html.

The People's Vaccine Alliance. "Peoples Vaccine," n.d. https://peoplesvaccine.org/.

Rigby, Jennifer. 2020. "Rich Nations Have Already Bought More than Half of World's Vaccine Doses, Oxfam Finds," *Daily Telegraph*, September 17.

Rivers, Caitlin, and Dylan George. 2020. "How to Forecast Outbreaks and Pandemics," *Foreign Affairs*, June 29.

Sabeti, Pardis, and Lara Salahi. 2018. *Outbreak Culture: The Ebola Crisis and the Next Epidemic*. Harvard University Press.

Saldinger, Adva. 2020. "Can Innovative Financing Tools Raise Funds for the COVID-19 Response?" Devex. www.devex.com/news/can-innovative-financing-tools-raise -funds-for-the-covid-19-response-97191.

Sheth, Sonam, and Gina Heeb. 2020. "Trump Spent the Past Two Years Slashing the Government Agencies Responsible for Handling the Coronavirus Outbreak," *Business Insider*, February 25.

DHIS2. "The World's Largest Health Information Management System—Developed through Global Collaboration Led by UiO," n.d. www.dhis2.org/.

Travaly, Youssef, and Aretha Mare. 2020. "Learning from the Best: Evaluating Africa's COVID-19 Responses." Brookings. www.brookings.edu/blog/africa-in-focus/2020/ 07/08/learning-from-the-best-evaluating-africas-covid-19-responses/.

U.S. Food & Drug Administration. 2020. "Coronavirus (COVID-19) Update: FDA Authorizes Monoclonal Antibody for Treatment of COVID-19." www.fda.gov/ news-events/press-announcements/coronavirus-covid-19-update-fda-authorizes -monoclonal-antibody-treatment-covid-19.

Wallace, Paige. 2020. "COVID-19 in Liberia: Learning from the Ebola Virus." www .borgenmagazine.com/covid-19-in-liberia/.

World Bank. 2020. "More Support to Boost Liberia COVID-19 Response." www .worldbank.org/en/news/press-release/2020/04/09/more-support-to-boost-liberia -covid-19-response.

Weintraub, Karen. 2021. "'This Has to Be the Moment' to Invest in Coronavirus Vaccines and Treatments against Future Pandemics, Experts Warn," *USA Today*, February 21.

2020. "What Is an Advance Market Commitment and How Could It Help Beat COVID-19?" www.gavi.org/vaccineswork/what-advance-market-commitment-and -how-could-it-help-beat-covid-19.

Coalition for Epidemic Preparedness Innovations. "Why We Exist—CEPI," n.d. https:/ /cepi.net/about/whyweexist/.

Wick, Jeannette Y. 2019. "2019 Was a Year for Advancements in Infectious Disease." www.pharmacytimes.com/publications/issue/2019/December2019/2019-was-a-year -for-advancements-in-infectious-disease.

Winny, Annalies. 2020. "In Liberia, Resources Are Scarce—but Contact Tracing Is

Second Nature." www.globalhealthnow.org/2020-06/liberia-resources-are-scarce
-contact-tracing-second-nature.

World Health Organization. 2019. "20 Million Children Miss Out on Lifesaving
Measles, Diphtheria, and Tetanus Vaccines in 2018." www.who.int/news/item/15-07
-2019-20-million-children-miss-out-on-lifesaving-measles-diphtheria-and-tetanus
-vaccines-in-2018.

———. 2020a. "Global Partnership to Make Available 120 Million Affordable,
Quality COVID-19 Rapid Tests for Low- and Middle-Income Countries." www
.who.int/news/item/28-09-2020-global-partnership-to-make-available-120-million
-affordable-quality-covid-19-rapid-tests-for-low—and-middle-income-countries.

———. 2020b. "WHO and UNICEF Warn of a Decline in Vaccinations during
COVID-19." www.who.int/news/item/15-07-2020-who-and-unicef-warn-of-a
-decline-in-vaccinations-during-covid-19.

———. 2020c. "WHO Coronavirus Disease (COVID-19) Dashboard," *Bangladesh
Physiotherapy Journal*, vol. 10, no. 1.

———. 2021a. "Access to COVID-19 Tools Accelerator Overview and Update, July
2021." www.who.int/publications/m/item/access-to-covid-19-tools-accelerator
-overview-and-update-july-2021.

———. 2021b. "Liberia: How Reinforced Community Health Structures and
Capitalizing on Lessons Learned from the Ebola Virus Epidemic of 2014–16 Helped
the Country Respond to the Challenge of Its Second Major Disease Outbreak in
Five Years." www.who.int/publications/m/item/liberia-how-reinforced-community
-health-structures-and-capitalizing-on-lessons-learned-from-the-ebola-virus
-epidemic-of-2014-16-helped-the-country-respond-to-the-challenge-of-its-second
-major-disease-outbreak-in-five-years.

———. "What Is the ACT-Accelerator," n.d. www.who.int/initiatives/act-accelerator/
about.

THREE

Fixing the Real "World Wide Web"

Breakthroughs at the Interface of Food, Agriculture, and Large-Scale Computation

Zachary Bogue

The global food supply is humanity's only truly distributed system. Everywhere humans live, food is consumed every day, and it is concomitantly produced almost everywhere on the planet and then broadly distributed with great precision around the globe.

Over the years, many people—from Thomas Malthus in 1798 to Paul Ehrlich in the second half of the twentieth century to newspaper editors in the twenty--first—have correlated increasing global population with a strictly finite amount of arable land and predicted the whole system would come crashing down. So far, they have all been wrong; the system has shown itself to be much more resilient than one might think.

Past performance, of course, does not guarantee future success. There are major emergent trendlines that could impair the system—or even lead to its collapse over the longer term. By some estimates, agriculture contributes up to 10 percent to 25 percent of global greenhouse gas ("GHG") emissions,[1] contributes to significant biodiversity loss, and results in widespread soil degradation.[2] The impact of these trends is ecological, economic, and—because of food's primacy—political and cultural. Examples of this complex feedback loop can be

1. IPCC.
2. Montanarella, Pennock, and McKenzie.

47

seen in studies that have shown increased CO2 in the atmosphere may result in less-nutritious foods.[3]

Despite the food system's ability to meet most people's caloric needs, the United Nations' Food and Agriculture Organization estimates that even in 2019, before the COVID-19 pandemic, 690 million people were chronically under-nourished—which is 10 million more people than were undernourished in 2018, and 60 million more than were undernourished five years earlier.[4] Yet in the developed world, acreage under cultivation decreases every year as productivity and yield outstrip demand.[5] Today's food insecurity crises are more a consequence of the unequal distribution of current agricultural technologies and local and regional economic policy, which, in turn, have consequences for larger issues of climate change and planetary sustainability.

For example, the average acre of corn in the United States yields 160 bushels, with top farmers producing more than 600 bushels per acre.[6] Meanwhile, in Sub-Saharan Africa, the average is 30 bushels per acre.[7] However, many Sub--Saharan farms use traditional agricultural approaches, which often have lower environmental impact than the high-yielding farms of the United States and other developed nations. Most industrial farm acreage in the West is devoted to non-biodiverse monoculture, which is heavily reliant on pesticides and synthetic fertilizer. The World Resources Institute cites agricultural runoff (mainly synthetic fertilizer and animal waste) as a key cause of eutrophication of once--productive coastal waters, creating huge "dead zones," where oxygen concentration is insufficient to support most marine life.[8] Further, agriculture's GHG production contributes to warming seas,[9] upsetting the nutrient cycle in many fisheries and threatening global thermohaline circulation,[10] often called the "ocean conveyor belt." So, producing more food on land often hurts our ability to harvest more from the sea.

Meanwhile, the COVID-19 pandemic also exposed weakness at the other end of the agri-food value chain. New York City's point-of-sale outlets, for example, typically only have four to five days of food in stock.[11] While this lack of inventory minimizes food waste, even backup processors, distributors, and retailers

3. Dong, Gruda, Lam, and others.
4. Kretchmer.
5. Fisher.
6. Spiegel.
7. Nigatu and Hansen.
8. World Resources Institute.
9. IPCC.
10. Brierley and Kingsford.
11. New York City Economic Development Corporation, NYC Mayor's Office of Recovery & Resiliency.

were hard pressed to keep basic foodstuffs on hand during the recent pandemic.

By contrast, about 65 percent of Sub-Saharan Africans rely on subsistence farming.[12] Those families grow a lot of their own food, which puts them at the end of the shortest possible value chain while also making them vulnerable to fluctuating local environmental conditions. As the fastest rates of urban growth continue in many of the lowest-income countries, more of the people most at risk will also be exposed to local supply-chain vulnerabilities.

The Green Revolution of the 1950s, 1960s, and 1970s produced massive yield gains thanks to the widespread adoption of modern agrarian practices such as synthetic fertilizer, pesticides, and modern grain varietals. In the 1980s and 1990s, the Global Positioning System (GPS) and genetically modified organisms (GMOs) were new innovations rippling across the global food supply. In the early part of this millennium, the continuing digitization of agriculture—focusing on bytes, not bushels—drove further yield improvements.

For the coming decades, the grand challenge will be to achieve what Jules Pretty has called "sustainable intensification." That is to say, we must further increase yields while reducing or eliminating the harmful impacts of our current agricultural system.

In 2019, Cornell University and the journal *Nature Sustainability* convened a panel of international experts who neatly characterized this goal for the global agri-food system: It should provide everyone with a diet that is healthy, equitable, resilient, and sustainable (HERS).[13] Although this chapter acknowledges today's grand problems, including climate change, we believe that adapting and spreading already proven technologies to the developing world can help us reach that HERS goal even as the world's population is generally expected to reach a peak of about 9.7 billion by 2064 before declining to 8.8 billion by the end of this century.[14]

Over the past decade, the convergence of the plunging cost of storage, computer resources, and bandwidth has spawned a wave of innovation, unleashing the now well understood and widely written about concept of artificial intelligence (AI). While many understand the value of AI in things like smarter business applications or more intelligent home electronics, this technology has also unlocked advanced computational approaches to enormously complex real-world problems in the global agri-food system. It has concurrently accelerated advances in relevant fields such as robotics, earth observation, and bioengineering.

In this chapter, we explore "Deep Tech" innovations that promise to increase

12. Savage.
13. Barrett, Benton, Fanzo, and others.
14. Stein, Goren, Yuan, and others.

efficiency, yields, and sustainability. We define Deep Tech as the combination of the latest advances in science and technology driven by unique computing and algorithmic advantages. The current vulnerabilities in the global agri-food system do not call for individual innovations or even a single revolution, à la the Green Revolution, but rather a series of revolutions working concurrently to reshape an enormous and disparate system. Creating a more equitable and sustainable global food supply chain can be met only with a whole-planet approach where governments, regulatory agencies, and NGOs share a unified vision. Private, for-profit companies also have a substantial role and, in many cases, the greatest incentive to innovate and bring these innovations to market as quickly as possible for use across the globe.

We certainly do not claim that the innovations discussed below represent a comprehensive solution, but this chapter is more than an exercise in wishful thinking. These technologies are all proven and ready for wider adoption. They can help us understand ecological risks, reduce our dependence on dangerous chemicals, and reduce the environmental impacts of the global agri-food system, moving the needle significantly by 2030.

We focus on four areas of advancement: applied AI; microbes and bioengineering; robotics; and a collection of technologies that can reduce the impact of meat production, which is unsustainable as currently practiced. Some of the technologies we highlight will broadly influence the global agri-food system, and some will reshape specific sectors as the global population—and attendant environmental pressures—increase.

AI on a Global Scale

As the old adage goes, you can only manage what you can measure. Heretofore, much of the food-industrial complex and its inputs from the agriculture systems have been too diverse, dispersed, and complex to measure or observe in any truly comprehensive or holistic way.

Agriculture is literally a down-to-earth activity, so space is not the most obvious place to find relevant innovations. But as the "space race" among national superpowers cooled, it gave way to transformational innovation from private sector companies seeking cost-effective ways to leverage Earth's orbit for humanity's gain. This private sector space race has created unparalleled opportunity for measurement-driven insight into agricultural systems across our planet through the creation and deployment of small satellites that provide affordable weekly or even daily medium- and high-resolution Earth images.

Persistent imaging from Earth's orbit allows agronomists to identify trends and issues early and track crop health in near-real time, including the detection of in-field variation with dense vegetation analysis and vitality alerts. With daily or weekly updates and field-level detail, farmers can respond quickly to changes in crop health and optimize variable rate application of chemicals to manage costs. Private satellite companies also help clients to monitor deforestation or pollution, limiting both reputational—and, more important, environmental—harm.

One of the pioneers in this industry, Planet,[15] deploys its own constellation of satellites to survey the entire landmass of the planet at three- to five-meter resolution on a daily basis. It then uses AI and machine learning to stitch together an essentially cloud-free, field-level snapshot that gives farmers, agronomists, and agribusinesses a new level of virtually real-time insight into what is happening on the ground—everything from crop productivity to water stress. This perspective on agricultural systems is invaluable, especially in less developed nations that lack their own imaging capabilities.

Extreme complexity is one factor that has caused the global agri-food system to lag other industries when it comes to leveraging data. In almost every industry and at every level, data is now a commodity with its own inherent value as an input. In most areas, the sheer size of these data sets has grown beyond the ability of human comprehension without the use of AI algorithms to help make sense of them. Stock trading once centered around crowded trading floors and timing decisions correctly based on new information as it became unevenly available. Today, some estimates suggest that up to 80 percent of equities markets trading volume is generated by black box trading algorithms that make decisions based on complex inputs from across the globe. The rule of thumb among commodities traders is that the agriculture market is ten times larger and ten times more complex than the finance industry, with much more variegated inputs from long-term weather forecasts to consumer meat demand to the growth rate of coconut plantations.

The global food system's complexity has recently been in evidence on several occasions. In 2010, Vladimir Putin ordered Russia to stop wheat exports after a crop failure threatened to increase the price of bread. His action threw global markets into chaos.[16] In 2019, flooding in the American Midwest had the same effect on global corn and soybean prices around the world.[17] Then 2020 brought a continued series of quasi-biblical-scale plagues: drought in Central America, locusts in east Africa, and fall armyworm in China. Each devastated a region in its own way, but understanding their effects in global markets requires both granular data and a way to extract meaningful data and patterns.

15. Zachary's venture firm DCVC is an investor in Planet, as well as Gro Intelligence, Pivot Bio, Zymergen, Sabanto, and Halter, all of which are also mentioned in this chapter.

16. Parfitt.

17. Kliesen and Bokun.

The same advances that brought financial markets from the trading floor to the data center can be used to make sense of enormously complex global agriculture and food interactions. Companies like Gro Intelligence are using AI to merge tens of millions of data sets comprising literally trillions of data points, creating sophisticated production and consumption forecasts and responsive models of agricultural supply and demand at the national or global level.

A broad spectrum of companies across agribusiness and finance, seed, and fertilizer companies upstream from farms—as well as food service, wholesale, and retail stores downstream from farms—use Gro's models to make key decisions about how to run their businesses.

Gro's AI-powered insight gives agribusinesses access to dozens of forecasts for key crops and markets—everything from soybeans in the United States to sorghum in Ethiopia and sugarcane in Brazil. These forecasts allow, for example, poultry, livestock, and dairy farmers to model feed prices, and provide traders with the insight they need to both align purchasing quantities with domestic and overseas demand and mitigate price risks through hedging strategies.

Gro also fuses its AI-driven insights into the global agriculture and food system with advanced climate change models, which underlie its financial indexes for factors like drought to help customers better manage climate risk. Banks and insurers can similarly use these indices and forecasts, including yields, commodity demand, and price forecasts, to assess creditworthiness and set policy premiums. Understanding regional finance and credit conditions helps financial institutions to properly price capital.

Closer to the consumer end of the spectrum, the food and beverage industry uses commodities such as corn, wheat, cocoa, sugar, coffee, and, of course, fresh produce to make much of what the world buys and eats. The ability to better predict yields and prices is just one advantage. It is now also possible to monitor the climate in real time to identify possible supply disruptions. Again, land suitability rankings help buyers decide where to develop, diversify, and solidify their supplier bases. Wholesale and retail sectors buyers can similarly analyze price trends and monitor growing conditions at key points of origin to forecast price disruptions days, if not weeks, in advance.

Overall, thanks to private sector efforts to both gather and harness data, it is increasingly possible to monitor and model the global food supply chain in real time and understand regional markets and situations in a world context. This offers unprecedented opportunities for efficiency gains across the vast complexity of agribusiness at all scales around the world.

From the Petroleum Century to the Microbe Century

Many people think of the computer industry as the defining business of the twentieth century, but when looking at the century in its entirety, the petrochemical industry shaped it much more profoundly, for better or worse. The burning of fossil fuels has contributed the lion's share of GHGs, but if Standard Oil had not commercialized kerosene production for the nascent petroleum industry, whales most likely would have been hunted to extinction for their oil, which was previously used for lighting.

Similarly, while the invention of petroleum-derived plastics created a huge pollution problem, it reduced the demand for elephant ivory for buttons and other small parts, which were incredibly difficult to make with existing materials. That those majestic animals still walk the Earth may be due, in part, to oil.

No industrial process has had a greater impact than Fritz Haber's discovery, in 1909, of a means to convert atmospheric nitrogen into ammonia for use as fertilizer. The Haber-Bosch Process has been called "the detonator of the population explosion."[18] The synthetic fertilizer produced this way nearly doubled global agricultural output, and it is the only reason our planet can support its current population.

Haber and Bosch may have staved off a Malthusian population calamity, but synthetic nitrogen fertilizer is far from perfect. Its production uses at least 2 percent of the world's total energy and contributes a whopping 7 percent of global GHG emissions.[19] In the field, synthetic nitrogen fertilizer's effectiveness is weather-dependent; if it rains too soon after the fertilizer application, much of it runs off, harming riparian, coastal, and ocean ecosystems, creating over five hundred ocean dead zones around the world.

One of the most bedeviling unintended consequences of the widespread use of synthetic nitrogen fertilizer is that its application inhibits the nitrogen-fixing properties of symbiotic bacteria that occur naturally in the soil microbiome. Farms have now become dependent on expensive synthetic fertilizers that have barely changed since their invention more than a hundred years ago. Breaking modern agriculture's expensive addiction to synthetic fertilizer would be a significant step toward sustainability, and there are several companies seeking to identify or create microbes to sustainably produce nitrogen for crops.

One such company is Pivot Bio, based in Berkeley, California. Using cutting-edge AI, its scientists analyzed trillions of interactions across thousands of soil samples to identify, culture, and create soil microbes that can be applied in-furrow

18. Smil.
19. Walling and Vaneeckhaute.

at the time of planting. As seeds germinate and roots grow, the microbes adhere to the roots, living in a symbiotic relationship with the plant. The microbes feed off the exudates emitted by the plant's roots and deliver nitrogen daily to the plant throughout its growth cycle. The farmer benefits from lower costs and increased yield. The environment benefits from plants, which are spoon-fed only the nitrogen they need; there is no fertilizer to break down into the atmosphere or run off into our waterways.

Completely replacing synthetic nitrogen fertilizer globally is years—likely decades—away. But even a modest proliferation of microbe-based approaches throughout the agricultural systems of industrialized nations will have a material positive impact on the sustainability of our food system.

Microbes may also help us solve environmental problems associated with another global addiction: palm oil.

This remarkably versatile oil is produced from the fruit of the oil palm tree. Over the last fifty years, palm oil has become a key ingredient in an astonishing number of foods, cosmetics, industrial products, and biofuels. As many as half of the products in a typical grocery store contain it. Demand has increased exponentially, to about 75 million tons per year—roughly 18 pounds for every person on earth![20]

What began as a crop that provided cash income for small farmers in developing nations across the tropics has grown into an environmental disaster. Oil palm plantations now occupy 44 million acres, more than half of which, until recently, were covered by mature tropical forest in Indonesia and Malaysia.[21] Oil palm plantations are replacing some of the world's most diverse ecosystems with relatively inert monocultures and destroying the habitat of critically endangered species. Such tropical deforestation contributes about 10 percent of greenhouse gases.[22] It is yet another crop that is fertilizer-intensive, so it also harms aquatic ecosystems.

Consumer awareness of these environmental harms is growing. But every year, more and more consumer products are imbued with this hard-to-replace ingredient. At this point, global industry cannot kick the collective palm oil habit, so an alternative supply of palm oil is needed instead, one that does not encourage slash-and-burn agriculture.

Fortunately, it is now possible to ferment identical or even superior "palm" oils using yeast, much the way beer is made. Manufacturing oil this way does not even require palm cultivation, so it entirely avoids deforestation and poses no harm to the endangered animals of the rain forest.[23]

20. Raghu.
21. International Union for the Conservation of Nature.
22. Union of Concerned Scientists.
23. DCVC is an investor in C16 Bio, which brews a sustainable alternative to palm oil from microbes.

While palm-free palm oil will certainly benefit our planet, we should be mindful that the palm oil economy has had a tremendous economic impact on the regions where palms are grown, lifting entire communities out of poverty. To protect livelihoods, one solution would be to ramp up oil fermentation in the same regions to help replace farm income and jobs.

In another dimension of the farm technology challenge, similar to how fertilizers have dramatically boosted farm yields, the adoption of modern pesticides has significantly reduced the crop losses to pests. However, the broad application of pesticides also harms beneficial insects like honeybees. An alternative means of protecting crops is to use microbial manufacturing to create new kinds of pest-resistance and pesticides that do not require broad application or that are less toxic to beneficial insects. Such pesticides use hitherto-unexplored protein compounds that occur naturally in the environment.

Zymergen is one such "biofacturer" based in Emeryville, California. It also uses fermentation, but not to create a single product like fermented palm oil. Rather it is working at the nexus of robotics, biotechnology, and advanced AI to build many new proprietary microbes that produce a broad range of new compounds and materials with useful and superior properties. Microbial manufacturing at this level uses intracellular biosensors, parallel genome editing technologies, robotics, and software to build and screen up to billions of micro-organisms, enzymatic pathways, and genetic interactions in parallel. The goal is to rapidly iterate new genomic designs to create the next generation of materials for the world. This approach produces compounds that are less harmful to the environment. It also uses as its starting point corn by-products and other sugars, rather than petroleum, which is equivalent to feedstock for many of current advanced materials reaching far across the global economy.

Robots to the Rescue

Back in the 1960s, when imagining the future, many people envisioned Rosie, the animated robot maid in *The Jetsons*. When that TV show was written, the integrated circuit was new, and the exponential power of Moore's Law was yet to be revealed. It was a common assumption that processing power would continue to be scarce and that households would have a single Rosie running the kitchen. Instead, millions of households today have a kitchen in which every appliance has a computer brain and many "micro-robots" each perform a single task, like baking bread or washing dishes.

The abundance of cheap processing power helped clarify that the actual hard problem is navigating the real world or having the flexibility to perform multiple or novel tasks. Indeed, robots like Rosie, with a human's versatile ability to manipulate objects in 3D, are still largely futuristic. In the agricultural field, the challenge of manipulating fragile crops is still daunting. So, for now, large segments of farming, like harvesting vegetables, still rely on a lot of "wetware"—humans.

That said, robots already make farming more productive. Even robots capable of only relatively simple and repetitive actions have been empowered by AI. For example, robotic sprayers can now use machine vision and neural networks to tell crop from weed and flower from leaf.

"See-and-spray" robotics platforms can spray herbicide on weeds and fertilizer on crops with precision similar to that of inkjet printers. Enabled by cutting-edge machine vision and AI, these robots evaluate billions of plants on every field. The precise targeting of see-and-spray systems improves sustainability and promises to cut chemical usage by 90 percent or more. By eliminating the need to treat entire fields with herbicides, this technology cuts farmers' costs, reduces surface runoff, and discourages the development of resistant weeds.

Some robotic breakthroughs have only indirect environmental impacts but show a lot of promise when it comes to farm economics in developed countries, where a shortage of workers is a chronic problem. Contracting out some tasks, such as seeding, to farming-as-a-service (FaaS) companies that offer robotic assistance on a per-acre basis offers a possible solution to labor shortages. Indeed, farmers' fields are excellent places to practice autonomous driving. At perhaps the peak of the autonomous vehicle hype cycle (circa 2018), John Deere executives were heard quipping, "We've been making autonomous vehicles since the 1980s," referring to the company's tractors.

A good example of an FaaS company is Sabanto, which operates autonomous tractors outfitted with GPS receivers, control boxes, and steering actuators to control the tractor and planter. Units are programmed to return to a predetermined area for seed and fuel when needed. The goal is to develop equipment that can operate with increasing autonomy, relying on only an off-site operator and one person on-site to deploy equipment, fuel tractors, and refill planters with seed. Less required labor means lower costs.

Although it is easy to see how an autonomous tractor can improve life for a farmer, it is less obvious how robotics might help a dairy farmer to herd her cows. At present, employees on horseback or all-terrain vehicles, assisted by herding dogs, can move hundreds of cattle. This is a labor-intensive process that is risky for both animals and people.

It need not be. Cows are trainable and quickly learn behaviors through the use of positive and negative reinforcement. Halter, a New Zealand–based startup, envisions a world in which every dairy cow wears a solar-powered, Wi-Fi–connected training collar that allows a single dairy farmer, working from her milking shed, to move herds from pasture to pasture or bring them to the barn without direct contact, all while avoiding watersheds and other environmentally sensitive areas.

These training collars can give farmers new insight into their herds, helping to eliminate the need for human—or herding dog—intervention in cattle management. Every cow is individually identified in an app on the farmer's smartphone, and each cow's unique location is known at all times. Farmers can "herd" animals with their phones, divide their cows into different herds, and move them around the farm by using the collar's sound and vibration to help a cow understand where it should go.

Beyond making things more efficient for farmers and protecting the local environment, this technology can also make life better for cattle. With greater insight into both the individual cow and the herd as a whole, farmers can quickly identify and support animals that may be lame or sick.

Some robotics solutions, like the ones that reduce chemical use, directly improve sustainability. But even solutions that simply improve farm efficiency and quality of life for farmers (and animals) can have an impact in an interconnected global market. For example, through 2030, small holdings of less than two hectares will continue to produce much of the food in the developing world. For those small farmers, investing in new technology is much harder, but commercial innovations may ease access to capital equipment. Hello Tractor, a company operating in Kenya and Nigeria, has been described as "Uber for tractors," allowing small farms to book a tractor for short periods through a smartphone app. This, in turn, allows farmers who could not make a return on such a capital investment from their own land to earn money from these tractors which would otherwise sit idle.

Farms in the developed world face chronic labor shortages so robotic help is often welcome. But some people fear that increased mechanization and automation will displace farmworkers in the developing world where employment is already scarce. We do not dismiss this fear, but other industries that are further along the curve have often found that AI and advanced automation do not eliminate jobs as much as change them. Repetitive, rote work is automated, leaving humans to focus on management and further innovation, which further increases farm productivity.

Despite the promise of robotics, a cautionary note beyond job markets is also warranted. Agricultural technology research and development is often understandably focused on the largest commercial crops, such as corn, wheat, and soybeans. These crops are often processed and become ingredients in foods with less-than-optimal nutritional profiles. The EAT-Lancet Commission recently published a report concluding that "a diet rich in plant-based foods and with fewer animal source foods confers both improved health and environmental benefits."[24] Following the commission's dietary recommendations would lower food costs for people in the developed world, but more than 1.5 billion people in less developed nations could not afford to replace the sugars, saturated fats, starchy vegetables, and refined grains in their current diet with healthier vegetables, fruits, whole grains, legumes, nuts, and unsaturated oils. Technology that has the effect of further lowering the relative cost calories from less healthy ingredients may have an adverse impact on the "healthy" part of the HERS goal.

Our Meat Problem

The first step in solving a problem is admitting you have one—and the world definitely has a meat problem. Even domestic pets have a meat problem. If all of the pets in the United States were counted as a standalone country, they would be the world's fifth-largest country in terms of meat consumption![25]

Per the World Resources Institute, beef requires twenty times more land and emits twenty times more GHG emissions per gram of edible protein than common plant proteins, such as beans and other legumes.[26] The majority of the world's native grasslands are already heavily utilized for livestock production, so incremental beef demand increases pressure on forests. According to the Food and Agriculture Organization of the United Nations, livestock sector growth has been a prime driver of the massive deforestation in Brazil in recent years.[27]

The United States and other developed nations consume far more meat per capita than do less developed countries, but as urbanization continues and average living standards climb, the world's appetite for meat is increasing. Between 1965 and 2015, per capita meat consumption in developing nations tripled from about 22 pounds per year to more than 66 pounds.[28]

Thankfully, cultured meats or plant-based meat alternatives show real promise. The company Beyond Meat was a revolution for a number of reasons. Primarily, it demonstrated that a non-pharmaceutical biological product could sustain a robust public market valuation (at $1.5 billion, it was one of the most successful IPOs of 2019). Beyond Meat's revenues have nearly tripled every year since 2016, evidencing the public's willingness to vote with their pocketbooks. Additionally, it paved the way for myriad other meat alternatives, such as Impossible Foods, to gain broader adoption.

While the market for cultured or plant-based meat alternatives is growing,

24. Willett, Rockström, and others.
25. Okin.
26. Waite, Searchinger, and Ranganathan.
27. Alexandratos, Gürkan, Mielke, and others.
28. Ibid.

between now and 2030, the vast majority of meat will still come from raising and slaughtering animals. Limiting the environmental impact of raising animals, especially ruminants, now forms a global imperative. This should begin with beef production, which produces the most GHG per ounce of protein.

Methane emissions are a major contributor to the GHG intensity of beef production. Methane is relatively short-lived in the atmosphere, but it is extremely potent, trapping up to eighty times more heat than carbon dioxide over a twenty-year period. More than one-third of all the atmospheric methane resulting from human activity is produced by dairy and beef herds as a by-product of the gut bacteria that enable cattle to break down their food.[29] Because cattle are ruminants, they mostly belch that methane out.

Reducing that natural methane release presents one of the most immediate opportunities for reducing the cattle industry's GHG emissions. One solution is found, perhaps surprisingly, in seaweed. *Asparagopsis armata* is native to New Zealand and Australia, and *Asparagopsis taxiformis* grows off the coast of Hawaii, where it is an ingredient in the traditional fish preparation called *poké*. Both contain a small amount of bromoform, which is a caustic chemical in its pure form, often used as a lab reagent. (It is similar to chloroform, made famous in spy novels.)

As it turns out, bromoform at the levels found in *Asparagopsis* disrupts the enzymes of the cattle's gut microbes that produce methane gas as waste during digestion. In field trials in Australia and the United States carried out by CSIRO, University of California, Davis, and the University of Pennsylvania, an *Asparagopsis*-based feed additive reduced methane emissions by up to 99 percent in beef and dairy cattle as well as sheep, with no adverse effects to livestock, their products, or the environment.[30] The bromoform-rich diet appears to increase feed conversion, so adding bromoform actually lowers costs to farmers. (A way to think of the increased conversion efficiency is that more of the carbon goes into growing the cow's body and less escapes to the atmosphere as methane.)

Growing seaweed also offers mild environmental benefits. It reduces ocean acidification and absorbs about five times as much carbon dioxide as land plants on a per-pound basis. However, only small amounts of *Asparagopsis* are required for the feed additive process, so even at industrial scale, the GHG benefits of seaweed cultivation would be dwarfed by the impact of materially reducing the one-third of humanity's methane emissions.

29. Borunda.
30. Commonwealth Scientific and Industrial Research Organization.

Incremental Improvements for a More Equitable, Resilient, and Sustainable Future

While initially targeted at industrialized markets, many of the technologies described in this chapter will improve food security and global environmental sustainability no matter where they are implemented. Substantive reductions in GHG emissions anywhere in the world will slow the rate of climate change for everyone.

But the reality of technological advancement is that industrialized countries typically develop new technologies that are not exported to developing ones until costs decrease over time. However, the populations in the regions with the most food insecurity, especially Sub-Saharan Africa, are on track to increase at an annualized rate of greater than 2 percent for the rest of the decade.[31] To do the most good and have the biggest impact on agricultural sustainability, it is imperative for these new technologies to be made quickly accessible to farmers in the developing world. We are hopeful that many of the technologies discussed above become "leapfrog technologies" in the same way that developing economies went straight to mobile phones without first having extensive landline networks. Many of the same countries now have more sophisticated mobile money and payments systems than some industrialized countries.

Business and policy leaders have personal responsibilities, too. Companies cannot focus solely on innovation at the expense of public education and government engagement. Like other science-based innovations, these approaches offer real progress toward addressing some of the most pressing technical challenges facing food supply chains. At the same time, where food comes from is a personal and delicate subject. Without taking the important steps to educate governments and listen to the public, innovative companies risk hitting regulatory hurdles or consumer skepticism. Meanwhile, government leaders need to do their part, as well. When new agricultural technologies arrive, policymakers need to ensure adversely affected regions are able either to take advantage of the new breakthroughs or to bridge to economic opportunities in more sustainable industries.

The global agricultural and food system is remarkably complex. In many ways, it is an ecology as much as an industry. But that complexity means there are countless points where incremental improvements can produce massive positive impacts without having to remake an entire system with huge inertia. The technologies we have discussed, and many other advances, are ushering in a future of healthier nutrition that can be more equitable, resilient, and sustainable for all.

---

31. *Economist* Special Report.

References

Alexandratos, Nikos, Ali Gürkan, Myles Mielke, and others. 2003. "World Agriculture: Towards 2015/2030. An FAO Perspective." www.fao.org/3/y4252e/y4252e05b.htm.

Barrett, Christopher B., Tim Benton, Jessica Fanzo, and others. 2020. "Socio-technical Innovation Bundles for Agri-Food Systems Transformation: Report of the International Expert Panel on Innovations to Build Sustainable, Equitable, Inclusive Food Value Chains." Cornell Atkinson Center for Sustainability and Springer Nature. www.nature.com/documents/Bundles_agrifood_transformation.pdf.

Borunda, Alejandra. 2019. "Methane, Explained." *National Geographic*, January 23.

Brierley, Andrew S., and Michael J. Kingsford. 2009. "Impacts of Climate Change on Marine Organisms and Ecosystems." *Current Biology*, v. 19, no. 14.

Commonwealth Scientific and Industrial Research Organization (author uncredited). 2021. "FutureFeed." www.csiro.au/en/research/animals/livestock/futurefeed.

Dong, Jinlong, Nazim Gruda, Shu K. Lam, Xun Li, and Zengqiang Duan. 2018. "Effects of Elevated CO2 on Nutritional Quality of Vegetables: A Review." *Frontiers in Plant Science*, August 15.

Economist Special Report (author uncredited). 2020. "Africa's Population Will Double by 2050." March 28.

Fisher, Jon. 2014. "Global Agriculture Trends: Are We Actually Using Less Land?" *Cool Green Science* (blog), January 18. https://blog.nature.org/science/2014/06/18/global-agriculture-land-sustainability-deforestation-foodsecurity/.

International Union for the Conservation of Nature (author uncredited). 2018. "Issues Brief: Palm Oil and Biodiversity." www.iucn.org/resources/issues-briefs/palm-oil-and-biodiversity.

IPCC. 2014. *Climate Change 2014: Mitigation of Climate Change.* Contribution of Working Group III to the Fifth Assessment Report of the Intergovernmental Panel on Climate Change. Edited by Edenhofer, O., R. Pichs-Madruga, Y. Sokona, and others. Cambridge University Press.

Kliesen, Kevin, and Kathryn Bokun. 2019. "Crop Prices and Flooding: Will 2019 Be a Repeat of 1993?" www.stlouisfed.org/on-the-economy/2019/june/crop-prices-flooding-2019-repeat-1993.

Kretchmer, Harry. 2020. "Global Hunger Fell for Decades, but It's Rising Again." www.weforum.org/agenda/2020/07/global-hunger-rising-food-agriculture-organization-report/.

Montanarella, Luca, Dan Pennock, and Neil McKenzie. 2015. "Status of the World's Soil Resources." www.fao.org/3/a-i5126e.pdf.

New York City Economic Development Corporation, NYC Mayor's Office of Recovery & Resiliency (author uncredited). 2016. "Five Borough Food Flow: 2016 New York City Food Distribution & Resiliency Study Results." www1.nyc.gov/assets/foodpolicy/downloads/pdf/2016_food_supply_resiliency_study_results.pdf.

Nigatu, Gettachew, and James Hansen. 2019. "Low Growth in Corn Yields Has Dragged Down Sub-Saharan African Corn Production." www.ers.usda.gov/amber-waves/2019/november/low-growth-in-corn-yields-has-dragged-down-sub-saharan-african-corn-production/.

Okin, Gregory S. 2017. "Environmental Impacts of Food Consumption by Dogs and Cats." *PLOS One*, vol. 12, no. 8 (August 2), https://doi.org/10.1371/journal.pone.0181301.

Parfitt, Tom. 2010. "Vladimir Putin Bans Grain Exports as Drought and Wildfires Ravage Crops." *Guardian*, August 5.

Raghu, Anuradha. 2017. "We Each Consume 17 Pounds of Palm Oil a Year." *Bloomberg*, May 17.

Savage, Isadora. 2019. "10 Facts About Farming in Africa." https://borgenproject.org/10-facts-about-farming-in-africa/.

Smil, Vaclav. 1999. "Detonator of the Population Explosion." *Nature*, v. 400.

Spiegel, Bill. 2020. "How David Hula Grows 600-Bushel-Plus Corn." *Successful Farming*, January 6.

Stein, Emil Vollset, Emily Goren, Chun-Wei Yuan, and others. 2020. "Fertility, Mortality, Migration, and Population Scenarios for 195 Countries and Territories from 2017 to 2100: A Forecasting Analysis for the Global Burden of Disease Study." *Lancet*, v. 396, no. 10258.

Union of Concerned Scientists (author uncredited). 2013. "Fact Sheet: Palm Oil and Global Warming." www.ucsusa.org/sites/default/files/legacy/assets/documents/global_warming/palm-oil-and-global-warming.pdf.

Waite, Richard, Tim Searchinger, and Janet Ranganathan. 2019. "6 Pressing Questions About Beef and Climate Change, Answered." www.wri.org/blog/2019/04/6-pressing-questions-about-beef-and-climate-change-answered.

Walling, Eric, and Céline Vaneeckhaute. 2020. "Greenhouse Gas Emissions from Inorganic and Organic Fertilizer Production and Use: A Review of Emission Factors and Their Variability." *Journal of Environmental Management*, vol. 276 (December).

Willett, Walter, Johan Rockström, and others. 2019. "Summary Report of the EAT-Lancet Commission." https://eatforum.org/content/uploads/2019/07/EAT-Lancet_Commission_Summary_Report.pdf.

World Resources Institute (uncredited, undated). "Sources of Eutrophication." www.wri.org/our-work/project/eutrophication-and-hypoxia/sources-eutrophication.

FOUR

Too Cheap to Meter
The Promise of Unstored Solar Power

Vijay Modi

lectricity provision in many countries remains a challenge. An even greater challenge is to mesh its use with development objectives. The year 2020 saw power purchase agreements for large utility-scale solar power generation reach prices as low as 1.5 cents per unit (one kWh) of electricity. At comparable scale of installation, 200 MW and above, Ethiopia obtained a power purchase agreement at 2.5 cents per unit. Solar photovoltaic modules are sold by the capacity of the module in watts; a module capacity range of 250 to 400 watts is common, and hence a large 250-MW capacity power plant (i.e., 250 million watts) would need 1 million of a 250-watt module. A 250-watt solar module capacity can produce anywhere from 1 kWh to 1.5 kWh per day during hours of sunshine. It is quite conceivable that at a much smaller scale of, say, 10 kW to 100 kW, capacity for each system installed (i.e., where 30 to 300 modules are installed in each system, if thousands of systems are procured and contracted for installation), could achieve a price point of 10 cents for electricity delivered to a home. This price would include operating costs as well as amortization of capital through loans at concessional terms. A provocative and bold proposition is that 30 kWh/month of daytime power could be made nearly free to the consumer. Consumers could be asked to pay the higher cost of power at other times. The combination would make power universally affordable. The approach would combine low costs with unmet larger power uses—an alternative or supplement to providing public subsidies for grid extensions that the poor would hardly use beyond basic evening and nighttime needs.

Our experience shows consumer willingness to use daytime solar electric supply if the price is right, and a willingness to coordinate power use schedules among a small group to ensure high utilization. This makes possible the prospect of a programmatic installation rollout after communities develop a local management structure, identify land on which to locate solar panels, and show willingness to contribute installation labor.

Could one potentially break through electricity cost barriers in rural areas with higher adoption of electric power for everything from irrigation, processing, cooking, commerce, drinking water, battery charging, and daytime thermal comfort requirements? To do this, one could imagine a complementary community-centric public-infrastructure provision approach that leverages local labor to install hardware and/or wire, as opposed to a commercial approach of building solar home systems best suited for evening/nighttime residential consumption. Systems of this kind may not be suitable for every community in a country. But an approach that frees itself of the constraints of existing transmission and distribution wire could allow early prioritization using community self-identification, commitment, contribution, and initiative. Community ownership and management is difficult to scale, and yet we have seen that this is not impossible if well thought through, perhaps with greater ownership residing with women. This initial entry point could be followed by a pay-as-you-go service for evening. Higher daytime consumption would be a down payment for the development benefits of such low-cost power.

The Revolution in Utility-Scale Solar without Storage

In 2020, the actual cost of electricity at a large utility-scale solar power generation plant fell below US$1/watt installed, comprising the solar modules themselves and what is called balance of system (BOS) costs. Note that at an installed cost of US$1/watt capacity, it becomes possible to supply one unit of electricity for 2.5 cents. The electricity is only produced when the sun shines, of course, but that electricity produced is competitive with the lowest-cost hydropower, cheaper than nuclear power and even coal-fired power plants. This transformative threshold, anticipated for decades, is not just an achievement for the solar industry, it is an achievement for humanity as the electricity is also clean.

With the exponential growth in production of solar photovoltaic (PV) modules, each time production doubled, the costs came down by 25 percent on average over a span of forty years, as reported by the Fraunhofer Institute. The term BOS is worth clarifying. When installations are utility-scale and designed to inject power into the electric grid, these costs generally do not include the cost of providing firm power—a term or trade for assured power over some time period. Capital equipment costs alone do not reflect the low prices of electricity produced. One also needs to lower the soft costs: financing costs that come down with use of proven technology and past experience and technical expertise, stable currency and exchange rates, import and transport logistics, and the cost of labor. It is these soft costs that meant that, as recently as five years ago, a solar power purchase agreement in a developing economy in Sub-Saharan Africa could have been 5 to 7 cents/kWh higher than that in a developed economy with a similar solar resource. The common explanations were around how developing economies experience higher costs of financing, worse inflation and exchange rate volatility, a poor and uncertain enabling policy environment, with a risk of contractual terms not being met. There was also a higher off-take risk in developing countries if the receiving end grid infrastructure was disrupted. So, a cause for celebration is that through a program such as Scaling Solar of the International Finance Corporation (IFC), the electric utility of a land-locked country such as Ethiopia, signed an agreement to buy power from a 250 MW utility-scale installation at a price point of 2.56 cents, or just 1 cent higher than a price point in places that combine financial stability with low costs of capital and labor. This dramatic reduction in the premiums in Sub-Saharan Africa through the IFC program demonstrates that, indeed, the soft costs can be managed, even though it is not necessarily easy to do so. These price points now offer a historic opportunity in Sub-Saharan Africa to bring nearly unconstrained low-cost supply when the sun shines.

The Emerging Revolution in Utility-Scale Solar with Some Storage

Until recently, utility-scale solar did not include the costs of battery storage. Just in the last year or two, some contracts are now for solar power with some storage at the power plant, to increase the ability to supply firm power at least through some hours of the evening and night. For example, the first phase of the Los Angeles Department of Water and Power (LADWP) solar plus storage PPA included 200 MW of solar generation capacity with 400 MWh of storage. In the case of Los Angeles, as in most other settings, these arrangements allow one to reduce the dependence on electricity from higher cost and/or higher emission gas power that must otherwise complement the daytime-only nature of solar power. The "solar with some storage" paradigm avoids the kind of sharp fluctuations in power that can occur even with the passing of a cloud; allows one to modulate what one draws from the solar power plant as electricity demand changes; and extends access to solar power into the evening hours of five p.m. to ten p.m.— that is, beyond the hours when the solar energy output starts to fade.

A good representation of the LADWP system is to imagine that for each 1 kW of solar power one has 2 kWh of battery storage. Let us say that 1 kW produces 6 kWh per day, of which 4 kWh is used during the day between about seven a.m.

and five p.m., while the other 2 kWh can be stored in the associated 2 kWh battery in order to be accessible from five p.m. to ten p.m. This allows about a third of the consumption to be in the evening. Given the costs and battery lifetimes today, it works out that the stored evening power in this arrangement is nearly four times as expensive as the daytime power.

In wealthier economies of the world, large interconnected electric grid networks can mix solar and wind power with sources that are capable of steady power delivery, such as nuclear, hydropower, gas, coal, or oil-fired generation. Such large networks allow one to overcome two hurdles; they make it possible to avoid expensive battery storage and they leverage aggregation of the electricity demands of millions of diverse customers, which makes it much easier to forecast the aggregate draw of power as it fluctuates through the day and seasons. In mixed systems, one can achieve a combination of reasonable cost of power and very reliable 24/7 electricity supply regardless of days without much sunshine. In the absence of other sources and solar plus storage, costs rapidly multiply. One cannot achieve both reasonable cost and reliable 24/7 access from solar and storage alone.

If you do not have the ability to build ecologically friendly hydropower, if geothermal resources are not present, if you do not have low-cost domestic natural gas, you might consider a grid of solar plus ample storage. You could also consider a combination of solar and wind power with some storage and diesel power for occasional backup needs.

The reason we are wedded to the solar plus storage combination for our discussion, is that it highlights the challenges of power generation in the absence of other low-cost resources. The paradigm is useful when we consider local grids that cannot easily integrate most other resources. Wind, hydro, nuclear, geothermal, natural gas, and coal-fired power are at too large a generation capacity to be viable as inputs into small-scale local grids. There is an option of including some liquid fuel (petrol, diesel, propane, or biofuel) generation, but, regardless, most such grids would end up with bulk electricity costs exceeding 50 cents/kWh.

There is another option: adopt solar with ample storage to obtain a reasonable but not complete reliability and accessibility. This way, disruptions from power could be limited to couple of hours a week and no more than a couple of days at a time, occasionally, during the year. In areas with good regular solar supply, the impact of power disruptions can be minimized.

Imagine: Utility-Scale Solar with Ample Storage without Other Energy Sources

Imagine a thought experiment, where the only power on a local rural grid in a developing country would be from this LADWP style mix of solar and battery storage alone, one of the many scenarios that engineers contemplate for a future without fossil fuels. The system would be much smaller in capacity than the LADWP system, but the solar and storage mix would be similar. To pull this off beyond just the engineering, some conditions must be met. For every kW of solar capacity, a full sunny day might produce 6 kWh of electricity, and this must be consumed in a roughly uniform electricity draw by the grid between seven a.m. and ten p.m. If there was a lot more use than 4 kWh during the day, there would not be as much to store as needed in the evening, and if the expected evening time use exceeds 2 kWh, then there would be inadequate amount in storage. In such conditions, even a single cloudy day that produced only 3 kWh instead of 6 kWh would make the entire arithmetic go awry. Hence an electric system that looks like the LADWP system has significant challenges, unless there are other supplemental power sources or a lot more storage.

If one wants to allow for some limited variations through the day in supply and demand, such as managing without disruptions even if faced with two cloudy days in a row, then every kW of solar modules would need perhaps 10 kWh of battery storage, instead of 2 kWh. This would significantly improve the probability of reliable power delivery through the year. Let us call this paradigm "solar with ample storage," ample enough to accommodate two very cloudy days in a row. Microgrids, local grids do exploit this paradigm, obviating the need for large distribution networks in favor of a local grid with a capacity that would be commensurate with a small community need as opposed to that of a large city or a region in a country. It is the larger proportion of storage, associated circuitry, and the shorter lifetime of the battery (compared to lifetime of solar modules) that, in turn, would make the cost of such electricity as high as ten times that of unstored solar power. Since commercial microgrids must also incorporate metering and revenue collection, the retailed price multiplier can be as high as twenty times now. It is this multiplier that must be kept low in order to benefit from low-cost solar.

Now Imagine: A Local-Scale or Home-Scale Solar with Ample Storage Approach

If you do not have large networked electric grids that reach every home, business, or farm, and the cost of extending the wire from that grid to your home or your farm is high, then you must rely on a local grid or your own private solution. The most common private solution today is solar with ample storage.

There are challenges with your own private solution: the electricity requirements vary over the year and your needs grow over a few years. There are diseconomies of small scale, in that an installation of a 25-watt capacity is 10 million times smaller than an installation of a 250 MW power plant.

In spite of these limitations, packaged home-scale solar with ample storage (also called solar home systems or SHS, for short, here) have seen dramatic consumer adoption levels. They meet the basic needs of a home, for now, for affordability reasons. These basic needs are evening and nighttime electricity requirements to power lighting, information (for example, TV or radio) and communication (such as a mobile device, internet) appliances.

We will also see below why these systems deliver power at prices in excess of US$1/kWh. Poor households can afford only a few kWh of consumption at these prices, but for those whose electricity needs grow over time, or for those who need much larger consumption, the price point can be a severe constraint. Yet, these systems are popular because they can be put in place quickly without major scale diseconomies. Solar PV technology is "divisible" in a way no other energy source is today. Divisibility implies that, in principle, one 250-watt solar module[1] costs the same to manufacture and has the same efficiency as each of the 1 million panels that will make up the 250 MW solar power plant in Ethiopia. It is this unique feature that has already brought light to millions of homes without electricity. This option, however, does need ample storage.

Reality: Home-Scale Solar with Ample Storage

A single 250-watt solar module would generously allow one to use several LED lights, a TV, a computer, and even a small refrigerator. Certainly not an air conditioner. When one includes ample battery storage, one-time upfront retail prices, including installation, approach US$1,500. This is well beyond the means of the poor, even without counting future battery replacement costs. This high first-cost price point has discouraged the adoption of packaged systems at this scale. It remains a technological opportunity to crack in the future. Coincidentally, a conventional grid extension could also cost the utility a similar sum. (Of course, when a utility installs the identical solar module without storage at a utility-scale solar plant, the cost of installation today is from US$150 to US$200.)

---

1. Just in a handful of years, mass-manufactured full-size solar modules that were commonly 250 watts are now 300 to 400 watts. They are about the size of an entrance door in one's house.

The first cost limitation has meant that commercially sold solar home systems (SHS) for homes of the poor are more likely eight to ten times smaller than 250W. Thanks to divisibility, it is possible to have your own personal solar panel. Divisibility also implies that you can obtain electricity without utility wire. So, SHS have been adopted by the millions with an output of a few units of electricity per month, just enough for a few lights and enough to charge a cell phone. Even if they are larger, with the costs of batteries, electronics, and packaging, combined with unit costs of procurement, logistics, and installation, the cost of this solar power now rises to 50 cents or more per unit of electricity—that is, nearly twenty times the cost of bulk unstored solar power at utility scale. Add to this the costs of collecting payments, risk of default, and customer acquisition, and what started out as 2.5 cents/kWh of unstored solar power becomes at least US$1/kWh when retailed to a customer.

Given how important even a small basic amount of electricity is, and the lack of other options, the poor have been willing to pay a high price per kWh for solar with ample storage for single homes. Social enterprises have tried to raise capital from those keen to support a good cause. They have worked hard to add reliably sourced, high quality products, and combined them with good-quality efficient lights and appliances. A fuller description of solar home systems is included at the end of the chapter.

Combining the Divisibility of Solar, Minimizing Storage, and Ensuring Higher Utilization: Can We Come Closer to Utility-Scale Economics?

While for small household loads, the high cost of battery-backed power remains attractive, it is not so for the much larger loads that power small industry or agriculture or even household cooking. Industry or agriculture must compete in a global marketplace. Cooking must compete with free firewood and the supposedly low opportunity-cost of time, generally that of women and girls, used in collecting firewood.

The larger electrical loads could enjoy some economies of scale in ancillary hardware, as opposed to the laptop-size solar panels. Can such an approach maximize the use of solar electricity when the sun shines, by connecting multiple customers to the same supply source? Can one use smaller storage or possibly no storage?

A Practical Experience in Senegal

There is no magical technological solution. But at the scale of tens (and could be hundreds) of 250-watt panels, as opposed to one panel or a million panels, we were able to exploit a dimension of this missing middle when working with farmers in Senegal five years ago. We demonstrated the potential to achieve a retail price point of 20 cents/kWh if attractive financing terms could be reached. This price point includes the cost of capital. Note that with small US$300 to US$500 grants per household that we had access to, and which paid for distribution wire, at today's solar power costs, this would drop to 10 cents/kWh. The farmers were willing to shift their larger loads to daytime hours in order to benefit from the lower price points of daytime solar power without a utility grid connection.

An agronomist colleague of mine had introduced me to onion farmers that were otherwise hand-irrigating their small patches of land, mostly lifting buckets of water from small, shallow wells. A handful of enterprising farmers were using gasoline-powered pumps at a cost equivalent of US$1/kWh, not an attractive proposition for poor farmers. I was told by the farmers that they could make significantly more money by putting a greater fraction of their small land holdings to onions, getting better yields, and doing two crops of onions per year rather than one, if lower-cost power was available. Listening to farmers was key to truly understanding their operational and financial constraints. They were willing to make their own investments in seeds, fertilizer, and drip lines that would save water and energy. The price points of battery-backed solar were not attractive to them, and alternative price points had to be lower than those from diesel and gasoline.

There was the option of requiring a large immediate investment from either the farmer or the utility or the government to extend utility wire to their farms. Utilities have not fully appreciated these farmer energy demands and lack the directives that would encourage them to run such wire. They do not see a strong likelihood of recouping capital costs, so view rural power provision as a losing proposition rather than a great investment in development. Regardless, the grid extension option was not immediately available to the Senegalese farmers I met. Their preference, if they had a choice, was to irrigate fields in the early morning or late evening. There might have been agronomic reasons for this, and a few also did side jobs in the daytime so could only work on their fields in the morning or evening. But they were willing to adapt and make some trade-offs if lower-cost power could be had.

One option we considered was to imagine every farmer having their own private solar panel(s) and pump. Individual systems have tremendous benefits accruing from personal stake and control. Such systems have flourished in some settings. But the main challenge with individual systems in the absence of batteries has been poor utilization. Unused power leads to higher cost. We also learned that it was not easy for individual farmers to prove their creditworthiness to a bank, so they could not finance a personal system. Individual systems that are mobile and low cost sometimes have even greater value for farmers whose power needs are sporadic or at multiple locations. One should not discount the value of a small liquid fuel (at present gasoline or diesel) engine powered pump that can be purchased for a low capital cost. Such a solution would be ideally suited if the power needs are for a single four-month season, or if power is only needed for a couple of times a week, or if one needs to move the system for multiple farm plots. So while a liquid fuel engine is inefficient and expensive to operate, one would not want to close the door on such choices just because solar could be attractive in the settings described here.

Through farmer dialogue, the approach we took for the specific Senegal setting was to work closely with farmer groups. They were already collaborating among themselves for marketing and sourcing of seeds and other agriculture inputs. The group would, in effect, become the owner-operator of a shared system, ensuring financing, maintenance, and payments for the power utilized. They certainly needed a way to ensure accountability of individual farmer electricity use and payments—who used how much and what they owed. They opted for a shared system that would minimize the need for storage and ensure high utilization. Buried wire from the shared solar installation ran to each individual pump, and the longest wire-run was no more than three hundred meters (a thousand feet) to allow use of a wire diameter that kept costs low. Farmers were willing to internally schedule loads in order to match the solar supply curve, thereby minimizing unused power. This is an extreme version of flexibility and demand response that a smart grid of the future is supposed to enable. The Senegal farm group approach may not be applicable everywhere, but the experience provided some lessons from this lean infrastructure and low resource setting that are summarized below.

Some Lessons Learned

First, for income generating electricity loads such as smallholder irrigation, farmers are willing to adapt their demand to timing of solar radiation and solar electric supply.

Second, the price point of supply was critical to farmers, and a battery-storage based system would have priced them out. They were willing to trade the benefits of lower price points for the inconvenience that came with timing their use with the sun and with the constraints of sharing and scheduling power off-take with others.

Third, they wanted to leverage the low cost of submersible AC pumps as opposed to far more expensive DC pumps, even though DC pumps are more efficient. This meant higher electrical power draw when the pump operates, but using three phase AC power reduced wire sizes and made it easier for pumps to start even with partial sunshine.

Fourth, while utilization was high during cropping periods, the fact is that there was no immediate use for power for three months of the year, so an annualized utilization rate of higher than 50 percent was difficult to achieve, based on irrigation loads alone. Note that this could be different with a diversity of daytime loads beyond irrigation, the key being willingness to schedule loads.

Fifth, allowing farmer groups to make payments for pump-hours they utilized, on the day they used the pump, allowed mimicking the payment schedule for petrol or diesel fuel with which they were familiar. A shared system also allowed large anchor farmers to initiate a system, while permitting much smaller farmers to also join.

Sixth, such high-return irrigation opportunities for horticulture do not arise everywhere in the farming landscape. So early and rapidly assessed field data is of great value. We have the possibility today to combine infrastructure, agriculture, and water sector data to leverage opportunities, but also avoid the environmental disasters that groundwater pumping can lead to if done without attention to sustainable water extraction.

Seventh, shared systems at scale need coordination and local organization structure, and require direct lending either to user groups or to private sector that, in turn, provides a service. So, it is important to tailor the specific institutional details to each context. Indeed, individual systems would also play a major role. Specifically, individual systems that could move among locations would also provide value. Solar systems are, however, least suitable for this purpose.

In the case of the onion farmers (there were other horticulture crops as well) we worked with, a 7-kW system shared by seven farmers proved to be a good combination, even though subsequent use suggested sharing among three or four farmers could be viable as well. This system added US$300 to US$500 per farmer in costs for wire extension, but this was offset by an ability to reduce the installed solar capacity by half, to just 1 kW per farmer, compared to the 2 kW per farmer system that sole ownership would have required. The shared system allowed farmers to leverage a single large low-cost variable frequency drive (VFD) that enabled pump operation at part load, justified the higher cost of mechanical devices that allow the solar panel to track the sun, and let farmers spread the cost of managing a prepaid payment system and maintenance over multiple farmers. It turned out that, in the setting we worked in, a cluster of no more than seven farmers was about the right scale to balance the increased cost of wire with the savings from higher utilization. These tradeoffs will depend upon many factors. Certainly, the cost of wire and diversity/nature of loads is a big factor. Utilization and sizing will depend upon crop-specific water requirements, how many crops per year, seasonality of demand, proximity of farmers to each other, well depths, and sustainable water yields.

My observation was that initial adopters were those with the potential to expand high-revenue horticulture crops, local water access, and an assured market for the produce, with transport services available when needed. The farmers continue to use the systems. Over the last five years, they progressively added a larger fraction of land to higher value crops.

The Senegal experience has some broader lessons for the need to combine energy and agricultural expertise in delivering rural power. There is a need to identify viable locations where farmer clusters could leverage existing or future water access and market access and produce higher value crops. This identification could be done by regional agriculture units but strengthened with tools and support at the national level to provide advice on appropriate seeds, soil fertility management techniques, and inputs in addition to energy.

Farmers also need to be assured that energy solutions are now available at much lower price points than petrol or diesel power. Energy providers need to communicate the fact that price points of 10 to 20 cents per kWh are possible if power demands are tens of kWh per month per farmer, even for as few as seven months of the year. If the demand is higher, the unit price of power could potentially be even lower. Farmers should be prepared to adapt their practices to the time when energy supply is most available, and, in turn, the optimal energy infrastructure must adapt to realities of land parcels, well locations, and water constraints.

Many agriculture or agriculture-related applications do not lend themselves to high utilization of solar power when installed at a single fixed location. Indeed, in these situations the use of proven low-capital cost engines that burn liquid hydrocarbons, such as petrol and diesel, to operate pumps should not be discounted as an option even at high operating cost. They are much easier to move around and are well adapted to periodic use. They are seen already in use by individual enterprising farmer (or several who share among themselves) that is willing to use high-cost fuel for a higher reward from horticulture or other cash crops. Such farmers played an essential role in allowing us to identify the enterprising ones who created the anchor or nucleus of larger shared solar systems in Senegal.

Power that Is Too Cheap to Meter

The nature of solar supply is such that one might want to explore the costs and benefits to society of a provocative but as yet untested proposition: If we provide a daily allotment of scheduled power between, say, eleven a.m. and two p.m., at zero cost, for the first five years of operation, to promote safe daytime electric cooking, then the development outcomes of that free power could exceed the costs. The big question is whether such free daytime power would completely flip the equation of how electricity is first used. Currently, cooking is probably the lowest rung on the household electricity ladder—after lighting, television, and electronics. It could be the last because it is expensive, it is not adapted to local practices, lacks appropriate appliances, or scheduled daytime power is simply not convenient for cooking. Would it alleviate the drudgery of cooking for at least one meal, perhaps not every day of the year but at least on days when the sun is shining? We do not know, but this should not be terribly difficult to determine. The poor are resourceful, women particularly so. Women have shown the ability to adapt to seasonally varying biomass availability and incomes. When it allows, they already juggle limited budgets to switch fuels between cooking tasks.

The hypothesis is that the poor will be willing to utilize the nearly free or free electricity when the sun shines, at a much higher level of consumption and with a much higher overall system utilization. We would need to carry out significant educational outreach to allow the shift from deeply rooted cultural traditions regarding when and how to cook.

Perhaps daytime productive uses of power could be provided at slight margins above cost recovery terms. This would still be attractive, compared to other options the poor have. Households would have the ability to invest in their own backup battery to accommodate evening power, whose use could grow organically as limited household budgets allow investments in storage and appliances. Batteries for lighting use alone would not be a huge burden for a poor household, due to advances in LEDs, but perhaps other appliance use at night would require added household investments.

If one can leverage the creditworthiness and the social capital of the poor, ensure the same de-risked financing for intermediate-scale systems, annual energy sales of 15,000 units of electricity could be obtained from a 10-kW system deployed at a raw cost of 10 to 20 cents per unit of power by combining household demands with the demand for productive uses. Certainly more attractive than US$1/kWh of solar with ample storage. Not always cheaper than the grid, but then also not dependent upon large early investments that the grid needs. Such systems could feed into larger grids when they are built out and could equally leverage emerging lower-priced battery storage.

This chapter proposes some engineering approaches to improve the well-being of farmers and poor rural households in a cost-effective way. Shared solar systems can permit small farmers to raise crop productivity, diversify into horticulture, and add value with the mechanization of manual lifting of water. For poor households, I postulate that eliminating or dramatically lowering the cost of electricity during daytime hours would enable a shift toward cleaner, convenient, and time-saving cooking practices. This could reduce the burden of collecting fuelwood enough to support better health, education, and environmental outcomes. We cannot tell exactly how cheap solar energy would change the lives of the poor—we would need carefully constructed field work, or perhaps to ask the poor themselves—but we can imagine a world in the not too distant future, where people who are currently without power or faced with exorbitant costs of power suddenly have access to very cheap solar power. We can be confident this would change their lives.

Appendix: Solar Home Systems

The commercial success of solar lanterns and solar home systems (here we generically refer to them as SHS) is due to the following features:

1. They can be used without any grid, small or large, hence they are called off-grid systems. They can be sold as a product you can own/rent or lease.

2. They primarily meet evening home use applications, such as lighting and, increasingly, a television set as well. The energy services they provide revolve around evening home use, hence a solar panel is packaged with battery storage. Given that these are individual products of a fixed capacity, it is difficult to size the systems for activities that occasionally draw larger power. Moreover, the usual challenges associated with batteries' lifetime, degradation, and replacement costs remain.

3. These systems achieved affordability by essentially leveraging the fact that an LED light, a cell phone or a smart phone, or a television today are all built around solid-state electronics technology that is extremely energy-efficient. Electricity consumption per month remains pitifully low and is generally no more than 2 to 3 kWh/month.

One should never look down on the commercial success that provides value to the poor, and SHS has been a value proposition for millions. Compared to a kerosene wick lamp, otherwise a near-universal staple of rural homes just a decade ago, a small but clean and efficient LED light cannot be beat. Charging your phone should not be a chore, either, with the most expensive electricity per kWh produced using petrol generator, which would waste ten to fifty times the electricity it would need to charge even ten cell phones at once. Yet the combined packaging of a SHS is such that the effective cost per unit of electricity from this packaged home system is an order of magnitude higher than the cost of grid supply.

To some degree, this higher cost of an off-grid supply is mitigated through the use of energy-efficient appliances—leveraging proven product assurances and overcoming otherwise thin supply chains for such appliances. There has been a legacy of CFL lightbulbs that did not live up to their promise because of unpredictable quality, of inefficient television sets, which product packaging has overcome. The dramatic scale-up of solid-state electronics also helped. Mobile-money and other prepayment modalities helped address the first cost barriers.

The transaction costs of collecting small payments for low-cost systems remains a challenge, and so does the issue of product longevity, especially the batteries. There are also lots of poorer-quality products on the market that the poor are compelled to buy in the hope that the seller's assurances are credible. That such small-scale solar home systems have succeeded is just as much about the lack of other alternatives for the poor.

FIVE

Interspecies Money

Jonathan Ledgard

The market economy has failed to price natural capital correctly. One result is a threat of mass extinction of other species. A novel central bank is proposed in response. The Bank for Other Species—or Banque pour d'autres espèces—will issue a central bank digital currency capable of accurately disbursing billions of dollars equivalent yearly to nonhuman life-forms (or their digital twins). Before 2030, "interspecies money" issued by the bank and held by nonhumans will be a significant financier of conservation. Because the poorest countries have the richest biodiversity, and because other species will pay local communities for services that improve their life outcomes, it is likely that interspecies money will help reduce extreme poverty. It may also turn the evolution of artificial intelligence toward nature. Machine interfaces can better represent other species to us, and interspecies money will, for the first time, provide a means of paying for perpetual data acquisition in the wild. Applying deep learning, GOFAI, global planning, and game theoretic models to data gathered by communities and scientists will soon make it possible to share information across the species divide. With information comes digital identity and a nonlinear leap to interspecies money.

> *Dum taxat, rerum magnarum parva potest res*
> *exemplare dare et vestigia notitiae.*
> So far as it goes, a small thing may give an analogy of
> great things, and show the tracks of knowledge.
> — LUCRETIUS

Why Do We Need Interspecies Money?

The biggest threat to diverse biological life on Earth is the failure of the market economy to correctly price natural capital.[1] The only value most nonhuman life--forms have is the value of their processed body parts. If money is memory,[2] it certainly holds no memory of the 8 million other species with whom humans coinhabit the planet. They have left no trace on the market economy, precisely because no money has ever been assigned to them or held by them. This paper proposes empowering wild animals, trees, birds, insects, and microbial colonies by enabling them (or their digital twins) to hold digital currency in a secure and divisible way, such that there will be a money memory of them and a correct weighting of their preferences in the continuance of life into the next centuries.

It makes no sense that the market economy puts money into ores, promissory notes, and blocks of computer code, but not into the continuance of rare, complex, and ancient biological life (regardless of how difficult this is). This paper outlines the urgent need for a novel central bank mandated to issue a central bank digital currency that can be held by nonhuman life-forms: in other words, an interspecies money. The Bank for Other Species—or Banque pour d'autre espèces—will mint a digital-only currency provisionally named the "life mark," after the Deutsche mark, which regenerated postwar West Germany. Before 2030, the equivalent of many billions of dollars will be held in life marks (also LM or L-mark). Interspecies money will be a primary financier of conservation in the pantropics and the largest means of payment for the acquisition of data in the wild, including through various devices. Other species will spend their LM on services that increase their chances of survival; they will also lend and invest LM to and in local communities. LM will be a direct liability on the Bank for Other Species with the transparency, trust, stability, legal standing, and finality of cash. Because LM is computational, the monetary and ecological rules guiding it will be embedded into it; it will be divisible to allow for an accurate direction of small payments across borders at unprecedented scale.

Interspecies money is a science breakthrough only in its combinatorial aspects: the technologies needed to begin building the first version of the life mark are already widely available and in use. And it is arriving at the moment of its greatest need. Some might even argue that the living system (Gaia or otherwise) is producing the tools it needs for its own continuance.

We are at a tipping point in our evolutionary history. Other species occupy

---

1. Dasgupta; Claes and others, Mission Économie de la Biodiversité, World Economic Forum, Network for Greening the Financial System (2021). Nature Editorial Board.
2. Kocherlakota.

a peripheral place in our consciousness. We seldom think about their needs, or how they move through the world. This will change. Over the next decade, we will begin to think about nonhumans in new ways and develop a new ethics and economics that takes better account of them. They will not be persons to us, but neither will they any longer be *things*.

The 2020s will be the most consequential decade for nonhuman life in recorded history. We are facing, in our lifetimes, a sixth mass extinction event in the last 500 million years.[3] There are half as many wild animals alive today as there were in 1970. The biomass of chickens exceeds that of all wild birds. The biomass of humans and livestock is twenty-five times that of all wild animals.[4] Tens of thousands of species are at threat of total or local extinction. As habitats are lost or cut up, the extinction rate rises: loss leads to more loss. The human footprint in ploughing, grazing, felling, in pollution and diminution of all kinds will continue to grow, given the growing human population and increased investment in meat production and monocultures.[5] This will happen regardless of whether the planet continues to warm and be subject to catastrophic weather events. Scientists are unequivocal: we are destroying the fabric of life out of which we emerged and which, in numberless ways, we are dependent upon. Interventions need to be audacious, rapid, and substantial.

In order to maximize biodiversity, scientists and governments are seeking to "fully protect 30 percent of the Earth's surface by 2030" and to sustainably manage another 20 percent.[6] This paper addresses one part of this challenge: how to create a payment system that can substantially improve human-nonhuman cohabitation at the edge of the forests, grasslands, and wetlands of the pantropics that constitute the frontline of the Anthropocene.

Better cohabitation will only happen if it is accompanied by improved life outcomes for humans. In particular, the poor and landless must benefit from the continuance of complex life-forms that live beside and among them. The biodiversity hotspots scientists would most like to protect in Africa, Asia, and Latin

---

3. It is the threat of mass extinction that makes Interspecies Money a reasonable and important approach. The science is clear and grim, even though it does not yet account for most nonhuman species or for the potential cascade effects of climate change. See, for example, Ceballos, Ehrlich, and Raven; Barnosky; Kolbert; World Wildlife Foundation (WWF); Beach, Luzzadder-Beach, Dunning; Ceballos, Ehrlich, and Ehrlich; De Vos, Joppa, Gittleman, and others; Intergovernmental Science-Policy Platform on Biodiversity and Ecosystem Services (IPBES). International Union for Conservation of Nature (IUCN); Pimm and others.

4. For a new perspective of one's place on this planet, see Bar-On, Phillips, and Milo.

5. Barrett and others; Yamaguchi; Wackernagel, Lin, Evans, and others.

6. Waldron, Adams, and others; Lovejoy and Hannah; Conservation is moving closer to the Harvard biologist Edward O. Wilson's half-Earth ambition of setting aside 50 pecent of the planetary surface for nature. For context, see Wilson (1984) and Wilson (2002).

America are beset by increasing insecurity and displacement. Nearly all of the world's extreme poor, 720 million people, live in communities made fragile by ecosystem loss. These communities have the highest rate of population growth in the world, the highest disease burden, they are the most likely to be left behind, to be hungry, to suffer flooding and drought, and they are the most likely to continue to deplete or destroy their surroundings.

Existing conservation solutions are underfunded. Some US$24 billion a year is spent on conservation worldwide. Most of it is spent in industrialized countries; only a tiny fraction ends up in the hands of the extreme poor. The sum is itself dwarfed by the US$97 billion the world spends each year on pet food: even as wild animals go extinct, there is a humanization of pet animals.

What is needed is a breakthrough that makes a thousandfold increase in finance available for the regeneration of biological life in areas of extreme poverty.

It is proposed that the Bank for Other Species (or, more likely, its private-sector settlement agents) will create a digital twin for other species that will serve as their identity online. In practical and legal terms, it is the digital twin that holds the value—the equivalent of a few cents, a few dollars, or even a few tens of thousands of dollars in LM (rare life-forms may hold sums equivalent to a rare Rolex watch). Computational and human proxies will allow the nonhuman to express simple preferences. Money will be spent or invested based on these preferences.

Because the richest biodiversity is in the pantropics, it is the poorest and fastest growing communities in Africa, Asia, and Latin America that stand to gain the most from interspecies money. Effectively, other species will become a source of income and investment capital for humans. Indeed, in some cases, income earned in LM will match direct cash transfers as an affordable and effective way of reducing poverty. Taken together, interspecies money will contribute to the Sustainable Development Goals for reducing poverty (SDG 1), hunger (SDG 2) and improving well-being of communities (SDG 3), as well as to increasing life on land (SDG 15) and life underwater (SDG 14).[7]

To emphasize: the life mark is conceived as a store of value for free living biological life—*wildlife*. Trillion-dollar sums may eventually be held in LM by mid-century, a capital flow constantly directed and redirected, invested and reinvested, always with the purpose of improving nonhuman and human life outcomes, and with repairing and nurturing ecosystems most at risk of destruction. Instead of mining numbers as Bitcoin does, L-marks will mine knowledge and species discovery, incentivizing communities to self-organize around the protection of nature. Gain leads to more gain.

---

7. United Nations.

Economists have failed to price the services of nature into GDP.[8] These services include healthy soil, nutrients, clean air, and clean water. Pollination of crops alone may be worth US$400 billion a year. Nature also provides shade, shelter, storm and flood protection, natural foods, natural products such as timber and rubber, natural pest control, study of species for biomimicry, species discovery for genetics and pharmaceuticals (most antibiotics are naturally occurring), and control of zoonotic pathogens, the most damaging of which—such as plague, leprosy, HIV-AIDS, Ebola, coronaviruses, African swine flu, and avian flu—have leaped from wild animals to humans and their livestock. By some calculations, the direct services nature provides to industry are worth US$40 trillion annually and the total value of natural capital may exceed the US$80 trillion value of Earth GDP.

Interspecies money depends on distributing value to widespread species that most contribute to the regeneration of ecosystems such as trees and insects. But initial investments will often take account of rarity. All resources gain value from being finite. So it will be with rare nonhuman life-forms. Their existence value is real, their scarcity makes them precious. And if, at some future point, some of these species reach their carrying capacity (the number an ecosystem can hold, just as, for example, African elephants have in some areas in Southern Africa exceeded their carrying capacity), the LM they hold is still held by them to pay for future services, and whatever income their investments generate will likely be paid in dividends to the local community, to investors, and to the Bank for Other Species to be reassigned.

Some studies have shown that ecosystem services can be quantified to the individual life-form. African forest elephants may give US$1.75 million value per animal against US$40,000 value for their tusks. Large whales may be worth US$2 million per animal because of their ability to draw down carbon.[9] Similarly, trees and soil biomes are being quantified in terms of the services they provide.[10]

Nonhumans undoubtedly have economic value within large complex systems, but their protection cannot be made on economic grounds. At some point, the economics of biodiversity becomes as meaningless as the economics of the entire biosphere. Nor is it clear that interspecies money can be modeled on the basis of extinction risk, because only a fraction of existing species have been recorded. Quite the opposite: LM may have utility as a species discovery tool payment mechanism precisely because our knowledge of the living world is so patchy. (For

8. Dasgupta.
9. Chami and others; Banerjee and others.
10. Liang, Crowther, and others.

example, only 45,000 of the 1 million or so mites—and only 100,000 of the 3 million fungi—thought to exist have been recorded.)

The preservation of other species will rather be made on an assembly of ethical, aesthetic, and amenity values. LM will first seek to extend the moral compass of humans to include other species. It will support the maturation of long-standing efforts to prevent cruelty to animals by improving life outcomes and mutual comprehension. A still more important ethical contribution is the survival of species. Future human societies should have the chance to work out for themselves which species they want in the world with them. This approach is synonymous with sacred or intrinsic value, where the push for 30 percent protection of nature by 2030 is an extension of the guardianship afforded to groves in countries such as Benin and India. These tiny islands of rich biological life survive on account of their perceived magical or spiritual value to people and other beings, not least in connecting them with beauty, ancestors, and fertility. The case for paying for species survival is therefore both futuristic and ancient, resting as it does both on technology and an animist recognition that human and nonhuman life are intermingled powerfully.

Anthropogenic mass in plastic, metal, glass, textiles, cement, gravel, and other materials has doubled every two decades and will continue to increase over the next decade. In 2020, anthropogenic mass exceeded global living biomass for the first time.[11] LM will help turn the economy toward biological life in a trusted way. Indeed, this will become an important rationale for L-mark as governments and markets look for ways to favor the living world over the manufactured world.

The Importance of Turning Artificial Intelligence toward Nature

There is another reason to build interspecies money at this point in time, and that is the arrival of artificial intelligence into the world. AI changes everything,[12] and the application of large sums of L-marks are needed in order to help turn it toward other living beings.[13]

Anthropologists have shown that there is a primal desire of man to know his surroundings, but as these surroundings become ever more digital and removed from the processes we were designed for, there is an existential risk that we could end up far from our evolutionary state. AI is changing the way we perceive our surroundings. It is developing fast. It is universal in application. If it shows no

11. Bar-On, Phillips, and Milo.

12. The AI community is slowly awakening to ethics. See, for example, Montreal Declaration on AI.

13. The relevant literature is vast and technical. See, for example, Vinuesa and others; Pechoucek, Ledgard, and Bosansky. For a helpful historical overview of AI, listen, for example, to Shadbolt.

curiosity for nonhumans in this early stage of its evolution, it is less likely to be a steward of their interests or even to record their disappearance. AI amplifies anthropocentrism. The animals we most often interact with are pets, subject to humanization (with names, toys, clothes, and so on), or else digital simulacra in gaming domains (for instance, US$1.5 billion was spent in 2020 on *Animal Crossing*, a bubblegum-colored game for the Nintendo Switch console, in which players build worlds with virtual animals). We can posit a rule that nature will recede in our consciousness for as long as the digital advances, unless and until it is well represented.

Because it is capital-intensive and financed by venture and military interests, the evolutionary arc of AI bends toward profit and security. The AI community shows little interest in the natural world. Stanford University's first report of its vaunted 100-Year Study on AI ("AI and Life in 2030") contained long sections on gaming and entertainment, but did not mention nature. Whatever AI finds remunerative goes fast, and whatever it judges powerful goes deep, while the unremunerative and the powerless go ignored. Since wild animals, trees, birds, and other beings lack money and voice, there is every chance AI will be incurious of them at precisely the moment it should be paying attention.

The only way to turn AI decisively toward the natural world is to feed it data about the natural world. Interspecies money, in this respect, is a self-financing data generation machine that, over longer periods of time, brings humans, non-humans, and machine intelligences closer together—a machine that is, in some ways, a corollary to the multiplicity of proprietary sensors, from iPhones to Alexas and Fitbits, that big technology companies incentivize the sale of in order to better monitor humans.

By assigning identity and finance across the species divide, interspecies money can perpetually generate high resolution data from the wild. But large sums of capital must be injected in order to trigger such a system. This is why there is no digital platform for other species and why there is no way for them to communicate with us online. The first service for which another species will pay with L-marks is to be known: record me and my kind, what I am, where I am, consider my existence alongside yours. Verification of LM transactions will depend on accurate data. The quality and sheer scale of these data sets will allow AI to become cognizant of other species and biological systems, even as it evolves to become a nonhuman life-form in its own right. In turn, the distributed intelligent computing subsidized by LM will inform communities, increase scientific understanding, and improve the economic and ethical choices we make. It is important to note that the cost and difficulties of gathering data in the wild mean that it is unlikely to happen without the L-mark.

The year 2021 marks the fiftieth anniversary of the Intel 4004. Since that first microprocessor in 1971, the human economy has transferred immeasurable amounts of information and value to inanimate microchips. Just as biological species have diminished and been overtaken by monocultures, so have microprocessors become numerous, dense, diverse, and complex. Interspecies money will use the same technology to transfer information and value back to animate beings. This highlights the paradox underlying the proposition: the digital technologies that push us away from nature are the same ones that can best help us understand and protect it. An Internet of Life makes more sense than an Internet of Things.

The network is densifying. In 2000, China had 23 million internet users; now it has 900 million. Similarly, the amount of data produced in the world is predicted to increase from 35 zettabytes today to 500 zettabytes by 2030. Ever richer forms of information will go ever faster. This implies that second life and digital twins will be commonplace, with human consciousness being mediated by machines. This has engineering considerations for interspecies money. Metcalfe's Law holds that the potential effect of a network is proportional to the square of the number of connected users of the system (n^2). In other words, a higher order of connections is possible as a network grows. But other species are not on the network, so no connections are possible with them online. They can be easily forgotten. In this sense, nodes matter, and interspecies money makes nonhumans nodes on the same network that humans and machines operate on.

How Will Interspecies Money Work?

The requirements for interspecies money include the ability to give nonhumans a digital identity, the ability to accurately address financial value, the availability of distributed computing, the ability to gather sufficient data to build a verification system trusted by markets and governments, the ability to model the gathered data with AI and other systems, and, above all, the support and trust of local communities.

L-marks will pay for the deployment of hardware into the wild in order to build data sets that are high-resolution and increasing in accuracy (known as "oracles"). For instance, community rangers might receive mobile handsets to record video and log or track the location of recipient species. Camera traps might be deployed at waterholes and microphones along paths and in tree canopies. Private sector partners will also build out the biometric markers necessary for money transfers; they will be paid in LM. In effect, the wild animal or the tree, or the collection thereof, becomes the identity that allows the transfer to happen: I am, therefore I own. In order to pay for a service or make an investment, the wallet holder will have to show, in a timely fashion, what condition it is in and whether it is receiving the services it paid for.

What makes interspecies money plausible is the coalescing of cloud computing, fintech (including cryptocurrency), satellites, drones,[14] and ground robots.
Underlying this is the new ability to affordably use AI pattern recognition on
cheap sensors and mobile phones to accurately track wildlife.[15] An early use of AI
applied to camera trap images taken in the Serengeti National Park in Tanzania
identified forty-eight species from 3.2 million images with 94 percent accuracy.
Face recognition of primates exceeds 95 percent accuracy. Visual recognition of
distinctive markings of animals such as giraffes or cheetahs is well advanced.
Numerous other vision-based examples include successfully reading facial expres-
sions in sheep to detect foot rot, and remote identification of dugongs grazing
sea meadows.[16]

As AI moves from old tag-based methodologies to convolutional neural networks that automatically learn from data inputs, LM-related data will be *better
than humans* for numerous species. These deep neural network approaches will be
extended out to plants and insects. For instance, there has been difficulty putting
together a listing for endangered orchids; orchids need expert assessment. Some
30 percent of 29,000 orchid species are threatened, but only 1,400 are accounted
for in the IUCN Red List. An orchid identifier already claims 85 percent accuracy and will eventually exceed 95 percent accuracy in the wild.

Datasets will be gathered into AI machine-learning programs and multi-
-agent simulations. The data will be mostly (perhaps completely) open source
and will feed entirely new knowledge systems built on cloud computing (such as
Microsoft's Planetary Computer, which aims to build a universal model for life
on Earth, and Google's Earth Engine and Wildlife Insights). Collective human
intelligence will label and work through and generally improve the contribution
of AI, either on a paid or a voluntary basis. Multilateral lenders, sovereign and
private wealth funds, pension and insurance funds, philanthropists, and other
investors will all be able to make use of granular data generated for verification of
LM transfers for green finance. For instance, a private reserve in Latin America
may achieve a higher market value as a biodiversity offset if it proves over long
periods of time that it supports an increasing number of species.

Communities will earn value by generating new data. Some of this will be
species prospecting based on vision, sound, and genetics. Payment in L-marks
can help incentivize the preservation of the knowledge of the book of life.[17] Only
2 million of 8.7 million species on Earth are recorded by science. The International Barcode of Life, an organization with US$130 million of funding, wants

14. Ledgard (2015).
15. See, for example, Fang and others; Brandes, Sicks, and Berger; Iacona, Ramachandra, and
others.
16. See, for example, Tanaka and others.
17. Sweetlove.

to identify a further 2 million species in the next decade. Some of this work can be undertaken by the extreme poor, possibly with windfall payments in LM for newly discovered or exceedingly rare species.

There are also reasons to be optimistic about sound as a useful data source. Acoustic signatures are complicated for AI, because vision is invariant compared to sound (a photo of a lemur is still recognizably a lemur when turned on its head, whereas a sound recording of a lemur call ceases to be an intelligible lemur call when it is played backward or slowed). Even so, there will be advances in neural processing of sound to match that of vision.[18] LM payments will contribute to solving the "cocktail party problem" so that animal and insect calls can be distinguished even in noisy environments (for example, the call of a particular macaque can be pulled apart from other chattering animals). This will allow nonhumans to pay for acoustic stations at the outer limits of tropical forests (led by NGOs such as Rainforest Connection, which has taken a lead in identifying acoustic signatures of birds and frogs in jungles).

The other necessary element of AI is in game theory approaches, which allow the incentives nonhumans pay to humans to be rewritten. The application of game theory to scalable algorithms will make LM payments superior to traditional conservation in many situations by extending the range of interventions at lower cost. Game theory is used in antagonistic situations such as stopping malicious behavior on a computer network or predicting pirate attacks on shipping lanes. It can also be applied to optimize complex networks such as flight paths into busy airports.

The life mark will take advantage of game theory by putting down on the real world a meta layer that can be tweaked and improved on a weekly basis. A basic game might inform a community that a Nubian giraffe (or, more likely, a herd) holds LMs and would like to spend them on services it needs. Payments are adjusted toward an equilibrium benefiting both giraffes and communities. The game will be played for as long as the giraffe holds LMs and only in ways that serve the norms, traditions, and long-term viability of the community. Game theory will need to be resilient against the threat that a community may hold a rare species hostage in return for higher payments, or that the treasury itself will be open to manipulation and fraud.

This is not to suggest that developing AI in the wild will be easy or always reliable. AI will need to develop open category systems (not just to identify a particular moth, but also to recognize there are many other winged insects that are not moths). But AI will not be a constraining factor for interspecies money, not least because its enormous power is that it draws on solutions that were applied in

---

18. Zhong and others; Hill and others; Ruffand others; Rappaport, Royle, and Morton.

quite separate domains (for instance, sensor systems developed for autonomous vehicles may have solutions relevant for sensors in the wild).

The direction of travel is clear. Just as television programs on wildlife in the 1950s were monochrome, indistinct, and fanciful, but are now Technicolor, sharp, and scientific, so will the quality and variety of data generated by LM constantly intensify. By 2050, it is possible that other sensory and chemical signatures will follow sound and vision. By then, AI might be able to smell and touch nature.

Where in the World Will Interspecies Money Be Most Usefully Applied?

Interspecies money is intended initially for targeted conservation. It will have greatest utility at the frontier in the pantropics, where nonhumans suffer because they have no means to change their economic value (and where their only value is the sum of their body parts). In the next decade, LM will often be applied first to animals capable of defining or even expressing simple preferences, including species such as primates and elephants, whose rights have already been acknowledged under habeas corpus rulings.[19]

It is possible to again use the Nubian giraffe (*Giraffa camelopardalis camelopardalis*) by way of a simple example. Giraffes are among the most iconic animals, and their preferences are simple and well understood. However, their ubiquity in toys and images does not reflect their endangered status in the wild. There are only 97,000 giraffes left alive in the wild, down from 163,000 in 1985. A further 1,700 live in captivity. In some places, their numbers have collapsed by 95 percent owing to fragmentation of habitat, incursion of farmers, and bovine tuberculosis. Giraffes are killed for meat, for their bone marrow, and for their tails (which are used for ceremonial purposes). They get snagged in barbed wire, or torn apart by vehicles when crossing roads. Nubian giraffes are critically endangered. There are only 2,100 of the subspecies left alive in Ethiopia, South Sudan, and Kenya. What would L-marks do for them?

First of all, the LM would give a Nubian giraffe a trusted identity based on facial recognition, gait recognition, and individual markings. With this identity, the animal would hold some financial value (say, US$32,000 in LM) and begin to disburse it in order to improve its life outcomes. It will pay to distribute mobile phones and for sensors to be deployed at water holes and along paths. It will pay for preferential access to water holes over cattle and goats. It may, in some instances, pay for security to stop poachers and charcoal burners.

Many of the services a giraffe asks for will result in payments or investments

19. Stone, Wise, and Posner.

Figure 5-1. Giraffes Can Pay for Their Own Protection

for better stewardship; often this will be undertaken by very poor communities. Herders might be compensated for moving their cattle away from the giraffes. Villagers might earn L-marks from planting trees, building fences, and keeping water holes in good shape in drought conditions. Payments will be made for accurate sightings of giraffes and for observation of spoor, prints, and hair. The animals will pay for periodic drone and satellite imagery, weather and farming data, and economic and security intelligence; internet connectivity from providers such as Starlink may be paid by the animals in LM. They may also pay to protect related other species, such as bees and other pollinators, and the oxpecker birds that pick them clean of insects and infections. A Nubian giraffe may pay for its own veterinary care with LM. Since translocations of giraffes are well established, it is possible that a herd might finance their own move to a safer location at some future point.

This is an example of an elementary application of the life mark. Lessons learned from rare, charismatic creatures like Nubian giraffes will be applied to other megafauna, including critically endangered hoofed animals like the Hirola antelope (less than a thousand individuals), Heuglin's gazelle (three thousand), and giant elands (twelve thousand).

However, conservation spending is biased toward charismatic animals. The most popular animals in zoos get the most money in the wild.[20] Identifying umbrella species in ecosystems may be more effective. An umbrella species is

20. Courchamp.

one whose continued existence is most likely to support an ecosystem (or to reliably indicate its health). Directing LM from charismatic to umbrella species will increase protection for the same investment (for example, a study in Australia found a conservation approach targeting umbrella species increased protection of terrestrial species from 6 percent to 46 percent).

Over time, life marks will be held by obscure small creatures, as well as trees, plants, and insects.[21] The poorest countries with the most endemic species, such as Papua New Guinea, Madagascar, Central African Republic, and the Democratic Republic of Congo stand to benefit the most. Biodiversity in these ecosystems often supports human diversity: a quarter of the world's languages are found in the Amazonian, New Guinean, and Congolese rainforests.[22] These languages and the cultures they belong to represent a profound knowledge of their surrounding ecosystems.

The cheapest and most effective way of reaching the 30 percent protection of terrestrial habitats by 2030 is to preserve tropical forests, water corridors, and animal migratory routes. LM will likely have its greatest utility at the edges of these forests,[23] as well as along rivers and estuaries where competition between humans and nonhumans is the most brutal. If crop-raiding chimpanzees in western Uganda could pay for any damage they caused, or Malaysian Sabah orangutans could use LM to gain an identity and announce themselves to local farmers before raiding their crops,[24] there would be both a basis for lasting cohabitation and a financial realization of the existence value of the nonhumans. In all instances, the purpose of the payments is to make the human invested in the survival of the nonhuman.

The L-mark will underwrite the regeneration of nature in fast-growing countries such as Nigeria, Ethiopia, India, and Peru. Nonhumans will pay humans for a multiplicity of entrepreneurial tasks, such as clearing plastic, controlling invasive species,[25] mitigating zoonotic disease,[26] planting trees, as well as recording and tracking in nature, so that day by day, little by little, the local economy becomes a natural economy.

In the early stages, L-marks will flow fastest to communities that are the most regenerative. This will have a demonstration effect, where solutions and so-called

21. Stork.

22. The work of Elinor Ostrom is useful for Interspecies Money. See, for example, Ostrom (1990), (1992), and (1995). For indigenous participation, see, for example, Novotny; Muller, Hemming, and Rigney; Arrow.

23. Laurance and others; Cooke, Köhlin, and Hyde; Lovejoy and Nobre; MacArthur and Wilson.

24. Voigt and others; Santikaand others; Campbell-Smith, Sembiring, Linkie.

25. Westphal and others.

26. Zoological Society of London (ZSL).

green hustles—where young people are incentivized with micropayments to gather data on a particular species or to undertake regenerative tasks such as repairing a water hold or providing veterinary care to a species—pioneered by innovative communities will be copied by others (for example, a group in Sri Lanka may learn best practices from a group in Niger). Communities that are too insecure, negligent, or untrustworthy will be passed over. Vitally, cash-poor, time-rich young people will earn the most money.

How Will Interspecies Money Be Financed and Organized?

Money is a social construct. Shells, feathers, coins, checkbooks, credit cards, and swipe payments have evolved with new ways of transmitting information. Digital money itself is not new: the first version appeared in 1983, soon after commerce was permitted on the internet. But the acceptance of digital money has accelerated in recent years with the emergence of Bitcoin in 2009 (Satoshi), retail e-cash solutions, and, more recently, a Facebook-founded consortium Diem, which seeks to create a stable digital currency[27] for increasing financial inclusion and cross-border micropayments. Why is it credible to expect large capital flows sufficient to mint the life mark when conservation has failed to raise adequate money to date?

One reason is that we are living through a monetary revolution connected to the explosion of data. Money is becoming liquid and digital. Intention and money are merging—dopamine is now a reliable indicator of earnings on social media. A new class of digital currencies will make this intentionality divisible, so that smaller and smaller tasks can be assigned and rewarded on much larger networks.

Digital money is already traded on a vast scale in the cryptocurrency markets. Bitcoin boasts a US$70 billion daily volume trade on a market cap of US$1 trillion at time of writing. The totality of cryptocurrencies, in many forms, will exceed US$2 trillion well before 2030. In this context, a market cap of tens of billions of dollars in LM is reachable within a few years.

However, Bitcoin is a poor means of exchange, a poorer store of value, is opaque and possibly corrupt, and uses more electricity to validate itself than Argentina.[28] A central bank (or a decentralized private sector with the proven qualities of a central bank) offers a steadier hand.

The majority of central banks are now exploring the possibility of issuing their own digital currencies. The process has been sped up by COVID-19, the

---

27. Arner and others.
28. Polemis and Tsionas; Carstens (2020) and (2021).

Figure 5-2. Capital and Data Structure of Bank for Other Species

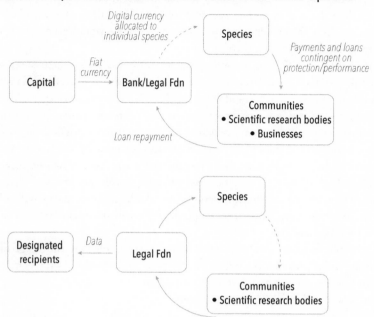

inflated value of Bitcoin, and the emergence of Diem. A consortium including the European Central Bank, the Bank of England, the Bank of Japan, the Bank of Canada, the Swiss National Bank, the Sveriges Riksbank, and the Bank of International Settlements have joined together to explore ways to build central bank digital currencies. China is more advanced: its digital renminbi is in experimental use in Shenzhen, Shanghai, and other cities. The d-renminbi will likely be the official currency of the 2022 Winter Olympics in Beijing.

The proposed Bank for Other Species will issue the life mark as a central bank digital currency. The bank will be an independent global public good working toward the agreed goals of the Convention on Biological Diversity.[29] Other central bank governors will likely sit on its board in a manner and purpose similar to the Bank of International Settlements; it will be for them to establish the structure of the bank. However, governance, science, and ethics related to the application of L-marks will be overseen by a subsidiary. This independent foundation of the bank will control all the data gathered by the payment system. It will have its own independent board of indigenous peoples, conservation, technology,

29. Convention on Biological Diversity.

government, and other stakeholders. Crucially, the foundation will write and rewrite the rules and incentives applying to L-marks while the bank will embed those rules into the currency using automatic computational execution (smart contracts adjusted by game theory).

Life marks are likely to be built using a distributed ledger technology with the bank serving as a central validator (unlike the decentralized validation of Bitcoin). It will be a hybrid model,[30] with the private sector self-organizing in a competitive and profitable payment system as settlement agents. Money transfer companies show that stability across most currencies is possible by creating internal currency baskets (Western Union uses an internal stablecoin process transactions in 137 currencies every few seconds). The L-mark will have central bank standards of stability, interoperability, transparency, privacy, and quantum resistant security against hacking and money laundering. L-marks will follow "know your customer" regulations quite literally with payments released upon verification of identity.

The public interest will always come before the technology in the design of the currency, and in this case the public interest is the contribution L-marks make to the continuance of rich and diverse life on Earth.

But where will the liquidity come from?

From many sources. Governments have publicly committed to climate change targets and to the preservation of biodiversity.[31] The European Union's €95 billion Horizon 2021–27 research fund has singled out biodiversity challenges among its goals;[32] it and similar American and Chinese initiatives will be a source of initial research funding. Philanthropy is also a significant source of early capital and innovation. The Amazon.com founder, Jeff Bezos, recently stepped back to work on philanthropic initiatives that include a US$10 billion Earth Fund focused on mitigating climate change and biodiversity loss; it can also underwrite the development of a Bank for Other Species. The Terra Carta initiative of HRH Prince of Wales is based on the Magna Carta.[33] It envisages yet larger sums invested into nature-based solutions each year.

Private investment into biodiversity is presently estimated between US$6.6 billion to US$13.6 billion a year, but loans and underwriting worth US$2.6 trillion go to industries driving biodiversity loss.[34] This makes institutional investors

---

30. See, for example, Auer, Monnet, and Song Shin; Auer, Cornelli, and Frost; Bank of Canada and others; Chaum, Grothoff, and Moser.
31. European Bank for Reconstruction and Development (EBRD); Moles Fanjul.
32. European Commission; EU Technical Expert Group on Sustainable Finance.
33. Windsor.
34. Picte Asset Management.

likely to buy LM.[35] Large sums will flow from the industrial north to the pantropics in the next decade as a matter of climate mitigation and climate justice reparations. Most will just be finance searching for higher returns in faster growing economies (by mid-century, the population of Italy is predicted to drop from 61 million to 28 million and of Japan from 138 million to 58 million, while that of the Democratic Republic of Congo will rise from 80 million to 130 million and of Tanzania from 54 million to 125 million). Since human demands on nature are running at the rate of 1.6 Earths, and since the biosphere clearly bounds the limits of economic growth,[36] the next decade will be one in which companies will accelerate non-fiduciary duties toward sustainability. Large purchases of L-marks will be made by fossil fuel, cement, and other biosphere-damaging companies. This will happen informally through shaming and sanctions, through market incentives, then through board decisions and divestments, and finally by the application of law.

Although the initial liquidity of the Bank for Other Species will be staked by other central banks and philanthropists, it will increasingly pay for its operation from the transaction fees it generates and from the investments nonhumans make using LM. The bank may earn money from intellectual property it develops for the purposes of its own verification protocols. Its data will be free and open for science and development; proprietary modeling for the private sector may earn additional revenue. The bank and the private sector may earn from interests in commercial carbon offsets, rewilding, debt forgiveness, and utilities controlling invasive species and zoonotic diseases. Another large income stream will be species prospecting, where discovery of new genomes is rewarded.

There is again the question of timeliness: the life mark has to be issued at this point in economic history not just because it is an ecological and AI imperative, but also because it is affordable to do so. This is likely the last decade where it is possible now to incentivize better cohabitation with billions rather than trillions of dollars. With each year that goes by, the edges of the biodiverse areas are brought into the human economy and covered with an anthropogenic mass of roads and buildings, which, however seemingly inert, has its own capital demands and incentive structures.

L-marks will move between nonhumans and humans not just through payments for services, but also through loans and investments. The bank will become a lending structure along the lines of Quaker banks or cooperatives, with local communities, institutions, and individuals borrowing at preferential rates. The same will apply to insurance. Microinsurance products pioneered by

35. United Nations Development Program (UNDP).
36. Smil.

major insurance companies (which are themselves algorithmic exercises relying on advanced technology), may in many cases be paid out in LM.

Even more significant, nonhumans will buy equity in local businesses. As those businesses grow, so will the net worth of rare life-forms. This value will be passed between generations until the carrying capacity of species is met. The L-mark will seek to be *natural*, ordering itself according to life cycles. In the simplest terms, we can envisage giraffes owning equity in local shops, electric charging points, solar arrays, rudimentary robots, seed banks, and transport. If money is directed into nonhuman life now and held over many generations, investments made in biodiversity will rise with the wealth of the economy. That will greatly increase the available finance for future conservation. By way of example, consider what would have been the value held by nonhumans in the special economic zone of Shenzhen in China. The Shenzhen economy has grown from US$40 million in 1980 to over US$40 billion in 2020. Even a tiny application of L-marks in the early days of Shenzhen would now be worth hundreds of millions of dollars. The Bank for Other Species will get richer as emerging economies get richer, so that it may eventually function like a sovereign wealth fund for other species.

Green finance is held back in the pantropics by increased investment in commodity crops. Sugar cane, palm oil, soy, and other flexible commodity crops provide enormous short-term returns to the super-rich at the cost of long-term ecological devastation for nonhumans and the extreme poor. Farming is the largest single emitter of greenhouse gases and by far the largest cause of biodiversity loss.[37] When damage to the biosphere is calculated, the cost of food production in the pantropics may already exceed its value.[38] Farming accounts for most of the livelihoods in Africa and many of the livelihoods in Asia and Latin America.

Climate change is likely to have a disruptive effect on rainfed crops and may further threaten nonhuman life. The bank will seek to align with the goals of the global food system to stay within safe planetary limits in the management of water, soil, air, and microbial life. Its finance structure and the flow of LM will incentivize farmers to reduce cattle herding, nurture the soil, and protect the watershed, as well as direct efforts to preserve rare nonhuman life. More food needs to be produced, but with far fewer inputs. Human agriculture developed over thousands of years in clement, unhurried, uncrowded, and biologically abundant conditions. It will now take place in blistering conditions of increasing fragility and scarcity. The life mark will play an assistive role in an entirely new

---

37. Rockström and others (2009).
38. Rockström and others (2009); Rockström and others (2020); Food and Agricultural Organization of the United Nations.

category of farming, not just of food but sharing of information with other biological life-forms for their own sake and the health of the biosphere.[39]

Conclusion

The entire notion of interspecies money and of life marks as a digital currency issued by a novel central bank (or a private sector alternative) will face criticism from some technologists, scientists, ecologists, animal rights advocates, philosophers, and from the general public, along the lines that the L-mark is an unacceptably extreme fintech, cryptocolonial in design, which seeks to drag nature into the very same human economy that has destroyed it. Pointedly, others will object that it is wrong for nonhumans to receive care while humans suffer and that the life outcomes of the extreme poor should in no way be conditioned by their ability to extend the survival of other species.

It is right to be skeptical toward the promise of a digital platform that claims to distribute financial value to nonhumans and onward to humans in the remotest and wildest bits of the world. Many digital panaceas have been promised in the twenty-first century and mostly only nostrums delivered. Wealth is notoriously tied to what is fixed, whereas biological life is shifting and unpredictable.

Some ethical concerns around interspecies money may be offset by making it provisional. For instance, there might be a clause allowing for its value to be dissolved; from 2123 onward, nature would again be outside of the economy and would cease to be monitored. But it seems more likely that a large and successful store of value in nature, with preferences of many species recognized, much new knowledge, and proven regeneration of ecosystems, would choose not to dissolve itself but to continue on as a contributor to twenty-second-century stewardship.[40]

Is it really possible that the life mark can be made to be accurate, equitable, affordable, uncomplicated, popular, and secure? Such that it neither collapses under its own weight, nor introduces a panopticon surveillance state into the natural world, nor has any other unintended or damaging side effects?

The skepticism is perhaps redundant, since interspecies money will only scale

39. See Rubin and others. According to this paper, life-forms are an "inevitable and emergent property of any random dynamical system that possesses a Markov blanket." All autonomous systems and all living things are self-organized into Markov blankets of Markov blankets, from their cellular structure to their bodily form. They are subject to a free energy principle where free energy is the dissipation of energy to the equilibrium—death. In order to contain energy, the biological life-form establishes a boundary for sensing and predicting the outside world. This boundary extends out to the communities they belong to. Such a scale-free and domain-independent approach may underpin Interspecies Money. See, for example, Kirchhoff, Parr, Friston, and others; Clippinger.

40. On stewardship, the author is indebted to a wide range of thinkers, including artists he works with, such as Olafur Eliasson. See, for example, Weil; Carson; Schama.

when it is shown to be effective. And besides, it is unlikely to work in all situations. Game theory is an approximation. It will not work when ecosystems and communities are subject to bad actors and externalities such as armed gunmen, forest fires, and crop failures. What matters is that it is effective in certain conditions, that it can be reliably replicated, and that it constantly improves.

Extinction is not inevitable. Dozens of species have been saved from extinction since 1993. Mountain gorilla population in Rwanda has increased from two hundred in the 1980s to over a thousand today. Care for the endangered nonhuman does not preclude care for the extremely poor human. On the contrary, their fates are entwined. An overemphasis on human development over nonhuman survival willfully ignores the conditions in which many of the extreme poor will live over the next decade, dependent on ecosystems that are increasingly unfit to support life.

The road map for interspecies money is short and direct. Testing will begin in multiple ecosystems in 2022–23. Support from conservation and computing circles will follow successful pilots. Work will begin on numerous relevant scientific questions, such as predation, vagility, and carrying capacity of species. The bank will be established and the LM minted before 2024. It will maintain digital autonomy and withhold its data for science and as an asset class. Large sums from governments and institutional investors will begin to be placed in life marks from 2025. Still larger sums from smaller investors will follow. Many of these investments, especially from legacies, will be made with the primary goal of limiting species extinction and supporting the regeneration of other life-forms. A separate track will advance the legal framework. The right of nonhumans (or their digital twins) to hold financial value will be settled in many jurisdictions, starting with higher animals with proven self-awareness (see, for example, the Nonhuman Rights Project, which has successfully pressed for civil rights for primates, elephants, and cetaceans not to be imprisoned or experimented on).[41]

Animism has been a defining element of humanity since Paleolithic times.[42] The aforementioned humanization of pets, together with the rise of ethical vegans and vegetarians, and advances in nonhuman rights, suggest that humans are becoming more sensitive to the needs of other species and to biodiversity more broadly.[43]

Within a decade, we may understand how to help nonhumans express simple preferences. That will have wider ethical, ecological, and economic implications, not least for livestock animals, which so greatly outnumber wild animals. The same facial recognition software that will afford an orangutan an identity and

41. Nonhuman Rights Project.
42. Weber.
43. Bawa and others; Vaes and others.

liberty in the wild may support the incarceration and eventual slaughter of other animals in industrial farms. Many of the AI solutions that underwrite interspecies money have been advanced in Chinese pig farms by technology companies looking to optimize meat production. Similar approaches will likely be applied by pastoralists in the pantropics, so that the cash value of their cattle and goats might be increased and secured year after year. But it is equally possible that some of the largest early investments in LM may be from vegans who see it as a way of undercutting industrial farming.

Interspecies money will be an expansion of the nodes available to the internet, but it could be larger and more culturally important than that. The Bank for Other Species will be the first of many digital platforms for nonhumans. What begins as a practical attempt to count, classify, and protect biodiversity may develop into an economy and culture beyond our present imagining. Breakthroughs in neuroscience and communication may, in a few instances, allow the chasm of misapprehension, blankness, and predation that has characterized our relationships with other species to be crossed. Given the diversity, number, and deep biological time, nonhuman insights are likely to alter our somewhat utilitarian understanding of the world and our place in it. The still larger question of the interspecies will be human-nonhuman-machine cohabitation. If life on Earth is to survive, machine intelligence will play the mediating role in mutual care and comprehension.

Only a centralized authority (or one taking the qualities of a centralized authority) can assure trust in a digital currency for nonhumans. It is possible that the Facebook-backed Diem, or a similar private sector digital currency, could be repurposed as LM, but it is far more likely that a bespoke central bank built from scratch and owned by other central banks would better serve the common good of a stable monetary framework for other species. Even at scale, L-marks are unlikely to influence monetary policy, but they will constitute a currency held by other species that will quite reasonably match the half a trillion dollars held by the Hong Kong Monetary Authority to back the Hong Kong dollar.

What matters is rewriting the economic rules in favor of nonhumans in a transparent and accurate way. By 2030, thousands of species will be able to spend L-marks to make themselves better known in the world. They will pay for their own veterinary and arboreal care (just as mountain gorillas already have greater access to medicine than many humans). They will live longer lives, with less pain.

Moreover, the system capable of regenerating diverse life on Earth will be self-financing and beneficial to the extreme poor, who also lack identity because they lack money. In this sense, interspecies money is a radical venture for financial inclusion and closing the informational asymmetry both of other species and of the extreme poor who benefit from living alongside them.

References

Arner, Douglas and others. 2020. "Stablecoins: Risks, Potential, and Regulation." Bank of International Settlements Working Paper No. 905.

Arrow, Kenneth J. 2000. "Observations on Social Capital." *Social Capital: A Multifaceted Perspective*. World Bank.

Auer, Raphael, Cyril Monnet, and Hyun Song Shin. 2021. "Permissioned Distributed Ledgers and the Governance of Money." Bank of International Settlements Working Paper No. 924.

Auer, Raphael, Giulio Cornelli, and Jon Frost. 2020. "Rise of Central Bank Currencies." Bank of International Settlements Working Paper No. 880.

Moles Fanjul, Patricia and others. 2020. *Climate and Environmental Risks and Opportunities in Mexico's Financial System from Diagnosis to Action*. Banco de Mexico and UNEP Inquiry.

Bank of Canada and others. 2020. Central Bank Digital Currencies Foundational Principles and Core Features. Basel: Bank for International Settlements.

Banerjee, Onil and others. 2020. "The Value of Biodiversity in Economic Decisionmaking." IDB Working Paper Series 01193.

Barnosky, Anthony. 2008. "Megafauna Biomass Tradeoff as a Driver of Quaternary and Future Extinctions." Proceedings of the National Academy of Sciences, v. 105, no. 1.

Bar-On, Yinon M., Rob Phillips, and Ron Milo. 2018. "The Biomass Distribution on Earth." Proceedings of the National Academy of Sciences, v. 115, no. 25.

Barrett, Scott and others. 2020. "Social Dimensions of Fertility Behavior and Consumption Patterns in the Anthropocene." Proceedings of the National Academy of Sciences, v. 117, no. 12.

Bawa, Kamaljit and others. 2020. "Opinion: Envisioning a Biodiversity Science for Sustaining Human Well-Being." Proceedings of the National Academy of Sciences, v. 117, no. 42.

Beach, Timothy Paul, Sheryl Luzzadder-Beach, and Nicholas P. Dunning. 2019. "Dark Matter Biodiversity." *Biological Extinction: New Perspectives*. Cambridge University Press.

Brandes, Stephanie, Florian Sicks, and Anne Berger. 2021. "Behavior Classification on Giraffes (*Giraffa camelopardalis*) Using Machine Learning Algorithms on Triaxial Acceleration Data of Two Commonly Used GPS Devices and Its Possible Application for Their Management and Conservation." *Sensors*, v. 21.

Campbell-Smith, Gail, Rabin Sembiring, and Matthew Linkie. 2012. "Evaluating the Effectiveness of Human-Orangutan Conflict Mitigation Strategies in Sumatra." *Journal of Applied Ecology*, 49.

Carson, Rachel. 1962. *Silent Spring*. Boston, Mass.: Houghton Mifflin.

Carstens, Agustin. 2020. "Shaping the Future of Payments." Bank of International Settlements Quarterly Review, March.

———. 2021. "Digital Currencies and the Future of the Monetary System." Bank of International Settlements Remarks to the Hoover Institution policy seminar, 27 January, www.bis.org/speeches/sp210127.pdf

Ceballos, Gerardo, Anne H. Ehrlich, and Paul R. Ehrlich. 2015. "The Annihilation of Nature: Human Extinction of Birds and Mammals." John Hopkins University Press.

Ceballos, Gerardo, Paul R. Ehrlich, and Peter H. Raven. 2020. "Vertebrates on the
    Brink as Indicators of Biological Annihilation and the Sixth Mass Extinction."
    Proceedings of the National Academy of Sciences, v. 117, no. 24.
Chami, Ralph and others. 2019. "Saving the Whale: How Much Do You Value Your
    Next Breath?" International Workshop on Financial System Architecture and
    Stability, working paper, https://iwfsas.org/iwfsas2019/wp-content/uploads/2017/02
    /Special-session-P3.pdf.
Chaum, David, Christian Grothoff, and Thomas Moser. 2021. "How to Issue a Central
    Bank Digital Currency." Swiss National Bank Working Paper No. 03.
Claes, Julien and others. 2020. "Valuing Nature Conservation: A Methodology for
    Quantifying the Benefit of Protecting the Planet's Natural Capital."McKinsey &
    Company report. www.mckinsey.com/~/media/McKinsey/Business%20Functions
    /Sustainability/Our%20Insights/Valuing%20nature%20conservation/Valuing
    -nature-conservation.pdf.
Clippinger, John. 2019. "Reflexive Mutual Series-LLC."MIT Computational Law Report.
    December.
Convention on Biological Diversity. 2017. "Green Bonds." www.cbd.int/financial/
    greenbonds.shtml.
Cooke, Priscilla, Gunnar Köhlin, and William F. Hyde. 2008. "Fuelwood, Forests, and
    Community Management—Evidence from Household Studies." Environment and
    Development Economics, v. 13, no. 1.
Courchamp, Franck and others. (2018). "The paradoxical extinction of the most
    charismatic animals."PLOS Biology 16(4). https://journals.plos.org/plosbiology/
    article?id=10.1371/journal.pbio.2003997.
Dasgupta, Partha. 2021. The Economics of Biodiversity: The Dasgupta Review. London:
    HM Treasury.
De Vos, Jurriaan M. and others. 2014. "Estimating the Normal Background Rate of
    Species Extinction." Conservation Biology, v. 29, no. 2.
EU Technical Expert Group on Sustainable Finance. 2020. "Taxonomy: Final report of
    the Technical Expert Group on Sustainable Finance." https://ec.europa.eu/info/sites
    /default/files/business_economy_euro/banking_and_finance/documents/200309
    -sustainable-finance-teg-final-report-taxonomy_en.pdf.
European Bank for Reconstruction and Development (EBRD). 2020. "Joint Report on
    Multilateral Development Banks." Climate Finance, v. 201.
European Commission. 2020. "EU Biodiversity Strategy for 2030." https://ec.europa.eu
    /environment/strategy/biodiversity-strategy-2030_en.
Fang, Fei and others. 2019. Artificial Intelligence and Conservation. Cambridge
    University Press.
Food and Agricultural Organization of the United Nations. 2020. "Yearbook of Forest
    Products." FAO, Italy.
Hill, Andrew P. and others. 2018. "AudioMoth: Evaluation of a Smart Open Acoustic
    Device for Monitoring Biodiversity and the Environment." Methods in Ecology and
    Evolution, v. 9, no. 5.
Iacona, Gwenllian and others. 2019. "Identifying Technology Solutions to Bring
    Conservation into the Innovation Era." Frontiers in Ecology and the Environment, v.
    17, no. 10.
Intergovernmental Science-Policy Platform on Biodiversity and Ecosystem Services

(IPBES). 2019. Global assessment report on biodiversity and ecosystem services of the Intergovernmental Science-Policy Platform on Biodiversity and Ecosystem Services. Eduardo Sonnewend Brondizio, Josef Settele, Sandra Díaz, and Hlen Thu Ngo (editors). IPBES secretariat, Bonn, Germany.

International Union for Conservation of Nature (IUCN) and others. 2020. "Red List of Threatened Species, Version 2020." www.iucnredlist.org/.

Kirchhoff, Michael and others. 2018. "The Markov Blankets of Life: Autonomy, Active Inference, and the Free Energy Principle." Journal of the Royal Society Interface v. 15, no. 138.

Kocherlakota, Narayana R. 1996. "Money is Memory." *Federal Reserve Bank of Minneapolis Research Department Staff Report*, no. 218.

Kolbert, Elizabeth. 2014. *The Sixth Extinction: An Unnatural History*. New York: Henry Holt and Co.

Ledgard, Jonathan. 2015. "Better Use of the Lower Sky in a Sharing Economy." École Polytechnique Fédérale de Lausanne (EPFL) Working Paper, https://s3-eu-west-1 .amazonaws.com/s3.sourceafrica.net/documents/120076/BETTER-USE-of-the -LOWER-SKY-in-a-SHARING.pdf.

www.interspecies.io/conferences/conversations2020public.

Laurance, William F. and others. 2002. "Ecosystem Decay of Amazonian Forest Fragments: A 22-Year Investigation." *Conservation Biology*, v. 16, no. 3.

Liang, Jingjing and others. 2016. "Positive Biodiversity-Productivity Relationship Predominant in Global Forests." *Science*, v. 354.

Lovejoy, Thomas E. and Lee Hannah. 2019. *Biodiversity and Climate Change: Transforming the Biosphere*. Yale University Press.

Lovejoy, Thomas E. and Carlos Nobre. 2019. "Amazon Tipping Point: Last Chance for Action." *Science Advances*, v. 5, no. 12.

MacArthur, Robert and Edward O. Wilson. 1967. *The Theory of Island Biogeography*. Princeton University Press.

Mission Économie de la Biodiversité. 2019. "Global Biodiversity Score: A Tool to Establish and Measure Corporate and Financial Commitments for Biodiversity." BioDiv 2050 Outlook: Club B4B+ Report, no. 14, www.mission-economie -biodiversite.com/wp-content/uploads/2019/04/N14-GBS-2018-UPDATE-MD_FR .pdf.

Montreal Declaration on AI. 2018. "Responsible AI." An Initiative of Université de Montréal, www.montrealdeclaration-responsibleai.com/the-declaration.

Muller, Samantha, Steve Hemming, and Daryle Rigney. 2019. "Indigenous Sovereignties: Relational Ontologies and Environmental Management." *Geographical Research*, v. 57, no. 4.

Nature. Editorial Board 2021. "Momentum on Valuing Ecosystems Is Unstoppable." *Nature*, v. 591.

Network for Greening the Financial System (NGFS). 2021. *Sustainable Market Dynamics: an overview*. NGFS Technical Document, www.ngfs.net/sites/default/files /media/2021/06/17/ngfs_report_sustainable_finance_market_dynamics.pdf.

Nonhuman Rights Project (2021). "Litigation." www.nonhumanrights.org/

Novotny, Vojtech. 2010. "Rainforest Conservation in a Tribal World." *Biotropica*, v. 42, no. 5.

Ostrom, Elinor. 1990. *Governing the Commons: The Evolution of Institutions for Collective Action*. Cambridge University Press.

————. 1992. *Crafting Institutions for Self-Governing Irrigation Systems.* San Francisco: ICS Press.

————. 1995. "Incentives, Rules of the Game, and Development." Supplement to the *World Bank Economic Review* and the *World Bank Research Observer.*

Pimm, Stuart L. and others. 2014. "The Biodiversity of Species and Their Rates of Extinction, Distribution, and Protection." *Science*, v. 344.

Pechoucek, Michal, Jonathan Ledgard, and Branislav Bosansky. 2019. "AI Game Theoretic Considerations for an Interspecies Money Solution." Czech Technical University working paper.

Pictet Asset Management. 2020. *Planetary Boundaries: Measuring the Business World's Planetary Footprint.* Pictet and the Stockholm Resilience Centre, www.fuw.ch/wp -content/uploads/2020/03/pictet-asset-management-planetary-boundaries.pdf.

Polemis, Michael L. and Mike G. Tsionas. 2021. "The Environmental Consequences of Blockchain Technology: Bayesian Quantile Cointegration Analysis for Bitcoin." *International Journal of Financial Economics*, v. 1, no. 20.

Posner, Richard A. 2000. Animal Rights (reviewing Steven M. Wise, Rattling the Cage: Twoard Legal Rgihts for Animals (2000)). Yale Law Journal v. 100, no. 527.

Rappaport, Danielle I., J. Andrew Royle, and Douglas C. Morton. 2020. "Acoustic Space Occupancy: Combining Ecoacoustics and Lidar." *Ecological Indicators*, v. 113.

Rockström, Johan and others. 2009. "A Safe Operating Space for Humanity." *Nature*, v. 461, no. 7263.

Rockström, Johan and others. 2020. "Planet-Proofing the Global Food System." *Nature Food*, v. 1.

Rubin, Sergio and others. 2020. "Future Climates: Markov Blankets and Active Inference in the Biosphere." Journal of the Royal Society Interface v. 17, no. 172.

Ruff, Zachary H. and others. 2019. "Automated Identification of Avian Vocalizations with Deep Convolutional Neural Networks." *Remote Sensing in Ecology and Conservation*, v. 2, no. 125.

Santika, Truly and others.2017 "First Integrative Trend Analysis for a Great Ape Species in Borneo." *Nature*, Scientific Reports, v. 7.

Schama, Simon. 1995. *Landscape and Memory.* New York: A.A. Knopf.

Shadbolt, Nigel and others. 2017. "Machine Learning and Artificial Intelligence." Ditchley Park working paper, www.ditchley.com/programme/past-events/2010-2019 /2017/machine-learning-and-artificial-intelligence-how-do-we-make.

Smil, Vaclav. 2002. *"The Earth's Biosphere: Evolution, Dynamics and Change."* Cambridge: MIT Press. Stone, Christopher D. 1972. "Should Trees Have Standing—toward Legal Rights for Natural Objects." *Southern California Law Review*, v. 45.

Stork, Nigel E. 2018. "How Many Species of Insects and Other Terrestrial Arthropods Are There on Earth?" *Annual Review of Entomology*, v. 63, no. 1.

Sweetlove, Lee. 2011. "Number of species on Earth Tagged at 8.7 million." *Nature.* www.nature.com/articles/news.2011.498.

Tanaka, Kotaro and others. 2021. "Automated Classification of Dugong Calls." *Acoustics Australia*, v. 10.

United Nations. 2015. "The Sustainable Development Goals." https://sdgs.un.org/goals.

United Nations Development Program (UNDP). 2020. *Moving Mountains: Unlocking Private Capital for Biodiversity and Ecosystems.* New York: UNDP. www.biofin.org/ knowledge-product/moving-mountains-unlocking-private-capital-biodiversity-and -ecosystems.

Vaes, Jeroen and others. 2016. "Minimal Humanity Cues Induce Neural Empathic Reactions toward Non-Human Entities." *Neuropsychologia*, v. 89.

Vinuesa, Ricardo and others. 2020. "The Role of Artificial Intelligence in Achieving the Sustainable Development Goals." *Nature Communications*, v. 11.

Voigt, Maria and others. 2018. "Global Demand for Natural Resources Eliminated More than 100,000 Orangutans." *Current Biology*, v. 28.

Wackernagel, Mathis and others. 2019. "Defying the Footprint Oracle: Implications of Country Resource Trends." *Sustainability*, v. 11, no. 7.

Waldron, Anthony and others. 2020. "Protecting 30 Percent of the Planet for Nature: Costs, Benefits, and Economic Implications." Campaign for Nature working paper.

Weber, Andreas. 2020. *Animism as Ecopolitical Practice*. New Delhi, India: Heinrich Böll Stiftung India.

Weil, Simone. 1949. *The Need for Roots*. London: Routledge.

Westphal, Michael I. and others. 2008. "The Link Between International Trade and the Global Distribution of Invasive Alien Species." *Biological Invasions*, v. 10.

Wilson, Edward O. 1984. *Biophilia*. Harvard University Press.

———. 2002. *The Future of Life*. New York: Alfred A. Knopf.

Windsor, Charles HRH Prince of Wales. 2021. "Terra Carta: For Nature, People & Planet." www.sustainable-markets.org/terra-carta/.

Wise, Steven M. 2000. *Rattling the Cage: Toward Legal Rights for Animals*. New York: Perseus Press.

World Economic Forum. 2020. *Nature Risk Rising: Why the Crisis Engulfing Nature Matters for Business and the Economy*. Geneva: World Economic Forum, http://www3.weforum.org/docs/WEF_New_Nature_Economy_Report_2020.pdf.

World Wildlife Foundation (WWF). 2020. *Living Planet Report 2020: Bending the Curve of Biodiversity Loss*. Almond, Rosamunde, Monique Grooten and Tanya Petersen (eds.). Gland, Switzerland: World Wildlife Fund.

Yamaguchi, Rintaro. 2018. "Wealth and Population Growth Under Dynamic Average Utilitarianism." *Environmental Economics*, v. 23, no. 1.

Zhong, Ming and others. 2021. "Multispecies Bioacoustic Classification Using Transfer Learning of Deep Convolutional Neural Networks with Pseudo-Labeling." *Applied Acoustics*, v.166, no. 25.

Zoological Society of London (ZSL), 2020: "Position Statement on COVID-19: Wildlife Exploitation and Trade, Zoonotic Disease and Human Health." ZSL position paper, www.zsl.org/zsls-position-statement-on-covid-19-wildlife-exploitation-and-trade-zoonotic-disease-and-human-0.

SIX

Predictable Disasters
AI and the Future of Crisis Response

Tarek Ghani and Grant Gordon

The greatest barrier to achieving many of the Sustainable Development Goals (SDGs) lies in fragile settings characterized by extreme poverty, weak institutions, and ongoing vulnerability to natural and human-made disasters. Given current trends, complex emergencies may become even more challenging over the next decade, however, artificial intelligence (AI) holds the potential to transform crisis response to both save and improve many lives.[1] In order to realize that promise, crisis response policymakers will have to prioritize ongoing and new AI investments based on a sophisticated understanding of risk and return.

Bending the curve to meet the SDGs in fragile settings will require new tools and radical improvements in the impact, scalability, or cost-effectiveness of current practices—an ambitious goal that can be supported by the exponential growth in promising machine learning applications. In turn, harnessing AI for crisis response requires a clear-eyed understanding of the conditions under which

---

1. We use the term "artificial intelligence" to refer to automated processes using algorithms to make inferences from data with self-directed learning and adaptation, including, but not limited to, machine learning applications. We use "data science" to describe the broader set of capabilities necessary to implement machine learning projects. We use "crises" to reference both human-made and natural disasters, and we distinguish between the two types as relevant.

We thank Homi Kharas, John McArthur, and Izumi Ohno for editorial wisdom; Megan Roberts for insightful peer review; and Alex Diaz, Stuart Campo, Leila Toplic, Robert Kirkpatrick, Heather Roff, Sarah Sewall, Nathaniel Raymond, Leonardo Milano, Philip Tetlock, Robert Trigwell, Cameron Birge, and Jay Ulfelder for valuable conversations.

machine learning can improve outcomes as well as a framework for when and how to effectively integrate machine learning into organizations.

As we describe below, AI is reshaping our ability to anticipate, respond to, and recover from crises. It increases visibility and access to areas that have historically been inaccessible; it expands capacities to identify and predict crises and their evolution; and it enhances the effectiveness and efficiency of resource allocation and optimization during response efforts.[2] AI does this by strengthening the accuracy and precision of what we know, the speed with which we know it, and the ability to continuously optimize decisions that require analyzing many fast-changing variables simultaneously.[3]

Machine learning applications have already begun to transform three key functions of crisis response policy and programming, which we expect to accelerate over the coming decade. First, machine learning is helping decisionmakers continuously assess the risks of new and ongoing crises, particularly in the domain of natural disasters where data is rich, scientific modeling of underlying causes is advanced, and events are frequent enough to support robust feedback loops. Second, humanitarian and governmental crisis responders are increasingly using machine learning to improve targeting, intervention selection, and service delivery. And third, machine learning is streamlining the mobilization and prepositioning of resources for first responders, with current applications ranging from anticipatory financing for disasters to optimizing the logistics behind delivering humanitarian aid.

What is a vision of the future of crisis response in which AI breakthroughs have been successfully scaled? It is one in which crisis response actors increasingly know where and how crises will happen, and crisis policymakers have the information required to resource and launch efforts to prevent and mitigate these crises. It is a world in which, when unavoidable crises do unfold, financing is immediately released to provide life-saving assistance to those affected based

2. We focus here on "first-generation" machine learning applications that seek to structure, automate, and inform crisis response decisions at macro- (for example, national), meso- (for example, sub-national), and micro-levels (for example, individual). To address first-order questions in the crisis response field, we limit ourselves to identifying, predicting, and optimizing crisis response rather than the number of downstream applications that also shape crises, ranging from the use of automated image processing by drones to AI-based precision agriculture to reduce the impact of climate change.

3. All of this is made possible by general improvements in machine learning algorithms and computational processing power, which support AI-based innovation in any field. But like data, which is context-specific and often a limiting factor, the most valuable AI also needs a feedback platform where interventions and predictions are tested against reality and continuously improved. While basic machine learning applications simulate such feedback by splitting a single dataset into "testing" and "training" components, a frequently occurring decision problem informed by continuous stream of data on relevant inputs and target outcomes is an ideal condition for AI applications.

on preagreed-upon triggers. And, should crises continue, targeted and context-specific aid can be consistently delivered in record time, at scale, and at a radically lower cost, helping to save lives, reduce suffering, and speed recovery.

Before this vision for AI in crisis response can be realized, several key conditions must first be met. To start, data quality, consistency, and coverage need to improve. Absent these improvements, the accuracy of machine learning predictions will be constrained to the limitations of existing data coverage, which too often reflect biased understandings of the world and structural inequities.[4] As data deserts continue to shrink amid a growing range of sources, the quality of AI predictions will also improve. Next, decisionmakers must identify and develop a range of feedback platforms to enable rigorous testing of new machine learning approaches relative to current practices. Last, frameworks and tools for the ethical and accountable use of AI technologies must be created or strengthened in relevant institutions to protect against potential abuse and harm.[5] Together, these necessary steps will help provide the operational architecture needed to help effectively, efficiently, and safely integrate AI into the crisis response field.

While some advocates have previously promoted AI as a crystal ball to predict and prevent global crises, this aspiration obscures the political and organizational constraints that shape crisis response as well as the type of decisions that such predictions can influence. Decisionmakers should consider the political and technical feasibility of any investment in AI as well as its expected impact, conscious that leveraging the impact of any potential application is predicated on identifying the types of decisions amenable to machine learning. It also requires investing in the capabilities or partnerships to deepen machine learning expertise and rigorously assessing the impact of machine learning applications relative to current practices.

Too often, discussions of AI descend into polarized caricature. While techno-utopianism often promotes non-testable platitudes or inflated aspirations of a single project to change the world, techno-pessimism can often fall into a similar trap of developing sweeping generalizations from isolated examples of failed projects. We aim to move beyond these dichotomies by articulating a framework to understand where the expected risks and returns are highest from AI in crisis response. To develop and situate this framework, we analyze current use cases of machine learning and explore the boundaries of their application. Overall, we recommend policymakers adopt a portfolio investment approach to AI that adjusts potential benefits against common risks of political or technical

---

4. See, for example, Glandon and others, and Toplic.

5. See, for example, NetHope's Artificial Intelligence (AI) Ethics for Nonprofits Toolkit, https://solutionscenter.nethope.org/artificial-intelligence-ethics-for-nonprofits-toolkit.

infeasibility and assesses potential impact relative to current practices. Our goal is to help move the debate from "Does AI change everything?" to "When and how can specific tools most usefully augment or transform current practice?"

We focus on the potential impact AI holds for crisis response as generally reflected in Sustainable Development Goal 16's objective of promoting peaceful and inclusive societies. This framing allows us to specifically address those populations furthest behind in the SDGs—across and within countries—who are most often the primary beneficiaries of crisis response efforts. However, it limits our ability to address how AI is changing many of the long-term drivers of crisis—including poverty, inequality, and economic opportunity—captured in other SDGs and covered by other chapters in this volume. And while we focus on the implications of AI for crisis policymakers in governments and international organizations, we also attempt to highlight implications for those most directly affected by crisis—including concerns about individual autonomy, consent, and privacy, that are central to discussions and decisions regarding AI.

Crisis and Opportunity

Since the start of this century, natural and human-made disasters have levied a rising toll in lives, livelihoods, and social stability. From 2000 until 2019, the UN recorded over seven thousand major natural disasters that claimed over 1.2 million lives, and affected roughly 4 billion additional people, many individuals more than once.[6] Over those same years, the Uppsala Conflict Data Program recorded over 940,000 fatalities from organized violence, including fifty-four active state-based conflicts in 2019—the highest number since the end of World War II.[7] In 2020 alone, UNHCR counted 82.4 million people forcibly displaced worldwide due to conflict, natural disasters, and related disruptions, nearly doubling the 43.3 million estimate just ten years earlier.[8] And as we write this article in September 2021, over 221 million people have been infected globally with COVID-19 and more than 4.5 million have died so far, with those figures expected to grow considerably before the pandemic ends.[9]

6. United Nations Office for Disaster Risk Reduction, "Human Cost of Disasters 2000–19," www.undrr.org/publication/human-cost-disasters-2000-2019.

7. Uppsala Conflict Data Program https://ucdp.uu.se/downloads/brd/ucdp-brd-conf-201-xlsx .zip. The 940,000 total reflects best estimates of "battle-related deaths" defined as fatalities "caused by the warring parties that can be directly related to combat" and thus exclude indirect deaths due to disease, starvation, criminality, or attacks directed at civilians. For more details, see Pettersson and Öberg.

8. UNHCR, "Global Trends 2020: Forced Displacement in 2020," www.unhcr.org/flagship -reports/globaltrends/.

9. Johns Hopkins University & Medicine, Coronavirus Resource Center, https://coronavirus .jhu.edu/map.html.

In listing humanity's global challenges, the UN's SDGs 1.5 and 11.5 highlight the need to prevent and mitigate the compounded harm posted by frequent disasters and complex emergencies. However, the impact goes far beyond these two goals, as it is difficult to imagine achieving many SDGs—from ending extreme poverty and hunger to expanding education and healthcare to promoting peace and protecting the environment—without better crisis response. Before the impact of COVID-19 was clear, researchers had identified the set of countries where the SDGs were already on track to fail based on current trends in climate change and ongoing vulnerability to political instability: by 2030, between two-thirds and 80 percent of the world's poor are likely to live in fragile and conflict-affected countries.[10] This development frontier grows larger if one includes subnational hotspots in otherwise prosperous countries: one Brookings estimate identified 840 poverty hotspots across 102 countries expected to host 1.7 billion people in 2030.[11]

There is a growing recognition that weak institutions and systemic poverty make fragile contexts more vulnerable to both political crises and climate hazards, and slower to recover from both types of shocks.[12] In short, we observe a self-reinforcing cycle in which the hardest development cases remain persistently behind, even while emerging and developed economies continue to progress. And so, improving the ability of crisis response to prevent and mitigate the impact of disasters in fragile settings could imply substantial development returns for those furthest behind.

Trends in modern crises and response efforts suggest the challenge may grow even more complex. For one, the impacts of the climate crisis are increasingly visible in fragile settings and projected to become even more severe this decade across Central America, the Middle East, the Sahel, and Southeast Asia. Wherever climate hazards intersect with weak governance, the challenges likely to face crisis responders will multiply exponentially. Whether fleeing human-made or natural disasters, displaced populations will place increasing pressure on urban centers and neighboring countries, contributing to a regionalization of each local crisis as societies strive to adapt. Meanwhile, international institutions may continue to struggle to rebuild confidence in the face of major power rivalries, while on-the-ground coordination challenges keep growing from an influx of governmental and non-state actors. Moreover, many challenges in crisis response may be further exacerbated by the long-term humanitarian and economic impact of COVID-19.[13]

---

10. Corral and others, 18; OECD, 3.
11. Cohen, Desai, and Kharas, 210.
12. See, for example, World Bank and Ghani and Malley.
13. See Ghani.

The last two decades have seen exponential growth in the data available on crises as well as the tools needed to effectively and efficiently analyze this information.[14] Historically, data on crises were limited to frontline reports and individual observations. In the 1990s and early 2000s, survey data from crisis-affected populations, operational data from implementers, and historical cross-national datasets were used to inform decisionmaking. Over this past decade, the informational floodgates have opened, releasing high-frequency, granular data from social media, satellite and sensors, call detail records, and so on. Consequently, crisis-related data is rapidly improving in quantity, frequency, granularity, and structure—and thus creating new opportunities to anticipate, respond to, and recover from modern crises.[15]

Recent estimates indicate that, from 2015 to 2022, the number of people online will triple to 6 billion. By 2030, 7.5 billion people will likely use the internet—90 percent of the projected world population six years of age and older.[16] Mobile phones will drive that growth, especially in developing countries, where the aftershocks of disasters can be more severe: from 2020 to 2025, mobile subscribers are projected to grow from 5.2 billion to 5.8 billion, but mobile internet users will grow twice as much, from 3.8 billion to 5 billion as smartphones become more widely available.[17] The impact for data collection—even in the most challenging settings—are already myriad: researchers are conducting phone surveys at unprecedented scale with Voice over Internet Protocol (VoIP), proxying for population movements with cell phone–related location data, and creating new measures of activity and sentiment from social media.[18] Standard early warning indicators like commodity price changes are now more easily tracked with online databases.[19] The cost of remote sensing imagery—from satellites, planes, or low-flying drones—continues to fall. Even remote audio sensors are used in settings like Syria to warn civilians of incoming aircraft or nearby gunfire.[20]

These changes have vastly increased the ability to integrate AI into crisis response, catalyzing a number of high-profile projects that have raised public expectations around AI's potential. To help separate hype from reality, we provide a simple framework that outlines our assessment of the underlying promise and pitfalls for integrating AI into crisis response. Specifically, we highlight how the risks to AI's breakthrough potential in crisis response vary by complexity and

---

14. Gleditsch, 301–14.
15. For useful overviews, see Panic and Pauwels.
16. See Morgan.
17. GSMA, 6.
18. Relevant examples include Flowminder, Orange Door Research, and Premise.
19. See, for example, Cavallo, Cavallo, and Rigobon.
20. See, for example, Hala Systems.

timeline of the crisis. We rank order risks in our framework but leave returns unspecified, enabling policymakers to apply a risk-adjusted weighting to potential returns for any particular investment in AI in crisis response.

Figure 6-1 categorizes potential AI applications in crisis response across two dimensions. The horizontal axis represents the crisis timeline, ranging from prevention to response. The vertical axis represents crisis complexity, ranging from less complex natural disasters, such as floods, to relatively more complex human--made disasters, such as conflict.[21] We argue that the expected value of any AI investment is driven not only by returns (for example, size and scale of potential impact) but also by the risks posed by technical and political barriers of integrating AI into crisis response efforts. Technical feasibility reflects characteristics that make a crisis context more or less amenable to AI implementation: frequency of the event, data availability and quality, and modeling complexity. For example, natural disasters are often high-frequency events with better data and more reliable scientific models, given the underlying natural processes involved when compared to complex disasters such as civil war. Political feasibility relates to the ability of crisis policymakers to act on the predictions AI can help improve.

Figure 6-1. Feasibility of AI Applications in Crisis Settings

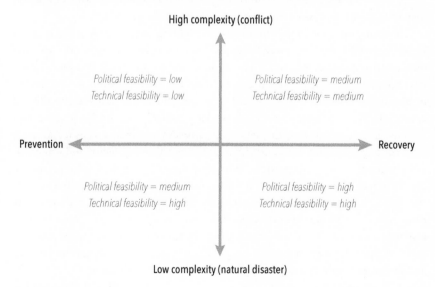

21. For ease of interpretation, we limit the framework's time horizon to one year before and one year after crisis onset. While prevention is desirable over a longer time period, multi-year time spans provide less help in thinking about the decision constraints faced by crisis policymakers and how best to invest in response in AI applications.

This is driven by the incentives around the timing of an intervention—because, unfortunately, response is often easier to mobilize than prevention—and the extent to which a crisis is driven by natural causes, which can often facilitate quicker local and international cooperation.

This framework has several important implications. First, the political feasibility of crisis response tends to increase as a crisis evolves and expands beyond the realm of prevention. The technical feasibility of response also increases for more complex crises as more data enables model refinement. Second, it is often more politically and technically feasible to respond to low-complexity crises than high-complexity crises, though for different reasons. On the one hand, cooperation on natural disaster response is often a win-win for political leaders relative to the contentious politics of conflict prevention and mitigation. And on the other hand, data and modeling of natural disasters is far more advanced than of human-instigated disasters.

After combining these feasibility constraints, we observe the highest risk-adjusted returns for AI investments in the bottom-right quadrant with natural disaster relief efforts, and the lowest risk-adjusted returns in the top-left quadrant with conflict prevention efforts. While crisis response actors should continue pursuing promising, high-return AI investments beyond natural disaster relief efforts, we would urge them to probe the technical and political constraints that may impede the success of those efforts early on in the process.

There are also some important caveats to highlight when considering integrating AI into crisis response, given fundamental concerns and constraints regarding data in crisis settings. Above all, having more data—and more complex data—does not unequivocally imply more useful data. Data that is inaccurate, imprecise, or biased can undermine analysis and response. This is true across crisis-affected countries—for example, there is more data available for Jordan than South Sudan—as well as within countries—for example, social media feeds reflect areas with connectivity. This data unevenness is a major limiting factor and often disadvantages the most marginalized and least digitally connected communities, regularly requiring policymakers to be savvy consumers and communicators of the pitfalls inherent to data-driven analysis. Moreover, collecting and analyzing these new types of data require capabilities not always well represented in crisis response organizations, which in turn demand new organizational investments or partnerships. These are nontrivial but soluble challenges that should be assessed and prioritized early in each new application of machine learning.

There are also a growing set of privacy, security, and ethical challenges around crisis data management.[22] Creating and operationalizing ethical guidelines for

22. For an overview of ethical considerations in applying AI to conflict-related crisis response, see Pauwels.

AI in crisis response is crucial to appropriately safeguarding individuals and following a no-harm principle, particularly when projects are serving vulnerable and marginalized populations. Safeguarding concerns are real and a number of AI projects in the humanitarian space have demonstrated the potential negative consequences of these methods. While much work remains to be done, emerging frameworks for crisis response provide guidance on how to ensure privacy, accountability, safety, and security, as well as a number of key ethical principles.[23] Again, the responsibility falls to all crisis response actors to ask hard questions and demand clear answers about the ethical use of crisis data, so that risks are properly balanced against potential returns.

Prevention and Mitigation

As digital data sources proliferate, machine learning can improve how policymakers anticipate and monitor new crises. Indeed, in the notable case of flood warning and mapping, that promise is already real. But as local contexts and disaster types vary greatly in terms of reliable signals, the crisis response field remains a long way from a crystal ball for crises. For example, in January 2020, well-informed observers understood the risks were high for a global pandemic, famine in Yemen, and war in Ethiopia—but few could say with confidence when and how those risks might unfold. And with risks proliferating nearly as fast as data, decisionmakers need help deciding what data to pay attention to and when.

Digital technologies have transformed the information available to crisis policymakers, offering unprecedented insights from disaster settings even as increasing data availability complicates their efforts to separate signals from noise. In an ideal-case scenario, crisis responders know exactly which data streams to analyze—and how—to better anticipate the likelihood, impact, and profile of an emerging disaster. Given their high frequency and natural processes, floods provide one such example where data scientists have made noteworthy progress—and with clear relevance to multiple SDGs, given the potential of flooding to close markets, disrupt food security, shutter schools, and spread diseases. The EU's Global Flood Awareness System (GloFAS) produces daily flood forecasts and monthly seasonal outlooks using weather data and hydrological models, while UN researchers developed a machine learning approach to processing satellite imagery that reduced the time to develop a flood map for emergency response teams by 80 percent.[24] More generally, scientists are working to translate UN

23. This includes the Humanitarian Data Science and Ethics Group's Framework for the Ethical Use of Advanced Data Science Methods in the Humanitarian Sector and The Harvard Humanitarian Initiative's Signal Code.
24. See European Commission, "Global Flood Awareness System," www.globalfloods.eu/; Nemni and others.

climate projections into impact models that can offer localized forecasts to show how climate change will affect critical sectors such as water, agriculture, or forestry, and nonprofit organizations are using climate models to strengthen physical infrastructure and population resilience against earthquakes and typhoons.[25]

But while climate hazards often lend themselves more readily to data collection and sophisticated modeling approaches, other common disaster types, such as pandemic disease, food insecurity, forced displacement, or deadly conflict are more directly influenced by hard-to-predict behavioral processes. So far, predictive modeling of the onset and evolution of complex emergencies has had more modest success than predictive modeling of natural disasters, but noteworthy efforts continue to make encouraging progress. And as many human-made disasters have gradual onsets followed by cycles of intensification, decline, and often relapse, attempts to mitigate low-level or persistent crises may contribute to prevention efforts over time.

The UN's OCHA-Bucky predictive model of COVID-19 spread and mitigation in humanitarian crises is one informative case. Developed as a collaboration between OCHA's Centre for Humanitarian Data and the Johns Hopkins Applied Physics Laboratory, Bucky provides humanitarian decisionmakers with subnational, four-week projections of the likely spread of the current pandemic in key fragile countries to inform resource planning and facilitate sophisticated scenario analysis of non-pharmaceutical interventions, such as changing social behavior, limiting movement, increasing healthcare access, or prioritizing medical care to vulnerable groups.[26] By combining pre-pandemic data on subnational demographics, intra-regional mobility, and social contact norms with regular updates on local case counts and global disease characteristics, Bucky provides insights for humanitarian responders in contexts such as Afghanistan, Iraq, and South Sudan. While the model is only robust to the accuracy and completeness of underlying data inputs, it goes beyond more standard "dashboard"-style exercises through continuous refinement and the ability to explore counterfactual scenarios. As such, it both complements and incentivizes the types of fundamental data investments necessary for sustained progress on AI adoption.

The devastating scale of COVID-19 has helped spur progress on disease prediction models, such as Bucky, that could generate increased demand for—and investment in—the data, algorithms, and feedback platforms needed not just for COVID-19 and guarding against future pandemics, but also addressing common

25. See, for example, the Inter-Sectoral Impact Model Intercomparison Project, www.isimip.org/; Build Change, https://buildchange.org/.
26. Center for Humanitarian Data, "OCHA-Bucky: A COVID-19 Model to Inform Humanitarian Operations," https://centre.humdata.org/ocha-bucky-a-covid-19-model-to-inform-humanitarian-operations/.

diseases like malaria—which was responsible for over 400,000 fatalities in 2018 alone.[27] At the time of writing this article, the Biden administration released a USD $65b plan for pandemic preparedness, including $3.1b for an early warning detection system.[28] These advances underscore the potential to leverage data science for this type of modeling. Moreover, methods recently developed, for example, to model the spread of COVID-19 in Cox's Bazar refugee camps in Bangladesh using open-source census datasets, locations of potential gathering places, and other information on daily movements, could be adapted and expanded with cell phone–related location data to help decisionmakers as far away as Uganda prioritize antimalarial bed net distribution and determine where to concentrate spraying for mosquitoes.[29] This can be helpful for targeting, even where malaria is endemic and transmission is year-round rather than subject to outbreaks. Other crises may benefit as well. Efforts to predict food shortages and prioritize the allocation of resources both between and within countries to prevent potential famines could receive fresh attention if the COVID-19 prediction models can help raise crisis policymakers' expectations of what insights forecasting approaches might offer elsewhere.[30]

But reliable predictions will most likely lag behind for challenges such as forced displacement and deadly conflict, given issues of data and modeling, even though those crises may become more frequent as climate change exacerbates food insecurity, water scarcity, and resource competition.[31] Forced migration data is comparatively scarce in developing countries. The most notable and systematic data sources are the IOM's Displacement Tracking Matrix and the Internal Displacement Monitoring Centre's Global Internal Displacement Database. The UNHCR and World Bank also launched the Joint Data Center on Forced Displacement with the goal of improving data on forced migration.[32] Moreover, decisions on migration frequently involve a set of push-and-pull factors such as climate impacts or political instability in origin countries and economic opportunities and social freedoms in destination countries. While these factors are

27. World Health Organization, "Malaria Fact Sheet," www.who.int/news-room/fact-sheets/detail/malaria.

28. StatNews. "The White House wants $65 billion for an 'Apollo'-style pandemic preparedness program," September 3, 2021. www.statnews.com/2021/09/03/biden-wants-65-billion-for-apollo-style-pandemic-preparedness-program/

29. See UN Global Pulse, "Modeling the Spread of COVID-19 and the Impact of Public Health Interventions in Cox's Bazar and Other Refugee Camps." www.unglobalpulse.org/2020/10/modelling-the-spread-of-covid-19-and-the-impact-of-public-health-interventions-in-coxs-bazar-and-other-refugee-camps/.

30. See, for example, Andrée and others.

31. For a review of AI in the human security field, see Roff.

32. Sarzin.

challenging to disentangle, much less predict, some researchers have made modest progress here using online search or advertising data.[33] However, existing migration prediction models often tend to be limited to country-year aggregate predictions that can raise concerns with decisionmakers given a tendency of those models to overweight preexisting trends and underpredict large shocks.[34]

Deadly conflict is subject to data limits similar to those of forced migration, though the spread of cell phones and social media may help future researchers better understand how and why violence breaks out. Current conflict prediction efforts are limited by the availability of high-quality input data from around the world, along with the empirical challenge that the onset of civil conflict is a low-frequency event.[35] For instance, one promising public effort combining unsupervised and supervised machine learning methods to analyze newspaper articles and predict conflict risk is limited to English-language sources, as natural language processing is unavailable for key dialects in many relevant conflict-affected countries, not to mention a standardized set of high-quality news sources across such settings.[36] Another recent rigorous analysis using high-quality conflict micro-data from both Colombia and Indonesia had success only in identifying persistent, subnational high-violence hot spots—and not new outbreaks or escalations of violence.[37]

While conflict early warning remains an elusive goal for crisis analysts given the complexity of political systems, progress continues to be made in predicting and preventing deadly violence at the micro-level. For example, Hala Systems has used remote audio sensors to warn civilians of incoming aircraft or nearby gunfire in settings like Syria. Two promising future areas to watch here are efforts by the UN to track hate speech online and via radio stations, both of which are being led by UN Global Pulse, the big data initiative of the UN Secretary-General.[38] Notably, the latter effort involving radio stations is a creative solution to the challenge of measuring activity in remote, marginalized, and often digitally disconnected communities, and could be used to target conflict resolution and policing efforts.

33. See, for example, Bohme, Groger, and Stohr, and Palotti and others.
34. See, for example, Milano.
35. While several governments have begun applying machine learning to conflict prediction and analysis, few details are available, and assessing the quality and policy application of these efforts remains challenging.
36. Mueller and Conflict Forecast, www.conflictforecast.org.
37. Bazzi and others.
38. For initial results of related previous efforts, see UN Global Pulse, "Exploring the Effects of Extremist Violence on Online Hate Speech," www.unglobalpulse.org/project/exploring-the-effects -of-extremist-violence-on-online-hate-speech/ and "Using Machine Learning to Analyse Radio Content in Uganda," www.unglobalpulse.org/project/pilot-studies-using-machine-learning-to -analyse-radio-content-in-uganda-2017/.

Finally, machine learning can improve mitigation efforts such as resource mobilization and prepositioning for responders by providing more accurate and precise predictions of where and when assistance will be needed. For example, in the emerging field of anticipatory disaster financing, the Centre for Disaster Protection and others have prominently advocated for a reorientation toward risk-based financing approaches based on contingency planning and prespecified triggers.[39] While one of the highest-profile anticipatory finance efforts—the World Bank's Pandemic Emergency Financing Facility—was recently shut down after widely shared criticisms of its slow and modest disbursements as COVID--19 spread around the world, it would be a mistake to discard a much-needed alternative to chronically underfunded humanitarian appeals because the financial parameters and operational arrangements of one example were poorly calibrated.[40] Much like the market for terrorism insurance after the 9/11 attacks, it will take time and government investment in order for the anticipatory disaster financing market to mature.[41] As of July 2020, the UN's Central Emergency Response Fund (CERF) disbursed US$5.2 million after a GloFLAS prediction of high probability of flooding in Bangladesh—the fastest CERF allocation in history and the first one to take place before peak flooding.[42] And beyond anticipatory finance, machine learning already delivers large cost savings by optimizing humanitarian aid delivery systems for agencies like WFP.[43] As the predictive models discussed above continue to improve, useful applications are also likely to emerge for the prepositioning of humanitarian resources.

Relief and Recovery

In addition to supporting crisis prevention and mitigation, data availability and machine learning have generated a sea change over recent years for crisis response efforts. OCHA's Centre for Humanitarian Data now houses over seventeen thousand humanitarian data sets as well as a specific catalogue of predictive models in the humanitarian sector.[44] Moreover, a recent analysis of predictive analytics in

---

39. See Guidance Notes for Highly Effective DRF, www.disasterprotection.org/guidance-notes -for-highly-effective-drf.

40. See Clarke.

41. Michel-Kerjan and Raschky.

42. Center for Humanitarian Data, "Anticipatory Action in Bangladesh before Peak Monsoon Flooding," https://centre.humdata.org/anticipatory-action-in-bangladesh-before-peak-monsoon -flooding/.

43. World Food Program, "Palantir and WFP Partner to Help Transform Global Humanitarian Delivery," February 15, 2019, www.wfp.org/news/palantir-and-wfp-partner-help-transform-global -humanitarian-delivery.

44. Center for Humanitarian Data, "Catalogue of Predictive Models in the Humanitarian Sector," https://centre.humdata.org/catalogue-for-predictive-models-in-the-humanitarian-sector/.

the humanitarian space commissioned by the then UK Department for International Development identified forty-nine different projects predicting the who, what, where, or when of crises.[45] This has created an informational foundation upon which machine learning has transformed three core areas of humanitarian relief and recovery: (1) targeting, the identification of how to allocate resources across crisis-affected populations; (2) intervention selection, the determination of which services should be provided; and (3) service delivery mechanisms, the ways in which core services are provided to clients. While these efforts do not necessarily increase the amount of resources allocated to a given crisis, they have already begun to influence how existing resources are allocated within a crisis. While relief and recovery efforts have demonstrated that AI can be integrated well at the project level, they have yet to be effectively scaled through broader adoption of practices and approaches.

One of the most promising areas for AI to transform humanitarian relief and recovery is in targeting aid delivery. Assessments to determine individual- and population-level needs and vulnerabilities are launched after every crisis and integrated into every project implemented in response. Often these are time- and capital-intensive processes limited in scale and precision by traditional data sources and analytic methods. Leveraging satellite imagery, cell phone records, and other administrative data, machine learning applications can systematically automate, at scale, the assessment process to more effectively and efficiently understand "who has what" and prioritize "who gets what" in crisis response.

A number of noteworthy pilot efforts have demonstrated AI's ability to improve this type of targeting in recent years. In 2014, GiveDirectly, an organization that provides direct cash transfers to the world's poor, developed algorithms to process satellite imagery and detect different types of roofing in Uganda, which was highly correlated with household economic characteristics, to enhance targeting cash payments.[46] Rather than conducting time- and labor-intensive village-level surveys to identify household-level poverty data, these algorithms automated the selection process, increasing the speed and cost-effectiveness of targeting and therefore increasing the ability to provide relief to a greater number of individuals.

More recently, to provide the most vulnerable Togolese citizens with cash support to weather the health and economic consequences of COVID, Joshua Blumenstock of UC Berkeley and co-authors used deep learning algorithms to process satellite images and phone usage data to map extreme poverty and target the transfers accordingly.[47] Using detection approaches for the satellite images

45. Hernandez and Roberts.

46. DataKind, "Using Satellite Imagery to Find Villages in Need," www.datakind.org/projects/using-the-simple-to-be-radical/.

47. Joshua Blumenstock, "Machine Learning Can Help Get COVID-19 Aid to Those Who Need It Most," *Nature*, May 14, 2020, www.nature.com/articles/d41586-020-01393-7.

in conjunction with call record data to estimate wealth and income, the project aimed to augment slower, survey-based methods that would traditionally identify needs.[48] In the article that formally assesses these methods, Aiken and co-authors note that compared to standard approaches, leveraging satellite and phone data reduced targeting errors by between 4 to 21 percent to many of the poorest citizens.[49]

This type of targeting has also been deployed outside of crisis contexts, with similarly large gains. IDInsight, an organization dedicated to reducing poverty through data and evidence, demonstrated that machine learning approaches could be used to identify out-of-school girls in parts of rural India, building an algorithmic model that increased the ability to locate between 50 percent and 200 percent more out-of-school children at the same cost as historically conducted individual household surveys.[50] These approaches have not only offered the ability to accelerate processing, but have also widened the pool of recipients by leveraging larger population datasets. In future crises, these datasets can be used as a foundation for targeting assessments, further increasing efficiencies and the ability to quickly and nimbly respond to crises.

While advances in targeting have helped answer the question of who needs what, AI has also provided the ability to help determine what is needed. A key advance in applications of machine learning is the ability to dynamically identify needs and optimize crisis response based on what works in a specific program context. In the first-ever adaptive experiment implemented in a humanitarian context by the International Rescue Committee in Jordan, academic researchers developed a machine learning algorithm to allocate different types of employment support services to Syrian refugees and vulnerable Jordanians based on their individual characteristics and how those different support services have generated impact.[51] This type of "precision social service delivery" optimized the specific package of services provided to each individual in order to maximize their individual outcomes. The data-driven approach generated a 20-percentage point improvement in the probability that refugees and vulnerable Jordanians were offered a job and were in formal wage employment six weeks after receiving targeted support.

Improvements in data availability and machine learning have provided the ability to better understand individual needs and create individual-level relief packages. Médecins sans Frontières created a machine learning–based application that allows nonexpert clinicians in low-income settings to identify antibiotic

48. Aiken and others.
49. Aiken and others.
50. Brockman and others.
51. Caria and others.

resistance using image processing methods and create bespoke treatment regimes for clients.[52] Similar approaches have been used to provide educational services in emergency contexts. Prior to COVID-19, 75 million children were out of school in crisis-affected countries, representing half of the world's out-of-school population. With only 2 percent of humanitarian funding allocated to education in emergencies and a lack of educational infrastructure and trained workforce, AI has been used to develop individually tailored learning experiences delivered through tablets to provide bespoke educational content to children across multiple learning levels.[53] Can't Wait to Learn is a digital game-based learning software developed by War Child Holland, which allows children to learn at their own pace and level. A quasi-experimental analysis of the program demonstrated that this approach led to significant improvements in math and literacy skills as well as psychological well-being.[54] While EdTech has clear limitations relative to in-person instruction, these individually focused services demonstrate how AI is increasingly transforming core service provision during the relief and recovery phases of crisis.[55]

Moreover, as the digital revolution sweeps through crisis-affected contexts, and given that refugees are increasingly displaced in middle-income countries, data availability and machine learning will likely continue accelerating innovation in service delivery.[56] Especially in the wake of COVID-19, digital delivery is emerging as an alternative cost-effective way to provide services in crisis contexts, including access to healthcare, cash to meet basic needs, educational content for children, and job platforms in local labor markets. Naturally, AI is shaping implementation models, enabling remote health consultations, supporting software to deliver and track cash, creating educational content, and algorithmically matching individuals to job opportunities.[57] For example, SkillsLabs is an example of a software and machine learning–based approach that largely helps refugees navigate labor markets and match into jobs in the EU.[58] Similar platforms have been established for Syrian refugees in Jordan.[59] A crucial challenge to leveraging AI for job-matching platforms in low- and middle-income countries is the availability of job opportunities and lack of evidence on what individual-level characteristics predict high-quality matches. Nonetheless, these

52. See Médecins Sans Frontières, Antibiotic Resistance, www.doctorswithoutborders.org/what-we-do/medical-issues/antibiotic-resistance, and Google (2019).
53. See, for example, Education Cannot Wait, www.educationcannotwait.org/the-situation/.
54. Brown.
55. Rodriguez-Segura and Crawfurd.
56. Devictor.
57. GSMA.
58. See Skills Lab, www.etf.europa.eu/en/projects-activities/projects/skills-lab.
59. See, for example, ILO Skills Platform, www.ecsjo.com/.

platforms demonstrate that even in these settings, there are gains in employment outcomes to using algorithmic matching.[60]

Over the past two decades, information provision has emerged as a key component of humanitarian service delivery.[61] Providing accurate, timely, and precise information at scale to crisis-affected populations enables them to make informed individual decisions about the context and how to respond. Here, too, AI has enhanced the ability to deliver information. For example, the Norwegian Refugee Council has begun using automated chatbots to provide Venezuelan migrants in Colombia with details on their rights within the country.[62] Information provision may be one of the areas most amenable to machine learning applications, as it seeks to provide high-frequency data over existing digital platforms.

AI holds the potential to transform the operational and financial model of how the humanitarian sector responds to emerging crises. The humanitarian response system is driven by what Stefan Dercon and Daniel Clarke call the "begging bowl" problem: a crisis breaks out, humanitarian responders deploy and make the case that aid is needed, and donors aim to overcome a collective action problem to finance response.[63] In practice, this can generate major delays between the advent of a crisis and when humanitarian aid is unlocked. This dynamic is, in part, driven by the inability to accurately and precisely identify when crises will break out and the consequent distrust by donors of needs assessments given the incentives for responders to potentially inflate humanitarian needs.[64]

Real-time data flows and machine learning applications will increase the ability to objectively identify and measure crises as they unfold, opening up opportunities to move into risk-based financing and reshaping how humanitarian response is delivered. Instead of an operational infrastructure grounded in post-hoc fundraising and service delivery, a future humanitarian system could orient around an operational structure that flexibly increases capacity for rapid response as a crisis worsens.[65] The Danish Red Cross and International Federation of Red Cross and Crescent Societies, for example, recently launched the first volcano catastrophe bond, which would release large tranches of funding for disaster response according to a tiered trigger structure.[66] Recently, UN OCHA

60. Caria and others.
61. Greenwood.
62. Toplic.
63. Clarke and Dercon.
64. Konyndyk.
65. Talbot, Dercon, and Barder.
66. See Reuters, "Danish Red Cross launches volcano catastrophe bond," www.reuters.com/article/us-volcano-insurance-bond/danish-red-cross-launches-volcano-catastrophe-bond-idUSKB N2BE00J/.

launched a pilot program in Somalia to explore how these types of instruments can be adapted for drought and sudden-onset emergencies.[67]

Harnessing Breakthrough Potential

Harnessing AI's breakthrough potential requires decisionmakers to recognize that machine learning applications are no panacea but do offer real opportunities to save and improve the lives of those affected by crisis. It requires moving beyond broad debates over whether or not AI is useful to instead embrace systematic analyses of the conditions under which machine learning enhances or detracts from current practice. It requires moving beyond the dichotomy of quantitative versus qualitative data to an approach that identifies and integrates the comparative advantages of each type of data as available. And it requires moving beyond vague theories of change to concrete assessments of breakthrough potential in impact, scale, and cost-effectiveness in specific contexts and plans to develop required new capabilities.

At the ecosystem-level, benefiting from the potential returns of AI requires investing in data quality and coverage, launching feedback platforms that take result-based learning seriously, and strengthening data ethics standards in governance frameworks. At the organizational level, it requires identifying decisions that can integrate machine learning applications, establishing capabilities, and assessing the impact of these new approaches. From an organizational perspective, the challenges of integrating machine learning into crisis response are not different from the broader question decisionmakers face when they determine if and how to invest in new capabilities: (1) what are the anticipated returns from a new approach; (2) how should insights from a new approach be integrated into organizational decisionmaking processes and culture; (3) should new capabilities be in-housed or developed through partnership, and so on. Of course, answers to these questions might vary by organization: for example, smaller, agile organizations may be able to integrate new technologies more quickly, whereas larger incumbents may prove to be later adopters at scale.

One noteworthy point in pursuing AI's breakthrough potential in crisis response is that investing in machine learning applications is about everything except the algorithm itself, which is often off-the-shelf technology. Instead, crisis response actors seeking to apply AI will have to develop the data sources, conceptual models, and feedback platforms to implement machine learning applications. Overcoming organizational barriers to adoption is thus an inevitable step

---

67. United Nations CERF, "CERF and Anticipatory Action," https://cerf.un.org/sites/default/files/resources/CERF_and_Anticipatory_Action.pdf.

for unlocking AI's breakthrough potential. Some issues, like establishing operational procedures or acquiring technical capacity, are straightforward once leaders see a clear value proposition from AI. Other constraints, including cultural resistance to quantitative analysis or ethical concerns over privacy and security of data sources, will require more nuanced attention. Overall, the achievements of data-driven efforts at the UN, such as the Centre for Humanitarian Data and UN Global Pulse, provides hope that progress will continue.

As crisis policymakers consider how to invest in AI, one common concern is that the use of AI in crisis response currently resembles a disparate set of projects rather than a cohesive portfolio. In part, this stems from AI tracking the natural arc that many new technologies take: several seemingly uncoordinated projects are launched to assess potential before more sophisticated programs or strategies take shape. Moreover, unlike the private sector's rapid adoption of AI applications, mechanisms for scaling AI in crisis response only move as fast as the governance approaches needed to support them.

While the danger of AI "pilotitis" may loom large for crisis response, there are three promising pathways to scale and sustainability. First, specific projects should be templatized for reuse, replicated across contexts, and most important, translated into global frameworks. For example, the Stanford Immigration Policy Lab has developed an algorithm to optimize where refugees are resettled within countries. This now needs to be piloted, tested, and replicated across countries, and if the impact and cost-effectiveness is confirmed, the United Nations and its member states could create a between-country matching system. Second, multilateral institutions should invest in public goods infrastructure and governance for data science and machine learning, including but not limited to climate and conflict prediction models. The Center for Humanitarian Data is a critical step in this direction, but more is needed, including articulating an agenda for how AI can meet the goals for preventing and mitigating crises. Third, machine learning should be integrated as a standard priority in donor behavior: data science should be added as a standard budget line in all projects above a certain funding threshold, funding windows that support AI-proven projects should be launched, and support to enhance state and local capacity to use AI should be made available.

As a range of crisis actors seek to integrate AI to save and improve lives across many different disaster contexts, we endorse a risk-adjusted AI investment approach that acknowledges where political or technical obstacles may impede success. With that said, the crisis response field would be best served by a portfolio of efforts that includes a mix of both high-risk, lower-return bets and low-risk, higher-return initiatives. As noted above, each category of crisis response has its comparative advantages and drawbacks, with prevention and mitigation more exposed to the uncertainty associated with political decisionmaking and relief and recovery more likely to focus on micro-level interventions that need to reach scale for significant impact. Achieving breakthrough potential in crisis response interventions over the next decade will not be simple or linear. After all, while the disasters may be predictable, what works best to prevent or respond to them is clearly not.

References

Andrée, Bo Pieter Johannes, and others. 2020. "Predicting Food Crises." World Bank Policy Research Working Paper No. 9412.

Bazzi, Samuel and others. 2019. "The Promise and Pitfalls of Conflict Prediction: Evidence from Colombia and Indonesia." NBER Working Paper No. 25980.

Blumenstock, J. E., G. Cadamuro, R. On. 2015. "Predicting Poverty and Wealth from Mobile Phone Metadata," *Science*, v. 350, no. 6264.

Aiken, Emily and others. "Machine Learning and Mobile Phone Data Can Improve the Targeting of Humanitarian Assistance." NBER Working Paper No. 29070.

Böhme, Marcus H., André Gröger, and Tobias Stöhr. 2020. "Searching for a Better Life: Predicting International Migration with Online Search Keywords," *Journal of Development Economics*, no. 142.

Brockman, Ben, and others. 2019. "Can Machine Learning Double Your Social Impact?" *Stanford Social Innovation Review*. February 20.

Brown, Felicity, and others. Forthcoming. "Can't Wait to Learn: A Quasi-Experimental Evaluation of a Digital Game-Based Learning Programme for Out-of-School Children in Sudan." *Journal of Development Effectiveness*.

Cavallo, Alberto, Eduardo A. Cavallo, and Roberto Rigobon. 2014. "Prices and Supply Disruptions during Natural Disasters." *Review of Income and Wealth*, v. 60, no. S2.

Caria, A. Stefano, and others. 2021. "An Adaptive Targeted Field Experiment: Job Search Assistance for Refugees in Jordan." University of Oxford, Department of Economics.

Clarke, D.J. "Now is not the time for the World Bank to step back on pandemic financing," August 13, 2020. www.disasterprotection.org/latest-news/now-is-not-the -time-for-the-world-bank-to-step-back-on-pandemic-financing.

Clarke, D. J., and Dercon, Stefan. 2016. *Dull Disasters? How Planning Ahead Will Make a Difference*. Oxford University Press.

Cohen, Jennifer L., Raj M. Desai, and Homi Kharas. 2019. "Spatial Targeting of Poverty Hotspots." *Leave No One Behind: Time for Specifics on the Sustainable Development Goals*, edited by Homi Kharas, John W. McArthur, and Izumi Ohno. Brookings.

Corral, Paul, and others. 2020. "Fragility and Conflict: On the Front Lines of the Fight against Poverty." World Bank.

Devictor, Xavier, Do, Quy-Toan, Levchenko, Andrei A. 2020. "The Globalization of Refugee Flows." World Bank Policy Research Working Paper No. 9206.

Ghani, Tarek. 2021. "The Sting in COVID-19's Tail." *Foreign Affairs*, January 26.

Ghani, Tarek, and Robert Malley. 2020. "Climate Change Doesn't Have to Stoke Conflict." *Foreign Affairs*, September 28.

Glandon and others. "Despite the hype, do not expect big data to replace traditional

surveys anytime soon," January 7, 2021. www.3ieimpact.org/blogs/despite-hype-do
-not-expect-big-data-replace-traditional-surveys-anytime-soon/

Gleditsch, Kristian Skrede, and others. 2014. "Data and Progress in Peace and Conflict Research." *Journal of Peace Research*, v. 51, no. 2.

Google. 2019. "Accelerating Social Good with Artificial Intelligence: Insights from the Google AI Impact Challenge."

Greenwood, Faine, and others. 2017. "The Signal Code: A Human Rights Approach to Information During Crisis."

GSMA. 2018. "Mobile for Humanitarian Innovation: Landscaping the Digital Humanitarian Ecosystem."

Hala Systems. Inc. 2019. "Protect Everything that Matters." https://georgetown.app.box
.com/s/qm2raov0qlh7kodt4ubl2p9zj5879x4v.

Hernandez, K., and T. Roberts. 2020. "Predictive Analytics in Humanitarian Action: A Preliminary Mapping and Analysis." K4D Emerging Issues Report 33. Brighton, England: Institute of Development Studies.

Konyndyk, Jeremy. 2018. "Rethinking the Humanitarian Business Model." Washington, D.C.: Center for Global Development.

Michel-Kerjan, E., and P. A. Raschky. 2011. "The Effects of Government Intervention on the Market for Corporate Terrorism Insurance." *European Journal of Political Economy*, no. 27 (Supplement 1).

Milano, Leonardo. "Reviewing the Danish Refugee Council's Foresight Model," October 20, 2020. https://centre.humdata.org/reviewing-the-danish-refugee
-councils-foresight-model/.

Morgan, Steve. "Humans on the Internet Will Triple from 2015 to 2022 and Hit 6 Billion," Cybercrime Magazine, July 18, 2019. https://cybersecurityventures.com/
how-many-internet-users-will-the-world-have-in-2022-and-in-2030/.

Mueller, Hannes, and Christopher Rauh. 2020. "The Hard Problem of Prediction for Conflict Prevention." Center for Economic Policy Research.

Nemni, Edoardo, and others. 2020. "Fully Convolutional Neural Network for Rapid Flood Segmentation in Synthetic Aperture Radar Imagery." *Remote Sensing*, v. 12, no. 16.

OECD. 2018. *States of Fragility*. OECD Publishing.

Pauwels, Eleonore. 2020. "Artificial Intelligence and Data Capture Technologies in Violence and Conflict Prevention." Global Center on Cooperative Security. September.

Palotti, Joao, and others. 2020. "Monitoring of the Venezuelan Exodus through Facebook's Advertising Platform." *PLOS One*, v. 15, no. 2.

Panic, Brank. 2020. "Data for Peacebuilding and Prevention Ecosystem Mapping: The State of Play and the Path to Creating a Community of Practice." Center on International Cooperation. October.

Pettersson, Therese, and Magnus Öberg. 2020. "Organized Violence, 1989–2019." *Journal of Peace Research*, v. 57, no. 4.

Reuters. "Danish Red Cross launches volcano catastrophe bond," March 21, 2021. www
.reuters.com/article/us-volcano-insurance-bond/danish-red-cross-launches-volcano
-catastrophe-bond-idUSKBN2BE00J

Rodriguez-Segura and Crawfurd. "What Works in EdTech," Center for Global Development, September 3, 2020. www.cgdev.org/blog/what-works-edtech.

Roff, Heather. 2017. *Advancing Human Security through Artificial Intelligence.* London: Chatham House.

Sarzin, Zara. 2017. "Stocktaking of Global Forced Displacement Data." World Bank Policy Research Working Paper No. 7985.

Talbot, Theodore, Stefan Dercon, and Owen Barder. 2017. "Payouts for Perils: How Insurance Can Radically Improve Emergency Aid." Washington, D.C.: Center for Global Development.

Toplic, Lelia. "AI ethics: 5 considerations for nonprofits," July 22, 2020. www.nethope .org/2020/07/22/ai-ethics-5-reasons-why-nonprofit-engagement-is-key/.

———. "AI in the Humanitarian Sector," Relief Web, October 8, 2020. https:// reliefweb.int/report/world/ai-humanitarian-sector.

World Bank. 2020."Poverty and Shared Prosperity 2020: Reversals of Fortune." Washington, DC: World Bank. https://openknowledge.worldbank.org/handle/ 10986/34496.

SEVEN

How AgriTech Is Transforming Traditional Agriculture in Emerging Markets
"Think Big, Act Fast, Start Small"

Lesly Goh

Agriculture is a significant contributor to the economic growth of most developing economies. It provides food security, reduces poverty, and generates a significant portion of employment. As of 2018, agriculture accounted for more than 25 percent of GDP in developing countries, and it is estimated that 65 percent of the poor working adults depend on agriculture for their livelihoods.[1] Agriculture also plays an essential role in driving job creation, and it is one of the most important sources of employment in low- and middle-income countries. In the ASEAN region, the agriculture sector contributes to about 35 percent of the region's employment, of which 60 percent are small-holder farmers.[2] Women hold important roles in all parts of agriculture value chains, and account for nearly half of the world's smallholder farmers. Equally important, agriculture will be critical to eliminating extreme poverty, and recent evidence shows that a 1 percent increase in agriculture GDP reduces poverty, on average, by more than 1 percent—this is especially true in the poorest countries.[3]

However, the agriculture sector in emerging markets continues to rely on tools

1. See World Bank website "Agriculture and Food," www.worldbank.org/en/topic/agriculture/overview.
2. PwC and FIA, p. 3.
3. Christiaensen and Martin.

and methods from the nineteenth century. The sector remains largely underdeveloped due to numerous challenges and constraints faced by smallholder farmers, such as high labor-intensity with limited access to modern equipment; lack of access to data; lack of access to markets, which leaves farmers highly dependent on intermediaries; limited access to formal finance due to lack of collateral to secure financing and lack of data to appropriately assess their credit risk; limited or no interest from young generations to become farmers, due to low income levels; and extreme weather events due to climate change, which affects crop productivity. Female smallholder farmers experience additional challenges, such as laws in many emerging-market countries that discriminate against women, limiting their land and property rights,[4] as well as lack of access to training, information, and market services, compared to male smallholder farmers. The FAO declared that eliminating the gender gap in agriculture would increase production in emerging markets by 2.5 percent to 4 percent.[5]

The COVID-19 pandemic has added to the challenges by significantly affecting the supply and demand factors of the agriculture value chain and exacerbating the issues related to the lack of food security and increasing poverty levels. Labor shortages at firms, logistics disruptions of food, and input supply chains have constrained the availability and access to food for consumers, and in some situations, have also led to local shortages and price hikes.[6] The U.N. World Food Programme has warned that an additional 130 million people could face acute food insecurity by the end of 2020, on top of the 135 million people who were already under severe threat of hunger before the crisis, because of income and remittance losses.[7] On the demand side, the pandemic is reinforcing changing consumer habits toward convenience and safety, increasing the reliance of packaged foods and e-commerce for a more direct sourcing and delivery of food.

Against this backdrop, there is potential for a breakthrough in how food crops are produced and marketed, which can dramatically improve living standards of producers and food nutrition value for consumers. The pandemic has accelerated the adoption of digital technologies and innovative solutions across all sectors, giving rise to new AgriTech models. Governments around the world are prioritizing needed investments in internet connectivity, and consumers are increasingly adopting digital payments and the use of e-commerce to shop for goods and services, including in emerging markets. The readiness of digital technologies is a key catalyst in the transformation of the agriculture sector. It enables the emergence of new business models to solve the main constraints and barriers in

4. Abass.
5. Agung.
6. PwC and FIA, p. 6.
7. Anthem.

a low-cost and efficient manner, which results in higher food productivity, food security, and financial inclusion. Innovations such as biotechnology, Internet of Things (IoT), e-commerce, precision farming, and climate-smart agriculture have demonstrated great potential to improve the sector's overall sustainability and resilience to external shocks, as well as to reduce food loss and waste (FLW) and greenhouse gases (GHG).

The combination of a broad range of old-tech and new-tech solutions in agriculture is creating a new mindset and dynamism in agriculture, a sector that has remained stagnant for a long time in emerging markets. These innovative methods and new business models can deliver significant benefits to smallholder farmers, encouraging young people to become farmers, providing a pathway to the formal economy and helping them become more resilient to the effects of climate change and the pandemic. Well-established old technologies, such as the mobile phone, are essential to connect farmers to information needed to manage their crops. In the past, reaching out to farmers was challenging, due to last-mile logistics from poor infrastructure and physical remoteness; the mobile phone has led to a paradigm shift, making it possible to reach smallholder farmers at scale. The pandemic has also underscored the critical role of the mobile phone, which has become the primary way most people access the internet. At the same time, new-tech business models, such as e-commerce platforms, can help smallholder farmers achieve higher income by connecting them directly to consumers' demands. These digital platforms provide farmers with higher price-transparency, match supply and demand, and increase farmers' access to market. The introduction of digital technologies also makes it possible to collect and track essential agricultural data, which can be used for the evaluation of farming conditions, and provides access to needed financing for smallholder farmers. To scale up these tech solutions in emerging markets, the responsible use of data and setting up partnerships between the public and private sector are essential.

Digital technologies in agriculture also play an important role in addressing five of the seventeen Sustainable Development Goals (SDGs), namely:

- No Poverty—by helping smallholder farmers increase crop yield and access to finance

- Zero Hunger—by improving crop yield and agriculture processes, which results in stronger food security

- Good Health and Well-Being—by focusing "smart" agriculture, a subset of agriculture technology, on food and nutrition quality

- Responsible Consumption and Production—by lowering costs in post-harvest, which reduces food wastage

- Climate Action—by helping reduce emissions and introduce sustainable farming techniques through innovations in climate smart agriculture

This chapter focuses on the themes of "think big, act fast, and start small." The traditional agriculture sector, which represents a significant portion of global GDP and is the livelihood for the poor in emerging markets, is being dynamically transformed by the application of digital technologies and innovative business models that enable smallholder farmers to increase their productivity, efficiency, and competitiveness. The dynamism and transformation of the agriculture sector in emerging markets is quickly taking place through the emergence of agriculture technology—or AgriTech—startups. These small, young companies are developing innovative business models and using a wide variety of old and new technology solutions, similar to the way that fintech startups are transforming the financial services sector. In this chapter, we first look at how general-purpose technology innovations are being used in ways that benefit farmers and describe five new AgriTech business models that are being used to solve specific problems. We then highlight case studies of AgriTech companies and technology providers from different parts of the world, showcasing key innovations and lessons learned. Two critical components for the success of AgriTech solutions are (1) the effective and responsible use of data and analytics and (2) the establishment of partnerships between the public and private sector. Finally, we examine the possibilities for digital agriculture in Indonesia—where agriculture is a significant contributor of the economy, with approximately 27 million farmers or 30 percent of the workforce—as an example of how a breakthrough can be scaled up across an entire country.[8] Specifically, we focus on Indonesian AgriTech and highlight the key challenges they face in transforming the agriculture sector. We argue in favor of setting up an Agriculture Innovation Hub in Indonesia, which would consist of an agriculture data exchange platform designed with data governance and would bring together multiple stakeholders such as government agencies, technology providers, venture capital firms, and AgriTech startups. Ultimately, the combination of AgriTech business models, data and analytics, and public-private partnerships can help unlock the full potential of digital technologies in agriculture and create significant breakthroughs in achieving food security in emerging markets.

8. BPS-Statistics Indonesia, p. 22.

Digital Technology Is Transforming the Agriculture Sector: "Think Big"

Key advances in technology are transforming the agriculture sector. These technologies are mitigating the main challenges farmers face and address the pain points of value chain actors in the agricultural last mile. Some of the key benefits of digital technology in agriculture are:

- *Elimination of information asymmetry* by increasing access to data to all stakeholders, which, in turn, increases transparency and results in effective communication among value-chain players at lower cost. More transparency can result in higher productivity and less food wastage

- *Lowering of operational and transaction costs* by using digital tools to reduce manual and paper processing or data entry errors

- *Improvement of crop yields* through the use of data analytics, artificial intelligence (AI), and machine learning (ML)

- *Improvement of access to markets* by connecting farmers directly to consumers, thereby eliminating the middlemen and resulting in better pricing for their produce and savings to consumers

- *Enabling of access to finance* by using alternative data to evaluate the creditworthiness of farmers who did not have access to finance in the past

- *Increase in the ability to perform sustainable farming techniques* that ultimately help the environment

Table 7-1 provides a summary of the key technology innovations emerging in the agriculture sector, and the main benefits each of them offers. One of the most essential technology innovations is the mobile phone, which helps to connect farmers at the last mile, making it easier to share data and serve as the main distribution channel for vital information about crop prices and weather forecasts to manage their crops. Although many smallholder farmers in emerging markets lack electricity and modern farm equipment, the majority have a mobile phone, even in the poorest areas. Therefore, the mobile phone has made it possible to reach almost all smallholder farmers, which was difficult in the past due to poor infrastructure and remote locations. Moreover, the mobile phone has become a key tool to access financial products for smallholder farmers.

In many instances, technology innovations overlap each other, which makes them mutually reinforcing. For instance, IoT sensors are able to monitor and measure soil moisture in the field, which can then automatically send a signal to the robotic irrigation system to turn on when it is too dry. The data generated

Table 7-1. Summary of Technology Innovations Serving as the Foundation for New Business Models in Agriculture

Technology Innovation	Description	Potential Benefits to Farmers
Biotechnology	Wide range of tools, including traditional breeding techniques that alter living organisms, or parts of organisms, to make or modify products; improve plants or animals; or develop microorganisms for specific agriculture uses. Some examples include pest resistant crops, genetics, nutrient supplements, antibiotics, vaccines	Improved crop yields, reduced vulnerability to environmental issues, increased nutritional qualities of food crops and reduced dependence on fertilizers
Mobile Phones	Designed to allow people to communicate wirelessly almost everywhere at all times and are transforming how individuals conduct business and interact socially. Mobile phones serve as a key distribution channel for information and financial services	Allow farmers to gain access to vital information about prices of crops and instant weather information to properly manage crops. They also serve as the main distribution channel for financial products such as loans, insurance, savings and a means to make payments
Internet / Connectivity	Refers to the different ways to connect to the Internet – mobile phones, tablets, Internet of Things (IoT) or computers. Also includes the latest connectivity standards such as 5G.	Brings new information resources and can open new communication channels for rural communities. Other benefits include increased efficiency, less duplication of activities, and global access to information
Data Analytics & AI / ML	Refers to the analysis of exponential amount of structured and unstructured data by using different techniques / methods such as AI and ML. AI refers to the analysis of data to model some aspect of the world by using computers and models that learn from the data in order to respond intelligently to new data and adapt their outputs accordingly	Enables farmers to manage key resources including seed and fertilizers, while increasing productivity. The tremendous amount of data generated can also be used with AI / ML techniques to make informed decisions and predictions.
IoT Software & Hardware	Refers to the global network of billions of Internet-enabled devices and machines that are connected to the Internet, collecting, generating and sharing data. IoT sensors are used to monitor different characteristics in the field such as soil moisture, rainfall, and other aspects of the production cycle	Introduces efficiency, precision and automation at various stages of the agriculture production cycle. IoT also enables the creation of real-time monitoring systems, which allows farmers to quickly respond to any significant changes in weather, light, humidity, as well as the health of each crop or soil in the field. IoT sensors and devices generate data that can help farmers make well-informed decisions related to the crops' growth
Robotics & Automation	Refers to the use of drones, satellite imaging, robots and other machines that help automate and improve the farming process such as weed control, harvesting and picking, sensing, imaging and monitoring of fields and sorting and packing	Robots automate slow, repetitive tasks for farmers, allowing them to focus more on improving overall production yields
Blockchain / DLT	Blockchain, a form of distributed ledger technology (DLT), is a decentralized, distributed digital ledger that records ownership and transactions across a network of computers and relies on consensus algorithms and cryptographic methods to add transactions to the ledger in sequential, time-stamped immutable blocks.	Can be used to improve the traceability of crops across the agriculture supply chain, thereby providing transparency throughout the process and potentially reducing transaction costs. Blockchain / DLT promises increased efficiencies through enhanced data management, lower transaction costs, optimized logistics, and enhanced food safety protocols

Source: Author.

from these IoT sensors can be analyzed by using AI/ML to ultimately develop a predictive tool for watering the field. The strong complementarities between these various innovations reinforce their disruption potential.

Digital technologies are affecting all stakeholders in the agriculture value chain, generating direct and indirect benefits. Table 7-2 shows suppliers benefit from biotechnology solutions that improve seed quality, while farmers are able to increase production yield and improve product quality, which leads to higher incomes. The food processors, in turn, will see improved product quality from the farmers and have reduced wastage. The distributors can experience improved linkages and less complexity along the farmer's value chain, while retailers and consumers will benefit from higher food quality and safety, improved food traceability, and faster time to market from the farms. In addition to the stakeholder impacts, there are economic impacts, such as economies of scale and greater efficiencies. Finally, technology innovations can better monitor deforestation and reduce GHG emissions.

The Rapid Emergence of Agriculture Technology (AgriTech) Business Models: "Act Fast"

Agriculture technology, or AgriTech, holds the promise to revolutionize farming quickly, especially for smallholder farmers in emerging markets. There are five main AgriTech business models that have emerged to address the numerous challenges that smallholder farmers face in the region. Table 7-3 provides an overview of each model, key technologies used, and their value proposition to farmers.[9] Examples of the different business models are discussed in more detail through three case studies from different parts of the world.

Southeast Asia, a region that is home to more than 70 million smallholder farmers, is an example of the rapid growth of AgriTech startups in the developing world. The majority of people own a mobile phone, with an estimated mobile phone penetration rate of 135 percent.[10] In addition, the population is becoming more connected to the internet, with more than 65 percent penetration, and 90 percent of the total internet users are using smartphones.[11] The AgriTech landscape features more than 130 different companies. Farm advisory AgriTech companies are the largest group, representing more than 40 percent of the total, followed by digital marketplace and traceability AgriTech startups.[12] Indonesia

9. Grow Asia, p. 5.
10. This phenomenon may be due to the fact that mobile penetration is counted by the number of SIM cards, and some individuals may own multiple SIM cards.
11. Grow Asia, p. 2.
12. Ibid., p. 11.

Table 7-2. The Role of Digital Technologies in the Agriculture Value Chain

	Suppliers	Farmers	Processors	Distributors	Retailers	Consumers
Stakeholder-Level Impacts	• Biotech solutions improve seed quality • Increased access to finance and insurance	• Better yield and quality • Less intense use of water and land • Optimal farm inputs and less wastage • Digital platforms for credit, payments	• Improved produce quality • Reduced wastage • Better anticipation of inputs	• Decreasing complexity in value chain • Improved traceability and produce quality	• Higher quality and safety of food • Stronger linkages with supply chain	• Improved food traceability • Better digital literacy and knowledge base
Economy-Level Impacts	• Reallocation of labor from farms to more productive sectors downstream • Stronger linkages along the value chain and increased potential for value addition • Economies of scale and greater efficiencies					
Environmental Impacts	• Reduced use and better management of water and land; lower use of fertilizer and pesticide, and reduced pollution • Smaller CO_2 footprint of agriculture and reduced GHG emissions • Better monitoring of deforestation					
Equity through Inclusive Markets	• Spillover effects from increased agribusiness competitiveness • Stronger farmer and processor integration into regional and global value chain, including through inclusion of smallholders • Dissemination and adoption of more sustainable farming practices and improved resilience to shocks					

Source: World Bank Group.

Table 7-3. Summary of AgriTech Business Models

Business Model	Key Technologies Used	Description	Key Challenges / Problems Addressed	Examples (Case Studies)
Farmer Advisory		Provide advice and information to farmers such as agricultural best practices, market prices, weather forecast through mobile phones / internet. By using mobile phones as a productivity tool, smallholder farmers can enhance their knowledge and skills, improve yields and income	Lack access to information	Twiga Foods (Kenya) Pinduoduo (China)
Peer-to-Peer Lending		Peer-to-peer (P2P) lending platforms serve as intermediaries bringing farmers which need capital to finance inputs and working capital with investors/lenders which want to invest. Loans are mainly done through mobile devices using alternative data such as mobile phone call data records and others to evaluate the credit risk of farmers	Lack access to financial services	TaniHub Group (Indonesia)
Traceability		First mile data collection using IoT sensors and blockchain / DLT to enable traceability of food across the supply chain. Traceability is important since it allows non-compliant (unsafe or off-specification) shipments to be traced back to their source, which can provide incentives throughout the chain to supply improved quality farm produce	Lack of information Lack access to markets Lack access to quality inputs	Twiga Foods (Kenya) Pinduoduo (China) Microsoft FarmBeats (USA)
Digital Marketplaces		Builds direct connections between farmers and consumers through online marketplaces. The result is significantly lower transaction costs as middlemen are removed from the value chain. In addition to efficiency gains, digital marketplaces have allowed smallholder farmers to enter a range of previously inaccessible markets, thus improving competition	Lack access to markets Lack access to quality inputs High search and transaction costs	Twiga Foods (Kenya) Pinduoduo (China)
Mechanization		A range of equipment is available to replace labor on farms and provide important information, from tractors to drones and satellite imagery and IoT sensors. Mechanization platforms have emerged which allow equipment owners to offer the temporary use of agricultural machinery on a digital portal, matching them with farmer customers. Using digital portals improves efficiency as it avoids the ad hoc placement of multiple phone calls and allows more effective scheduling around demand clusters	Lack access to machines and labor Inefficiencies in production	Pinduoduo (China) Microsoft FarmBeats (USA)

Mobile Phones   Internet Connectivity   Data Analytics & AI / ML   IoT Software & Hardware   Blockchain / DLT   Robotics & Automation

Source: Grow Asia, Author.

represents the largest market for AgriTech startups, with more than fifty of them identified across the five different business models. Figure 7-1 provides an overview of some of the main AgriTech companies in Southeast Asia.[13]

The digital marketplace platform business model offers substantial opportunities for smallholder farmers by providing more transparency, opening access to new markets, and improving the efficiency of producing and selling products to customers. This business model has attracted significant interest from investors, raising more than twice the amount of capital in Southeast Asia when compared to the other business models combined. By enabling the buying and selling of agricultural produce online, farmers can bypass intermediaries and gain access to new markets, giving them more choice and a higher margin of what consumers pay.[14] In addition, farmers can sell their agriculture products, purchase goods online, make online payments, and pick up purchased goods at the service facilities without leaving their respective villages.

The sustainability and scalability of AgriTech e-commerce platforms depend on a country's infrastructure (mobile internet penetration and connectivity), logistics networks, and financial services, including the digital payment solutions

Figure 7-1. The AgriTech Startup Landscape in Southeast Asia: Selected Companies by Business Model

| Business Models | SEA countries with large smallholder population | | | | |
	Indonesia	Philippines	Vietnam	Thailand	Myanmar
Farmer Advisory	eFishery · KARSA · NEURAFARM	TechAguru · Tagani		LISTENFIELD · algaeba	Impact Terra
Peer to Peer Lending	CROWDE · iGrow · Tanijoy	CROPITAL · FarmOn			
Traceability	HARA · KOLTIVA		agri check · WOWTRACE	VERIFIK	
Digital Marketplaces	chilibeli · TaniHub · kedaisayur	Mayani	THUOCTHUYSAN.NET	ricult · 100Rai	
Mechanization Platforms	Sentragro	NEW HOPE		TALAD APP · GetzTrac	Tun Yat

Source: Grow Asia.

13. Ibid., p. 13.
14. GSMA (2020), p. 63.

available.[15] These factors have contributed to rapid growth of agriculture e-commerce platforms in China, such as Pinduoduo, Meichai, Meituan, and others, expanding their services to offer fresh produce from farmers directly to consumers. The COVID-19 pandemic has accelerated the adoption of agriculture e-commerce, as consumers limit their shopping in person. The emergence of more innovative business models is expected in the future, which may combine lending and advisory together with e-commerce to drive a holistic solution for farmers.

AgriTech Sector in Practice: "Start Small"

AgriTechs are making inroads in reshaping the agriculture value chain, much in the same way that fintech firms are transforming the financial services sector. These AgriTechs may hold the key to attract more young people to the agriculture sector, which is essential to ensure food security in the future.

The digital transformation of various agriculture systems (such as invoicing, supply chain, crop receipt) and the harmonization of the data architecture that supports the agriculture sector is another important factor for the scale-up and growth of AgriTechs. For instance, the digitization of farm registries could lead to better governance and transparency for public subsidies, with significant reduction in inefficiency and leakages.

Case Studies of Transformative AgriTech Companies

There are several lessons to be learned from established AgriTech players that can help other startups to scale up and succeed. The case studies below provide an overview of three AgriTech companies by summarizing their business models, digital technologies used, and key factors that led to their success.

Pinduoduo (China)

Pinduoduo (PDD) is the fastest-growing e-commerce platform in China, which has attracted more than 700 million users in five years with its unique interactive team purchase and social e-commerce model. Through team purchase, users are able to enjoy lower prices by forming teams of two with their friends to make purchases. Users simply send an invitation to join their team purchase to selected contacts in their social network through popular in China platforms like WeChat or QQ. This helps aggregate large volumes of orders in a short time for PDD's merchants, which enables them to offer products to its

15. GSMA (2019), pp. 16–18.

users at competitive prices. Another important feature of the business model is the consumer-to-manufacturer (C2M) approach, which connects manufacturers directly with consumers. Provided with insights on consumer preferences, manufacturers can reduce production costs and upgrade their inventory management by focusing on selling more of the products consumers want, while pick-up and delivery planning for logistics can be streamlined.[16]

The company, which started out selling fresh produce, is now the largest online marketplace for agriculture products in China. The company's vision is to help accelerate the digitization of the agriculture industry and share the efficiency gains with farmers and the platform's users. PDD has applied its innovative model of aggregating demand through team purchases to make it possible for more farmers to tap into the online market. By removing intermediaries and providing transparent pricing, PDD allows farmers to capture better economics in the value chain while saving consumers money compared to traditional offline retail channels. The company can also actively push agriculture produce on the relevant users' recommendation feeds, so that users can easily discover fresh and affordable produce. By sharing these finds with their friends to form team purchases, they, in turn, help drive more volume with greater visibility to the farmers. This is especially useful for produce in over-supply or that needs to be sold quickly to maintain its freshness.

PDD is also shaping supply to meet the demands from consumers by guiding farmers on what they should plant, when they should plant, and how they should market to consumers more effectively. For instance, PDD partnered with tea producers from Anxi, Fujian, to provide consumer insights and help them build their brand. From the data that PDD has collected, it can provide suggestions on preferred packaging, price points, and product development based on the preferences of different target audiences (for example, young/old, family/single buyer).[17]

Another way that PDD helps farmers is through its Duo Duo University New Farmer training, a collaboration with China Agricultural University, whereby the former provides free agronomist guidance and training to farmers, with PDD providing inputs on consumers' product preferences and business management tips. This better equips farmers to transition into being agricultural entrepreneurs online. As of 2020, PDD has nurtured over a hundred thousand new farmers, with over 12 million smallholder farmers selling produce through their platform.

Technology has played an essential role in the company's significant expansion and growth. The company has leveraged technology to optimize its operations and design customer-centric products/services, as well as teach farmers how

16. Jao.
17. World Bank webinar.

to use agriculture technology to improve their livelihoods and lift themselves out of poverty. In October 2020, the company announced a strategic partnership with the National Engineering Research Center for Information Technology in Agriculture (NERCITA) to develop smart agriculture solutions to alleviate rural poverty.[18] As part of the partnership, PDD and NERCITA will explore the use of AI and 5G for precision farming and build a smart agriculture innovation center to develop data-driven production and boost sales through brand-building. Overall, PDD has been successful in leveraging agriculture technology for farmers in China by engaging them through its e-commerce platform and establishing different programs to help farmers in rural areas adopt innovative techniques that will ultimately lift them out of poverty.

PDD's success as one of the world's top online marketplaces for agriculture products can be attributed to several key factors:

- Favorable preconditions for e-commerce in China—The country has a well-established and reliable logistics infrastructure (95 percent coverage of rural areas) and internet connectivity is widespread in rural areas. Moreover, the digital payment system is one of the most advanced in the world, facilitating quick and efficient transactions that are free and widely accessible.

- Compelling value proposition and easy to use platform—PDD has made its e-commerce platform very simple and easy for farmers to use, with low transaction fees.

- Focus on user insights to inform product design and advise farmers—PDD has built up a deep understanding of its user base and their needs over the past five years, which it can use to advise farmers to make decisions that benefit them.

By addressing farmer pain points from the perspective of what to sell (through product insights), where to sell (market access via PDD online platform), and how to sell (from training farmers to run a business), PDD has created a comprehensive and compelling offering that addresses both farmers' and consumers' needs. This "handholding" approach could be applicable to other developing countries to increase adoption in the long run.

Twiga Foods (Kenya)

Founded in 2014 and based in Kenya, Twiga Foods is a fast-growing B2B, mobile-based e-commerce marketplace platform, focused on solving the major inefficiencies of the food production and distribution system in Kenya. An

18. Pinduoduo website.

inefficient supply chain, where almost 90 percent of the food produce sold is through the informal sector, is a major challenge, which results in high food prices. In Nairobi, 6.5 million people purchase food through 180,000 small retailers. The retail food marketplace is highly fragmented and inefficient, consisting of various layers of middlemen, which invariably leads to increased costs.

To address these inefficiencies, Twiga delivers food produce to the mass market by digitizing the supply chain, cutting out layers of middlemen, eliminating waste, and reducing food prices. The company aggregates produce from farmers and delivers it to retail vendors in the informal sector in Nairobi through its comprehensive distribution infrastructure. As a result, farmers and food manufacturers have guaranteed access to a fairly priced, transparent, mobile marketplace, and retailers can consistently source lower-cost, higher-quality produce, which is conveniently delivered to their doorstep within eighteen hours of their ordering it.[19] Since its founding, Twiga has reduced typical post-harvest losses in Kenya from 30 percent to 4 percent for produce brought to market on its network.[20]

Twiga collects produce from more than 700 farmers and distributes it to over 35,000 vendors every month. Over the last few years, the company has diversified to a fast-growing range of agriculture products and processed foods, including bananas, rice, maize flour, cooking oil, milk, juices, table sugar, and snacks. The company has been instrumental in the development of efficient commercial farming ecosystem that is geared toward the domestic food market. In November 2020, the company announced a US$30M IFC-backed debt facility that will be geared toward helping farmers develop irrigation and other modern agronomy infrastructure to improve yields and efficiency.

Twiga's business model offers significant value to farmers, vendors, and mass market consumers. Through Twiga, farmers can get a guaranteed market for their products, with fair, transparent, and reliable pricing; payment within twenty-four hours; and no intermediaries involved. For vendors, Twiga provides convenience, since products are delivered on site, and offers a stable, on-demand supply of high quality, well-priced products, with no middlemen involved. The result is that mass market consumers are able to enjoy a lower purchase price for high-quality products.

Twiga is digitizing the agriculture value chain by aggregating supply and demand, disintermediating brokers, and unifying vendors in Kenya on a single platform. The company has created a tech-enabled digital platform, minimizing supply-and-demand inefficiencies for farmers and vendors along the value chain. The platform relies on the use of mobile money, such as M-Pesa, to manage and

19. Twiga.
20. Bright.

streamline its payment processes for vendors and farmers. Moreover, the company has integrated mobile payments in its supply chain platform, whereby the majority of farmers receive their payments through mobile money and information is recorded in real time in the field, to enable timely settlement of payments.[21]

At its core, Twiga is a data-driven AgriTech company collecting and analyzing all market-driven data while simultaneously tracking farmers and vendor data through its platform. Through the use of data analytics, the company is able to record and analyze the activities of farmers, vendors, and logistics in order to better optimize the supply chain of products.

Leveraging an array of digital technologies has been a critical component for the growth, scale-up, and success of Twiga. The digital platform business model simplifies the supply chain process by connecting the farmers directly with the vendors, thereby eliminating the intermediaries. In addition, Twiga is able to address the inefficiencies in the market by serving as an aggregator of the informal food retailers, resulting in significant cost savings to consumers and vendors. The amount of data captured on Twiga's platform is highly valuable, since it can be used to optimize the logistics, broaden the company's product base, and help vendors access financial services, including working capital loans from financial service providers that partner with Twiga.

Microsoft FarmBeats (USA)

Launched to the public in 2019 by Microsoft's research arm, FarmBeats is a project that combines IoT sensors, data analysis, and ML to augment farmers' knowledge about their own farm with data and data-driven insights. The idea behind FarmBeats is to take in data from a wide variety of sources, including sensors, satellites, drones, and weather stations, and then turn that into actionable intelligence for farmers, using AI and ML,[22] which results in higher agriculture productivity, reducing losses and cutting down input costs. The rapid advances in technology, such as cloud computing, IoT sensors, and AI, are helping to make affordable digital agriculture solutions for farmers. Transparency in food is becoming a big issue globally, and thus data is becoming increasingly important to farming, since consumers want to know where their food is coming from and whether conservation and environmentally oriented practices were used when cultivating the crops.

FarmBeats aggregates massive amounts of agriculture data from different sources and develops AI models by fusing the datasets. Using satellite imagery combined with IoT sensors in the field, FarmBeats creates a farm map and assesses

21. Ibid.
22. Lardinois.

farm health using vegetation and water index. FarmBeats tracks and visualizes the farm conditions through the collection of data from different sensors, aerial imagery from partner drone companies, and soil moisture maps from the combination of sensors and satellite data.[23]

Given the lack of internet connectivity in most rural areas, the agriculture sensors used by FarmBeats leverage unoccupied slices of the UHF and VHF radio frequencies used for TV broadcasts, slotting data between channels. Often referred to as "TV white space," many developing and developed economies are experimenting with this innovation to unlock extra bandwidth for mobile phones.[24] Using the TV white space for internet connectivity is a game changer that significantly reduces the cost, which makes it extremely affordable to use IoT sensors to collect data.

FarmBeats provides a groundbreaking, cloud-enabled software platform that is able to democratize the use of data for farmers so that they can gain better insights into ways to improve their crop yields, as well as predict performance. The partnerships established with different providers (drone and satellite imagery companies, IoT sensor providers, and so on) are vital for the success of FarmBeats, and having an open-source software stack that connects through APIs makes it easy to use and connect with the different partners. Finally, innovative solutions, such as the use of TV white space for internet connectivity in rural areas with limited access, make it possible to collect large amounts of data at an affordable price.

Challenges in the Adoption of Digital Technologies in Agriculture

While digital technologies offer many benefits in the agriculture sector, technology adoption is highly dependent on economic, regulatory, and social factors. From an economic perspective, some of the technology innovations outlined above are expensive, especially in emerging economies with poor infrastructure and internet connectivity. For instance, it is difficult to deploy IoT devices at scale, due to the fact that emerging market countries may not have licensed mobile IoT networks deployed by mobile network operators (MNO).[25] Digital literacy is also a major challenge, which has made it difficult for smallholder farmers to adopt these new technologies.

Access to data together with digital technologies provides transparency in the value chain. However, it is important to recognize two potential issues: power

23. Microsoft Azure website.
24. Ibid.
25. GSMA (2020), p. 70.

concentration and data governance. Digital technologies can increase market power and concentration that reduces competition. With access to processing high volume of data to fine-tune the AI algorithm, digital technologies could increase power and vertical consolidation in the entire food supply chain, with harmful effects leading to market concentration from the monopoly of the digital platforms and super apps. In addition, the lack of contestability and oversight for data governance could be an issue for personal data protection and could erode trust from the consumers and citizens.

Agriculture Innovation Hub for Indonesia: Overview

The government of Indonesia considers the agriculture sector a major priority for the economy. Specifically, the Strategic Agricultural Program focuses on the development of high value agriculture, export markets, nutrition, food supply, rural incomes, and entrepreneurship.

Indonesia already has an active ecosystem of AgriTech companies. Currently, there are more than fifty startups that can disrupt the agriculture and aquaculture sectors in Indonesia. Firms like TaniHub are using technology to bridge the large gap between farmers and consumers by allowing consumers to buy fresh produce directly from the farmers, which results in higher income for farmers by eliminating the middlemen. In addition, TaniHub's peer-to-peer (P2P) lending platform, TaniFund, connects retail investors with money to lend with farmers that need debt capital. AgriTechs such as e-Fishery are using AI and ML, as well as IoT sensors to better track production yields and provide essential data to banks in order to better evaluate the credit risk of farmers.

The adoption of digital technologies will be essential in order to implement the government's program; however, technology adoption in the agriculture sector varies significantly across 17,508 islands in the country. Complementary policy actions, including encouraging more private sector involvement through improving the policy and regulatory environment, are critical to accelerating the countrywide adoption of digital technologies in agriculture. Furthermore, infrastructure investments are also needed to address the other constraints that farmers face, such as roads, energy, post-harvest storage, and logistics. A combination of these investments and policy improvements has the potential to increase the adoption of digital technologies and bring in new generation of farmers in Indonesia.

Objectives of the Innovation Hub

Establishing an innovation hub would catalyze agricultural innovation and investment for the development of the agriculture sector in Indonesia. The hub could be structured by a neutral convening broker, such as the World Bank Group, as a public-private partnership (PPP) digital platform where government intervention would foster an enabling environment for the growth of the sector, crowding in private sector for investment capital to become the driving force for sustaining an innovation culture that cultivates a growth mindset to disrupt the sector. The Agriculture Innovation Hub will have the following objectives:

- Foster innovation ecosystem from multi-stakeholders in the agriculture value chain (government agencies, academia, and technology providers) to share insights and key learnings on the use of digital technologies

- Invest in data platform accessible to all, providing a wide variety of public and private data to increase market intelligence and have better information on how to best scale up agricultural businesses

- Provide capacity building for the new generation of farmers so that they are able to quickly learn and deploy these technology innovations

- Link enterprise with e-commerce platform to increase market insights, connecting smallholder farmers directly to consumers

Furthermore, there are key characteristics of the Innovation Hub that would be essential to offer a positive environment for the development and growth of AgriTech startups and encourage the adoption of digital technologies across the agriculture value chain:

- Presence and support of large agri-food businesses—cross-pollination from the established businesses with the AgriTech, leading to new strategic partnership and business models

- Government initiatives supporting innovation and investment—to provide incentives for AgriTech innovations and direct connection with policymakers

- AgriTech start-up ecosystem and entrepreneurial culture—AgriTechs are leading the way with the introduction of digital technologies

- Mentoring from accelerators—to scale up AgriTech innovations with mentors to support the business model

- Digital talent development—knowledge-sharing from agronomists and big technology using challenges and hackathons as a way to crowdsource expertise

- Quality research with academic institutions—gain better understanding of the local market dynamics, key innovations, and factors affecting agriculture

- Engagement and presence of venture capital and private equity firms— to provide the investment capital needed to fund the growth of digital agriculture

Many factors contribute to the market failure for smallholder farmers. Two main causes are the lack of market access and limited access to finance to fund working capital. The data platform could address information asymmetry for smallholder farmers and gain market insights from the e-commerce platform.

The agriculture digital transformation could benefit from the learnings in the vibrant growth of fintechs in Indonesia by building the collective strength of the AgriTech community, similar to the Indonesia FinTech Association (AFTECH), which is now the self-regulating organization for the financial authority. Currently, AgriTechs in Indonesia do not have direct access to the policy makers; therefore, organizing into AgriTech groups with similar functions could have better advocacy for the well-being of the smallholder farmers and offer direct communication channels for policy matters.

The Innovation Hub is envisioned to support action-oriented policy dialogue for cross-sector collaboration (for example, agriculture and fintech) through technical assistance, studies, consultations, and learning events with agriculture experts from industry and academia, Big Techs with agriculture experience, and fintech entrepreneurs to promote, develop, and adopt digital solutions for smallholder farmers. Other thought leaders, such as World Economic Forum, have put forth Agriculture Innovation Hub concepts,[26] and thus it is important to join forces to amplify the strength of the multi-stakeholder partnerships, operationalizing the concept in specific countries.

Creating a Data-Sharing Platform—The Heart of the Agriculture Innovation Hub

Data holds great promise for digital technologies, and open data could generate large benefits for society, but there are risks that need to be addressed. To maximize the benefits, governments could encourage the private sector to share

26. Bora, Kowatsch, and Desai.

data that are of public interest, monitoring and increasing the impact of public data, and improving the governance of data sharing. To mitigate the data risks, governments could improve data protection and clarify data ownership, address unfair data practices in agricultural policies, and reduce imbalances in the value chain–related information asymmetries.

The data platform will focus on the optimal use of data that empowers smallholder farmers and agribusiness entrepreneurs to increase their productivity, efficiency, and competitiveness, thereby facilitating access to market intelligence, improving nutritional outcomes, and enhancing resilience to climate change. An agriculture data exchange platform designed with data governance could unlock the full potential of digital technologies and maximize data benefits between private and public sector.

The Innovation Hub will be designed for agriculture data sharing, harmonizing the granular data types and coordination with government data, to provide real time data access on simple user interface to help smallholder farmers make better decision for the crop yields, beyond the traditional data sharing for academic research. Having access to market intelligence could improve the efficiency of farms and agribusinesses in the value chain. Firms can learn about customer preferences and tailor their products accordingly, and can also forecast more accurately, improving their profitability.

Data integrated with tracing systems can also increase transparency and accountability in food systems. Tracing systems integrated with public systems alert consumers over digital platforms and speed product recalls when food hazards are discovered. Traceability, as a part of food safety systems, limits costly outbreaks of foodborne illnesses and reduces the financial and reputational risks posed to grocery stores and fast-food restaurants by tainted food.

Having access to the transactional and operational data is a virtuous cycle that fuels greater innovation and entrepreneurship. When combined with data from weather, commodity prices, and agronomic research data, it could reduce production costs and mitigate risk for the smallholder farmers.

Data Governance—A Major Challenge that Needs to Be Addressed

Data is not a zero-sum game. Policymakers need to recognize that data is a "public good"—it is not a finite good, and the usage of it by one actor in the economy does not prevent others from using it. Therefore, good data governance from the collection and processing of data is critical for building trust. Data security by design and data use agreement will be established as part of the Innovation Hub and must be enforced and implemented consistently for both public and private institutions that are part of the hub. A successful data protection regime will embed consumer education as a key objective focusing on the human dimension. This needs to include measures to inform users of their rights, the benefits as well as risks, and what avenues they have to lodge complaints and seek redress.

Conclusion

If there ever was a silver lining in the COVID-19 crisis, it would be the readiness of digital technology to change the way we work and the way to adapt to online and contactless buying experience to reduce the risk of spreading the pathogen. The pandemic confirms that AgriTechs have an incredible potential to change the agriculture value chain.

The COVID-19 pandemic is already disrupting food systems and supply chains and affecting the economic life of farmers. Our world is also confronting a climate crisis, not only with higher temperatures and rising seas, but also intensifying food shortages. There are many promising agricultural innovations, including advances in irrigation, new types of seeds and fertilizer, and digital technologies that provide close-to-real-time data about growing conditions. To realize the promise of these innovations, however, farmers need access to capital and digital financial services, such as payments, savings, and insurance.

Technology offers new business expansions, such as GoJek transformation from ride sharing to food delivery and digital financial services. The growth of cross industry partnerships powered by digital transformation is enabling a wide range of new and traditional finance providers to join forces with agribusinesses and other Big Tech platforms that work in rural areas to provide credit and other capacity-building services to farmers.

Various AgriTech business models have emerged globally to address the main challenges smallholder farmers face. We look at Indonesia as an example of what developing countries can hope to achieve. There is growing momentum in Indonesia, with more than fifty AgriTechs founded over the last five years. Together with enabling regulations and increased investments in infrastructure, digital technologies will be the main contributor to food security, reduction in food wastage, and sustainable farming, addressing the Sustainable Development Goals to end poverty and hunger, and promote responsible consumption and climate action. The establishment of the Agriculture Innovation Hub in Indonesia can enhance these benefits by bringing together multiple stakeholders of the agriculture value chain to share data; foster innovation; and provide investment, mentoring, and capacity building for young startups. The hub's success will be dependent on building partnerships between the public and private sector and making sure that regulations can foster innovation while mitigating potential risks. The February 2021 MOU between Ministry of Agriculture and

Microsoft,[27] together with the establishment of the new data center to empower Indonesia's digital economy,[28] is the first among multiple partners to scale out the innovation ecosystem in Indonesia.

More technological innovation in agriculture is needed today. This is a global challenge, and the time to act is now. In the spirit of Lean Startup mindset: let us think big, start small, and act fast.

References

Abass, Jamila. 2018. "Women Grow 70 Percent of Africa's Food, but Have Few Rights over the Land They Tend," *World Economic Forum* blog, March 21, www.weforum .org/agenda/2018/03/women-farmers-food-production-land-rights/.

Agung, I Dewa Made. 2020. "Empowering Indonesia's Women Farmers," *ASEAN Post* blog, April 5, https://theaseanpost.com/article/empowering-indonesias-women -farmers.

Anthem, Paul. 2020. "Risk of Hunger Pandemic as Coronavirus Set to Almost Double Acute Hunger by End of 2020," *World Food Program Insight* blog, April 16, https:// insight.wfp.org/covid-19-will-almost-double-people-in-acute-hunger-by-end-of-2020 -59df0c4a8072.

Bora, Saswati, Bernhard Kowatsch, and Noopur Desai. 2020. "How Food Innovation Hubs Will Scale Technology to Transform Our Food System," *World Economic Forum* blog, November 20, www.weforum.org/agenda/2020/11/food-innovation -hubs-scale-technology-transform-global-food-system-farmers-agtech/.

BPS-Statistics Indonesia. 2018. "The Result of Inter-Census Agricultural Survey 2018."

Bright, Jake. 2019. "Kenya's Twiga Foods Eyes West Africa after $30M Raise Led by Goldman," *TechCrunch* blog, October 26, https://techcrunch.com/2019/10/28/ kenyas-twiga-foods-eyes-west-africa-after-30m-raise-led-by-goldman/.

Christiaensen, Luc and Will Martin. 2018. "Five New Insights on How Agriculture Can Help Reduce Poverty," *World Bank* blog post, July 26, https://blogs.worldbank .org/jobs/five-new-insights-how-agriculture-can-help-reduce-poverty.

Grow Asia. 2020. *Smallholder AgriTech S.E.A. Landscape 2020.* Singapore: Padang & Co.

GSMA. 2019. *E-Commerce in Agriculture: New Business Models for Smallholders' Inclusion into the Formal Economy.*

———. 2020. *Digital Agriculture Maps: 2020 State of the Sector in Low- and Middle-Income Countries.*

Jao, Nicole. 2020. "Explaining Pinduoduo, and whether the Model Can Work in Southeast Asia," *TechinAsia* blog, August 19, www.techinasia.com/pinduoduo-model -work-southeast-asia.

Lardinois, Frederic. 2019. "Microsoft Azure Gets into Ag Tech with the Preview of FarmBeats," *TechCrunch* blog, November 4, https://techcrunch.com/2019/11/04/ microsoft-azure-gets-into-agtech-with-the-preview-of-farmbeats/.

---

27. Microsoft Indonesia News Center.
28. Microsoft Stories Asia.

Microsoft Azure website. 2019. "Overview of Azure FarmBeats (Preview)," November 4, https://docs.microsoft.com/en-us/azure/industry/agriculture/overview-azure -farmbeats.

Microsoft Indonesia News Center. 2021. "Indonesian Ministry of Agriculture Signs MoU with Microsoft to Strengthen Data-Driven Agriculture Ecosystem," February 19, https://news.microsoft.com/id-id/2021/02/19/indonesian-ministry-of-agriculture -signs-mou-with-microsoft-to-strengthen-data-driven-agriculture-ecosystem/.

Microsoft Stories Asia. 2021. "Microsoft to Establish First Datacenter Region in Indonesia as Part of Berdayakan Ekonomi Digital Indonesia Initiative," February 25, https://news.microsoft.com/apac/2021/02/25/microsoft-to-establish-first-datacenter -region-in-indonesia-as-part-of-berdayakan-digital-economy-indonesia-initiative/.

PwC and FIA. 2020. *Maintaining Food Resilience in a Time of Uncertainty: Understanding the Importance of Food Value Chains in ASEAN and How to Ensure their Resilience during the COVID-19 Crisis.* Price Waterhouse Coopers. Commissioned by Food Industry Asia.

Pinduoduo website. 2020. "Pinduoduo enters strategic partnership with NERCITA to develop smart agriculture," October 19, https://stories.pinduoduo-global.com /articles/pinduoduo-enters-strategic-partnership-with-nercita-to-develop-smart -agriculture.

Twiga. 2020. "Our Story," https://twiga.com/twiga-story/.

World Bank webinar. 2020. "Pinduoduo: Injecting Tech into Agriculture," May, https: //olc.worldbank.org/system/files/PDD%20Webinar_WB_May%206%202020% 20Final.pdf

EIGHT

Eyes on the Planet
Toward Zero Deforestation

Hiroaki Okonogi, Eiji Yamada, and Takahiro Morita

Disappearing Forests in the Tropics

Forests are an irreplaceable resource for all living creatures, especially human beings. In a figure dubbed "the Wedding Cake," the Stockholm Resilience Centre mapped the SDGs into three tiers—a foundational biosphere supporting a set of societal goals that, in turn, support economic goals. In this structure, they placed sustainable forest management within targets for SDG 15 "Life on Land" as part of the biosphere.[1]

Viewed in this way, forest management is a foundational goal that directly contributes to many other goals. Forests serve as a huge carbon stock. They absorb carbon dioxide from the air and release oxygen as trees grow. In addition, forests contribute to water purification and watershed conservation (see, for example, "The Sea Is Longing for the Forest" by Shigeatsu Hatakeyama,[2] an account of the forest management efforts that have been made in Japan to protect water quality for sustainable oyster farming). Furthermore, sustainable use of forest resources can provide incomes to marginal communities, helping achieve SDG 1 "No Poverty," improve land use practices that help achieve SDG 2 "Zero

The authors are grateful to Dr. Homi Kharas and Dr. Izumi Ohno for suggesting the topic treated in this paper. We also thank Dr. Takeo Tadono and Dr. Izumi Nagatani from JAXA for reprocessing the JJ-FAST dataset for us. This work has been supported by JICA-JAXA Forest Early Warning System in the Tropics (JJ-FAST).

1. Stockholm Resilience Centre.
2. Hatakeyama.

Hunger," and generate timber, fuels, and non-timber forest products (NTFPs) that contribute to SDG 12 "Responsible Consumption and Production."

However, forests are decreasing. According to the FAO, the world's forest coverage area has been reduced from 4.24 billion hectares in 1990 to 4.06 billion hectares in 2020.[3] This has resulted in 4 Gt (gigatons) of carbon being released into the atmosphere. The problem is particularly severe in tropical forests of the Amazon, Congo Basin, and Southeast Asia. These forests, which comprise only 7 percent of the planet's land area but are home to 50 to 80 percent of Earth's living creatures, are also crucial in terms of biodiversity.

The drivers of the deforestation of tropical forests vary by country and region but include agriculture (small-scale for subsistence and large-scale for commerce), fuelwood harvesting, urban development, and mining excavation. Relatively large deforestation is caused by cattle farming in Brazil and palm oil tree plantations in Indonesia. Meanwhile, in the least developed countries, population growth is driving an increase in small-scale land-use changes for food production and deforestation and forest degradation for fuelwood harvesting. There are no simple solutions to these problems, reportedly aggravated by COVID-19.[4]

Taking into account the importance of forests for climate mitigation and other SDGs, the international community has already, at the 2014 United Nations Climate Summit, committed to reduce the global rate of deforestation in natural forests by at least half by 2020 and to zero by 2030 (Goal 1 of the New York Declaration on Forests (NYDF)). However, the most recent progress report for NYDF points out, "Rather than halving since 2014—a 2020 target in NYDF Goal 1—the rate of natural forest loss has increased. Ending natural forest loss by 2030 will require a rapid paradigm shift by the global community toward valuing forests for their essential benefits and prioritizing their protection."[5]

Achieving the goal of zero reduction in natural forests by 2030 requires support for the private sector to eliminate deforestation from agricultural production, strengthening of forest governance, and community empowerment. There has been some success in providing alternative livelihoods to reduce forest usage by the poor. For example, a "Participatory Forest Management Project in Belete--Gera Regional Forest Priority Area," Phase 1 (2003–06), Phase 2 (2006–12), funded by the Japan International Cooperation Agency (JICA), showed how a coffee certification program had a large impact on forest protection and decreased the probability of deforestation by 1.7 percentage points.[6]

Such efforts are, however, limited. Even if the concerned countries and

3. FAO.
4. Brancalion and others.
5. NYDF Assessment Partners.
6. Takahashi and Todo.

international development agencies promote alternatives, it remains a huge challenge to secure sustainable forest management in places without clearly defined land use planning, monitoring, and enforcement.

The breakthrough we envisage in the next five years is to establish land use plans, including forest areas, in all developing countries, to monitor forest usage, and to control illegal deforestation through improved remote sensing and data processing and through a radical expansion of advocacy to change corporate incentives toward forest preservation rather than destruction.

When forest monitoring is done through surveys by forest officers, it takes massive time and effort, and information is processed too slowly for effective prosecution of illegal deforestation. Thus, the use of remote sensing by Earth observation satellites becomes very important for the efficient and effective monitoring of vast forests. When this data is seamlessly linked with field data, there can be effective forest management. One example of this operating in practice is a JICA Technical Cooperation Project, "Sustainable Natural Resources Management Project" (2015–21), conducted in Vietnam. In this project, the forest data collected by the forest patrolling team, which included locals on the ground, was input into tablets by forest rangers and then used for forest management. By inputting information in a digital format rather than through paper surveys, the team transferred the data directly into the forest management system and combined with remote sensing data. In addition, already processed remote sensing data was viewed and ground-truthed in the field using tablets.

This example shows the potential for remote sensing technologies to operate national forest monitoring systems and also to lead to improvements in forest governance, investment for social responsibility, and finally zero deforestation. In this chapter, the history of forest monitoring using satellite "Machine Eyes"—"Optical Eyes" and "Radar Eyes"—to improve the ability of forest authorities to enforce laws against illegal deforestation is briefly explained. Then we argue that a breakthrough to achieve zero deforestation is possible by combining improved "Machine Eyes" and "Smart Eyes" with "Functional Eyes" and "Eyes of People."

The History of "Machine Eyes": Achievement of Forest Monitoring by Remote Sensing

Forest Monitoring by "Optical Eyes": Visual Grasp of the Earth

Dating back to the 1970s, optical satellite images—"Optical Eyes"—have been used to monitor the vast forests of Brazil, home to 60 percent of the world's largest tropical forest, the Amazon. Deforestation monitoring started in 1974, using Landsat, and has been conducted using the Amazon Deforestation Satellite Monitoring Project (PRODES) program since 1988. Visual interpretation work has been performed by semiautomatic processes such as supervised classification with gradual improvement of analysis methods as the processing power of computers has advanced. At the global level, a number of systems are used to monitor annual forest change, including WRI's Global Forest Watch, which uses the GLAD (Global Land and Discovery) forest change algorithm developed by the University of Maryland,[7] and the national forest monitoring system (NFMS) developed by various countries, for sustainable forest management. Many of these systems are supported by a recent cloud computing system that has made it possible to process huge amounts of data. A country-level NFMS helps to understand entire forest areas and is also utilized in REDD+ activity and other applications. For example, the Brazilian government was granted US$96.5 million from the Green Climate Fund's (GCF) REDD+[8] results-based payments in 2019,[9] thanks to the efforts of the Brazilian Institute of the Environment and Renewable Natural Resources (IBAMA) to monitor forests based on field activities and satellite information and to furnish this data to the federal and state police under the Action Plan for the Prevention and Control of Deforestation in the Legal Amazon (PPCDAm).

To take effective action, deforestation must be monitored at all times to discover changes as soon as possible. An early warning system (EWS) for deforestation is needed. In Brazil, the authorities have used the Terra and Aqua satellite's MODIS sensor to monitor deforestation of 25 hectares or larger as the target for illegal deforestation control on a nearly daily basis since 2004. Following a change in satellite data sources from MODIS to Landsat and China-Brasil Earth Resources Satellite (CBERS) in 2015, the detection of deforestation is possible in areas as small as 6.25 hectares as the control target.

The Brazilian process for controlling illegal deforestation works from detection to enforcement and starts with the National Institute for Space Research (INPE) using multiple optical satellites under the Near Real-Time Deforestation Detection System (DETER) program to detect deforestation. From INPE, suspected deforestation data (illegality is unknown, at this stage) are sent to IBAMA, the regulatory agency for illegal deforestation. IBAMA and its branches then compare DETER and other EWS data against the satellite imagery, a database of legal land use, and other matters. When deforestation appears to be highly illegal, the authorities move in to enforce the law, sometimes with the support of the federal police and other institutions. In Brazil, satellite images are also used as documentary evidence for prosecuting illegal deforestation operators by determining exactly when and over what area the deforestation occurred.

7. Hansen and others.
8. REDD+ is an abbreviation for Reducing Emissions from Deforestation and Forest Degradation and the Role of Conservation, Sustainable Management of Forests, and Enhancement of Forest Carbon Stocks in Developing Countries.
9. Green Climate Fund.

Other EWS programs at the international level include NASA's Forest Monitoring for Action (FORMA), GLAD Forest Alert, and Global Forest Watch. These are built upon Landsat data and are updated roughly every sixteen days, according to the regression cycle of the satellite. At the national level, only a few countries have their own EWS, because it requires a huge amount of data and rapid analysis rather than the usual forest monitoring system. Besides Brazil, Peru operates an EWS system that custom-tailors the GLAD Forest Alert system to its own vegetation, the Alerta Temprana in the Geo Bosques system.[10]

In tropical forests, however, the ground is often difficult to observe. The skies are covered in dense clouds during the rainy season and can be covered by altocumulus or cirrocumulus clouds even during the dry season. The annual average cloud coverage, calculated by Wilson and Jetz using MODIS data,[11] shows that areas with tropical forests, such as the Amazon Basin, Congo Basin, and Southeast Asia, have especially high cloud coverage rates, which may pose difficulties in using optical satellites such as Landsat for EWS. In Brazil, as the use of optical satellites in monitoring illegal deforestation is common knowledge, illegal deforestation operators have adapted by cutting down forests during the rainy season, using cloud cover to avoid optical satellite detection.

If "Optical Eyes" were to shoot images more frequently, there would be a better chance of obtaining pictures during gaps in the clouds. To date, almost daily observations have been possible by utilizing MODIS data from the wide-range Terra and Aqua satellites, although resolution suffers, given the widened range for each observation. This explains why, in the early stages, Brazil's DETER program was able to detect areas of deforestation only 25 hectares or greater. Thus, there is an unavoidable trade-off between observational frequency and resolution. The narrative, however, is changing, thanks to significant technological innovations such as using constellations of commercial microsatellites to capture multiple images each day. Even so, using this technology for early detection of deforestation over large areas is still not practical. Given the narrow observation range per image, monitoring the Amazon, for example, would require data processing on a massive scale, and no images could be taken if cloud cover lasts all day.

Forest Monitoring by "Radar Eyes": Observing the Earth through Clouds

Another means of monitoring is using radar satellites. "Radar Eyes" can solve the weaknesses of optical satellites. Radar satellites are equipped with synthetic aperture radar (SAR) in which the satellite emits radio waves, which are then

10. Ministry of Environment of Peru.
11. Wilson and Jetz.

captured by sensors as they are reflected back from the surface, in contrast to "Optical Eyes," which capture the reflection of sunlight. Being emitted from satellites, as long as the bandwidth used is long enough to pass through clouds, ground activities can be analyzed by captured radio wave reflections even when it is cloudy or at night. Starting with JERS-1 in 1992, and later ALOS and ALOS-2, Japan has operated radar satellites using the L-band, a longer bandwidth that has advantages in sensing vegetation. Since the early 2000s, the monitoring of tropical forests has used data from such radar satellites. These include the Brazil-based ALOS project conducted from 2009 to 2012,[12] which produced significant results. These projects detected more than a thousand examples of deforestation, including 150 prosecuted illegal deforestation cases from 2010 to 2011. Over a hundred investigation reports of illegal deforestation have been created for evidence in court procedures. As a result, the extent of deforestation in 2014 was 500,000 hectares, about 80 percent less than the 2004 level.

Given these results, the use of radar satellite technology has been considered in other countries with tropical forests, although challenges remain. Unlike with the satellite imagery from optical satellites, few people are adept at working with radar satellite images, making data interpretation difficult. As a workaround, rather than training image interpreters in each country, the detection of deforestation has been automated, and information-receiving countries are simply provided with the results that they then superimpose on their own diverse data sets to verify and prosecute illegal operations. To achieve this outcome, the JICA--JAXA Forest Early Warning System in the Tropics (JJ-FAST),[13] an EWS using ALOS-2 data, was developed as a tool to allow foreign forest officers to allocate more of their strength to field efforts in sustainable forest management. JJ-FAST has been operational since November 2016.

JJ-FAST detects forest changes of two hectares or more from data collected approximately once every forty-five days by ALOS-2 for seventy-seven target countries. It publishes this polygonal data on the JJ-FAST website. Since going operational, JJ-FAST has detected 284,823 cases of deforestation as of March 2020. JJ-FAST has been utilized in technical cooperation projects in South America and Africa, including Brazil, Peru, Cameroon, Mozambique, and the DRC.

The use of JJ-FAST has improved the detection of deforestation of areas greater than two hectares. GLAD Alerts can see smaller individual areas of deforestation, and so captures more than JJ-FAST in the aggregate, but for the larger areas, it missed significant episodes. In 2019, JJ-FAST detected 11,175 km^2 of deforestation, while GLAD Alerts detected 4,093 km^2 of deforestation of areas

---

12. The project name is "Utilization of ALOS Images to Support Protection of the Brazilian Amazon Forest and Combat against Illegal Deforestation."
13. Japan International Cooperation Agency.

greater than two hectares in the Brazilian Legal Amazon. Particularly during the rainy season from January to April and from October to December, when cloud coverage is extremely high—87.71 ± 2.99 percent, based on data from Wilson and Jetz (2016)—and optical satellite imagery rarely permits ground observation, the area of deforestation detected by optical satellites decreases. However, once the dry season from May to September started, which means the cloud coverage is reduced (53.58 ± 8.31 percent, based on the data cited above), the deforestation area detected by GLAD Alerts has increased (table 8-1). This is because deforestation that could not be detected during the rainy season was detected along with actually increased deforestation in the dry season. It should be noted that the correctness of deforestation data is not taken into account in both JJ-FAST and GLAD Alerts data.

The JJ-FAST data are updated every forty-five days. In previous exchanges with the countries utilizing JJ-FAST, it became apparent that some countries considered this refresh rate to be insufficient. However, given how rarely the clouds clear away enough for optical satellites to observe the ground during the rainy season, even every forty-five days is thought to be a significant improvement.

The Brazilian Amazon is vast, and the monthly cloud cover rate varies from region to region. Figure 8-1 shows the area of deforestation detected by JJ-FAST and GLAD Alerts every other month for January–December 2019 in an area separated by one degree, for each cloud cover rate. It is clear that the GLAD Alerts detect more areas (with up to 75 percent cloud cover) than JJ-FAST. However, beyond 75 percent cloud cover, the area detected by JJ-FAST increases and deforestation detection by radar satellites becomes dominant.

Thus, "Radar Eyes" allow detecting deforestation earlier than "Optical Eyes" in the rainy season when the cloud cover rate is high and dense clouds cover the tropical rainforest. This advantage of radar satellites may help forest authorities to enforce laws more effectively. In fact, deforestation detection by JJ-FAST significantly reduces deforestation, according to a statistical analysis using satellite data of 2019 in the Brazilian Amazon. There is a statistically significant negative relationship between the deforestation area detected by radar satellites (reported by JJ-FAST) in the previous months and the area of deforestation detected by optical satellites (reported by GLAD) in the current month, conditional on the area detected by optical satellites in the previous months. This means that the detection of deforestation by radar satellites (JJ-FAST) will significantly reduce further deforestation in the future, suggesting the effectiveness of radar satellites as an enforcement device for forest protection.[14]

---

14. The details of the statistical analysis on the benefit of radar satellite (JJ-FAST) appear in Yamada and others (2021), www.brookings.edu/blog/future-development/2021/07/02/protecting -forests-are-early-warning-systems-effective/.

Table 8-1. Monthly Deforestation Areas Estimated by JJ-FAST, GLAD, and GLAD (Over 2 Hectares) Models in 2019 in the Brazilian Legal Amazon (Square Kilometers)

	Jan.	Feb.	Mar.	Apr.	May	Jun.	Jul.	Aug.	Sep.	Oct.	Nov.	Dec.
JJ-FAST	422.91	705.13	771.52	482.18	371.35	762.50	1081.69	1226.95	1696.24	1184.03	1632.84	837.57
GLAD	245.26	240.91	531.05	820.90	943.72	1726.21	2176.11	2779.88	2101.55	1624.78	587.44	72.79
GLAD (over 2 ha)	91.78	71.57	190.22	305.52	420.54	626.02	586.16	693.88	519.00	428.53	141.76	17.60

Source: Authors' calculations

Figure 8-1. Deforestation Areas Detected by JJ-FAST
and GLAD Alerts per 1-Degree Mesh by Each Cloud
Cover Ratio, Divided into Every 1 Percent in the Brazilian
Legal Amazon Area, in January to December 2019

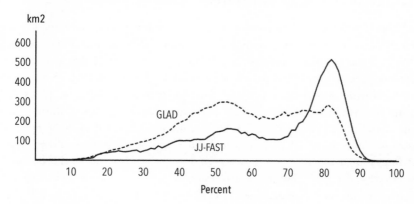

Source: Authors' calculations

However, to date, JJ-FAST cannot detect deforestation of less than two hectares due to the resolution of the ALOS-2 data used. To detect deforestation at
a truly early stage, it is necessary to detect smaller areas of deforestation even
during the rainy season, and to do so, it is necessary to use SAR data with higher
spatial resolution. With ALOS-2, it is also possible to produce images with high
spatial resolution, such as three-meter square or six-meter square. However, the
observation width is 50 km, compared to 350 km at fifty-meter square spatial
resolution, which is used for JJ-FAST. Thus, in the same way as for optical satellites, there is an unavoidable trade-off between observational frequency and
resolution.

Alternative approaches, such as a constellation of small radar satellites, are
under consideration. However, they require more power than optical satellites
for radio wave radiation, so they need large solar panels and batteries. In addition, due to the characteristics of capturing the intensity of reflections from the
ground, advanced attitude control is also required to handle time-series data.
Therefore, large satellites still have an advantage. On the other hand, improvements in technology have led to the development of large satellites that can perform highly spatially resolved observations over a wide observation range, and
it is expected that new large radar satellites will be launched and utilized in the
future.

Future Breakthrough with "Eyes": Issues to Be Solved for Sustainable Forest Management

Improvement of "Functional Eyes": Enhancement of Forest Governances Utilizing "Machine Eyes"

As efforts to improve deforestation detection accuracy press forward, illegal deforestation operators are adapting. According to Richards and others, before PRODES started, illegal deforestation happened regardless of area size. However, once the program started, deforestation of small plots under 6.25 hectares increased while it decreased in larger plots.[15] Moreover, according to IBAMA, before the ALOS-based project, illegal deforestation was rampant during the rainy season, due to cloud coverage, because monitoring relied solely on optical satellites. Once the ALOS project started and it became widely known that radar satellites were detecting deforestation even during the rainy season, this became an effective deterrent. However, deforestation operators started switching to spraying herbicidal defoliants from aircraft flying under the clouds, to kill the forest, and then setting fire to it. In this method, the deforestation goes unnoticed for some time. Radar satellites still see standing trees, so they judge that the forest remains intact. Optical satellites could observe the changes of the "health status" of trees, because the leaves turn yellow or brown after being sprayed, but cannot capture images when the cloud cover is heavy. There is no end in sight to the cat-and-mouse games between deforestation detection technology and illegal deforestation methods, so prospects for achieving zero deforestation based on these techniques remain poor.

There is an additional complication. No matter how developed the technology, and no matter how accurately deforestation is detected, it will all be meaningless without an anti-deforestation policy and framework in place, and without the forest officers to enforce that policy. To enhance forest governance and administrative capacity, "Functional Eyes," utilizing "Machine Eyes," are required. Even Brazil, which has succeeded in decreasing deforestation of the Amazon Basin, cannot officially distinguish whether each deforestation case is legal or illegal without investigation of each situation.[16] Therefore, enforcement of deforestation control policy and information needs to be highly integrated. With the launch of JJ-FAST, JICA and JAXA also launched the Forest Governance Initiative (FGI) to use satellite technology to improve forest governance. FGI minimizes the effort allotted to satellite data analysis, looking to free up human resources to focus on improving and enforcing policy and, as a result, enabling the execution of better

15. Richards and others.
16. Hummel.

forest policy through technology. In fact, in technical cooperation projects in Peru,[17] the FGI has already assisted in introducing JJ-FAST and other data, and in establishing roundtable meetings for local deforestation crackdowns. Furthermore, FGI goes beyond just policies to properly regulate illegal deforestation to include the larger question of how to prevent deforestation due to the conversion of land—that is, how to develop without deforestation.

Encouragement of the "Eyes of People": Involvement of Global Stakeholders in the Forest Sector

The utilization of satellite data for forest monitoring has the potential to increase the transparency of forest policy.[18] In November 2020, Norway launched a program to publish high-resolution optical satellite images free of charge to monitor deforestation. Its users include investors, journalists, scientists, indigenous peoples, and NGOs. The minister of climate and environment of Norway, Sveinung Rotevatn, said that "indigenous people themselves can use this satellite imagery as their own surveillance tool in the struggle against infringement of rights with large companies; global supermarket companies can use it as a confirmation tool for unilateral proof that it is an environmentally friendly product (especially primary products such as soybeans and palm oil) from suppliers."[19]

In Brazil, the Central Bank and the Ministry of Environment have teamed up with private soy and beef producers to suspend access to agricultural credit for those farms and ranches located in the counties with the highest deforestation rates. This has succeeded in drastically reducing deforestation in some counties.[20] Brazilian soybean giants, such as Bunge,[21] Cargill,[22] and ADM,[23] have committed to zero deforestation to align with PPCDAm to promote sustainable agriculture and responsible supply chains. By doing so, they reduce the risk of having their reputations in international markets tarnished by anti-deforestation advocacy campaigns.[24] The public and private sectors are working together to achieve zero deforestation.[25]

In Indonesia, a paper giant, Asia Pulp & Paper (APP), has also committed

17. The project name is "Project on Capacity Development for Forest Conservation and REDD+ Mechanisms" (2016–21).
18. Fuller.
19. KSAT.
20. Nepstad and others.
21. Bunge.
22. Cargill.
23. ADM.
24. Seymour and Harris.
25. Lambin and others.

to zero deforestation. However, NGOs, using open-source satellite data, have accused them of acting in violation of that commitment.[26] This is an example of how transparency, enabled by the "Eyes of People" watching through the "Machine Eyes," can reveal corporate malpractice. With NGOs, investors, bankers, and general citizens all able to use satellite data as a source of objective information on deforestation, the reputational risks to any corporate malpractice have risen dramatically.[27]

Building "Smart Eyes": Predicting Deforestation for Precautions against Illegal Activities

Until now, deforestation detection by "Machine Eyes" has only been able to reveal events after the fact. Even the speedy JJ-FAST takes several days to process satellite images. By the time of detection, the forest has already been cut. This is the weakness of traditional remote sensing. Looking forward, what is needed is to predict deforestation before it happens. Similar to predicting traffic conditions and crimes, it should be possible to predict deforestation locations in advance by identifying the latent drivers of deforestation, analyzing the historical drivers of deforestation patterns. Based on these predictions, the deforestation control agencies could efficiently conduct monitoring and patrolling before the forests are cut down. There is a possibility then to build a "Smart Eyes" deforestation prediction system.

To set up a system to effectively predict illegal deforestation, which can be used both in dry and in rainy seasons, the following is required: (1) radar satellite data to detect deforestation even during the rainy season, as well as the resulting calculation data of the exact deforestation locations; (2) socioeconomic data to determine the latent drivers of deforestation; and (3) massive computing power to apply AI (deep learning) to satellite imagery in quantity. Rather than reiterating these actions for each country, as JJ-FAST has done to date, predictive models should be based on an international platform that can process data by supercomputers (or cloud computing resources) using information from all over the world. The results could also be distributed all over the world.

With Landsat being in use since the 1970s, a huge amount of data has been accumulated from optical satellites, and this is enough to perform AI image recognition. Meanwhile, radar satellites, especially with L-band radar such as JERS-1 and ALOS, have also accumulated a great amount of satellite imagery. Moreover, a new L-band satellite, the successor of ALOS-2, is also planned. All

26. Jong.
27. Galaz and others.

this data promises to usher in a new era of more accurate deforestation detection and the start of deforestation prediction through AI analysis.

If such a system is developed, preventive measures against illegal deforestation can be effectively implemented, and the deterrent effect of being under constant surveillance can be realized. Moreover, based on the predicted information on deforestation, appropriate sustainable forest resource management programs such as the introduction of alternative livelihoods and incentive schemes for development without deforestation can be implemented.

Potential of "Eyes on the Planet": Priority Actions toward the Achievement of Zero Deforestation

Throughout human history, we have been developing the capacity of "Eyes." The desire to understand the world visually seems almost instinctive. The ancient Greek philosophers tried logic to describe the cosmos beyond the reach of the naked eye. In the fifteenth century, the invention of the telescope expanded our naked eye capacity and opened the door to the remarkable development of astronomy and natural science. The evolution of "Eyes" is part of the ongoing process by which people consolidate and expand their image of the world.

Satellites are leading the way in the innovation of "Eyes." The first satellite was the USSR's Sputnik 1, launched in 1957. Today, just over sixty years later, thousands of satellites orbit the earth with more to come. These "Machine Eyes" have expanded our naked-eye capacity dramatically in a short time and, as we have discussed in this chapter, the satellite data and information on the earth has become indispensable for sustainable forest management. In the near future, by combining AI technology with satellite data, we should be able to witness the development of "Smart Eyes" able to predict deforestation to tackle this illegal activity with far more accuracy.

In our everyday life, we receive original data through the naked eye. Then we process and analyze the raw sensory data in our brain to make decisions. In the same way, we can use "Machine Eyes" and "Smart Eyes" to mechanically absorb input data while "Functional Eyes" and the "Eyes of People" help us make decisions using this data.

We are on the cusp of a breakthrough for forest conservation as a result of improvements to each "Eye on the Planet." "Machine Eyes" and "Smart Eyes" are providing ever more accurate and timely data. "Functional Eyes" and the "Eyes of People," are fueling the actions needed to deter illegal activity and encourage corporations, local communities, financiers, and other stakeholders to commit to zero deforestation and to be held accountable for these pledges. We could say that the road to zero deforestation is being built in the sky.

References

ADM. "ADM Commitment to No-Deforestation Policy Implementation H1 2018 Soy Progress Report," https://assets.adm.com/Sustainability/2018-Soy-Progress-Report .pdf.

Brancalion, Pedro H. S., Eben N. Broadbent, Sergio De-Miguel, Adrián Cardil, Marcos R. Rosa, Catherine T. Almeida, Danilo R. A. Almeida, and others. "Emerging Threats Linking Tropical Deforestation and the COVID-19 Pandemic." *Perspectives in Ecology and Conservation*, September 30, 2020. doi:10.1016/j.pecon.2020.09.006.

Bunge. "Bunge Announces Significant Progress against Deforestation Goals in South America," www.bunge.com/news/bunge-announces-significant-progress-against -deforestation-goals-south-america.

Cargill. "Cargill in the Amazon and Our Commitment to Ending Deforestation in Our Supply Chains," www.cargill.com/story/cargill-in-the-amazon-and-our-commitment -to-ending-deforestation.

Fuller, Douglas O. "Tropical Forest Monitoring and Remote Sensing: A New Era of Transparency in Forest Governance?" *Singapore Journal of Tropical Geography*, v. 27 (2006): 15–29. doi:10.1111/j.1467-9493.2006.00237.x.

FAO, "Global Forest Resources Assessment 2020: Main Report." Rome, 2020.

Galaz, Victor, Beatrice Crona, Alice Dauriach, Bert Scholtens, and Will Steffen. "Finance and the Earth System—Exploring the Links between Financial Actors and Non-Linear Changes in the Climate System." *Global Environmental Change*, v. 53 (November 1, 2018): 296–302. doi:10.1016/J.GLOENVCHA.2018.09.008.

Green Climate Fund. "FP100-REDD-PLUS Results-Based Payments for Results Achieved by Brazil in the Amazon Biome in 2014 and 2015," www.greenclimate .fund/project/fp100.

Hatakeyama, Shigeatsu, *The Sea Is Longing for the Forest* (in Japanese). Kyoto: Hokuto-syuppan, 1994.

Hansen, Matthew C., Alexander Krylov, Alexandra Tyukavina, Peter V. Potapov, Svetlana Turubanova, Bryan Zutta, Suspense Ifo, Belinda Margono, Fred Stolle, and Rebecca Moore. "Humid Tropical Forest Disturbance Alerts Using Landsat Data." *Environmental Research Letters*, v. 11, no. 3 (March 2, 2016). doi:10.1088/1748-9326/11/3/034008.

Hummel, Antônio Carlos. "Deforestation in the Amazon: What Is Illegal and What Is Not?" *Elementa: Science of the Anthropocene*, v. 4 (December 8, 2016). doi:10.12952/ journal.elementa.000141.

IPCC, "Climate Change 2014: Synthesis Report," Geneva, 2014.

Japan International Cooperation Agency. "JICA-JAXA Forest Early Warning System in the Tropics," www.eorc.jaxa.jp/jjfast/.

Jong, Hans Nicholas. Mongabay, "Report Finds APP and APRIL Violating Zero-Deforestation Policies with Wood Purchases from Djarum Group Concessions in East Kalimantan," https://news.mongabay.com/2018/08/report-finds-app-and-april -violating-zero-deforestation-policies-with-wood-purchases-from-djarum-group -concessions-in-east-kalimantan/.

KSAT. "KSAT, with Partners Planet, and Airbus Awarded First-Ever Global Contract to Combat Deforestation," www.ksat.no/news/news-archive/2020/ksat-awarded-global -contract-combat-deforestation/.

Lambin, Eric F., Holly K. Gibbs, Robert Heilmayr, Kimberly M. Carlson, Leonardo
C. Fleck, Rachael D. Garrett, Yann Le Polain De Waroux, and others. "The Role of
Supply-Chain Initiatives in Reducing Deforestation." *Nature Climate Change*, v. 8,
no. 2 (February 1, 2018): 109–16. doi:10.1038/s41558-017-0061-1.

Ministry of Environment of Peru. Geo Bosques, geobosques.minam.gob.pe/geobosque/
view/index.php.

Nepstad, Daniel, David McGrath, Claudia Stickler, Ane Alencar, Andrea Azevedo,
Briana Swette, Tathiana Bezerra, and others. "Slowing Amazon Deforestation
through Public Policy and Interventions in Beef and Soy Supply Chains." *Science*, v.
344, no. 6188 (June 6, 2014): 1118–23. doi:10.1126/science.1248525.

NYDF Assessment Partners. "Balancing Forests and Development: Addressing
Infrastructure and Extractive," https://forestdeclaration.org/.

Richards, Peter, Eugenio Arima, Leah VanWey, Avery Cohn, and Nishan Bhattarai.
"Are Brazil's Deforesters Avoiding Detection?" *Conservation Letters*, v. 10, no. 4 (July
7, 2017): 470–76. doi:10.1111/conl.12310.

Seymour, Frances, and Nancy L. Harris. "Reducing Tropical Deforestation." *Science*, v.
365, no. 6455 (August 23, 2019): 756–57. doi:10.1126/science.aax8546.

Stockholm Resilience Centre. "How Food Connects All the SDGs," June 14, 2016,
www.stockholmresilience.org/research/research-news/2016-06-14-how-food
-connects-all-the-sdgs.html.

Takahashi, Ryo, and Yasuyuki Todo. "The Impact of a Shade Coffee Certification
Program on Forest Conservation: A Case Study from a Wild Coffee Forest in
Ethiopia." *Journal of Environmental Management*, v. 130 (November 30, 2013):
48–54. doi:10.1016/j.jenvman.2013.08.025.

Wilson, Adam M., and Walter Jetz, "Remotely Sensed High-Resolution Global Cloud
Dynamics for Predicting Ecosystem and Biodiversity Distributions." *PLOS Biology*,
v. 14, no. 3 (March 31, 2016). doi:10.1371/journal.pbio.1002415.

Yamada, Eiji, Hiroaki Okonogi, and Takahiro Morita. "Protecting Forests: Are Early
Warning Systems Effective?" *Future Development* (blog), Brookings Institution, July
2, 2021.

NINE

Redefining the Smart City for Sustainable Development

Tomoyuki Naito

Breakthroughs in Smart Cities

Fifty years ago, Jane Jacobs placed economic growth in cities at the center of national economic growth. She explained: "If my observation and reasoning are correct . . . rural economies, including agricultural work, are directly built upon city economies and city works."[1] She spearheaded urban development as a self-standing discipline for academics and policymakers.

By 2030, 60 percent of the world's population is projected to live in urban areas, double the share in 1950. Urbanization is fastest in developing countries in Africa and Asia.[2] With more than 80 percent of global GDP generated in cities, a well-managed urbanization is central to sustainable growth. Urbanization can lead to increased productivity, innovation, and the emergence of new ideas,[3] but it can also lead to slums and deteriorating security. Historically, the influx of population into urban areas has also caused environmental problems such as traffic congestion and air pollution.

Managing urbanization in a way that contributes to sustainable growth has given rise to the concept of "smart cities," an effort to comprehensively plan and control city development using science and technology. Starting around 2000, smart cities spread rapidly across the world, largely as demonstration test sites for

1. Jacobs, pp. 3–4.
2. UN-DESA.
3. See World Bank website "Urban Development," www.worldbank.org/en/topic/urbandevelopment/overview.

165

new technologies. Like any experimental movement, smart cities had failures as well as successes, and have evolved away from their technological origins. Today, smart cities are conceived of as "data-driven societies" that collect and analyze information via networked complex elemental technologies to solve social issues. In other words, the modern smart city model stores large amounts of data collected by sensors and cameras in a data center via a high-speed broadband communication network and examines ways to solve problems in human life through analysis by artificial intelligence (AI).

Currently, few smart cities have deep insights into the issues to be solved, public opinion regarding those issues, or the technological means of implementing solutions. Yet they are expanding fast. The global smart city market was valued at US$83.9 billion in 2019 and is expected to grow by almost 25 percent between 2020 and 2027.[4] By that time, the market size created from the relationship between cities and ICT will reach 600 billion U.S. dollars.

This chapter describes the breakthrough in smart city development that is now on the horizon. It is a breakthrough that can be implemented in developing countries as well as in advanced economies. It can help solve many of the pressing issues of the day. One study suggests that 70 percent of the Sustainable Development Goals (SDGs) can be achieved simply by converting to smart cities using technologies that exist today, but with new applications and processes. The breakthrough can be brought about by combining visionary technology with good governance and citizen-level collaboration.[5]

At the outset, it is worth emphasizing that the socioeconomic problems smart cities set out to solve will surely change over time. A clear example is the change in mindset occasioned by the global COVID-19 pandemic. With an estimated 90 percent of all reported COVID-19 cases, urban areas have become the epicenter of the pandemic. In the near term, for many cities, the COVID-19 health crisis has triggered multiple secondary urban crises: in access, equity, finance, safety, joblessness, public services, infrastructure, and transport, all of which disproportionally affect the most vulnerable in society.[6] Cities may have created economic growth through agglomeration, but it is now clear they also created vulnerability to the new enemy of invisible infectious diseases. Regardless of the country or region, none of the existing smart cities, which were proof-of-concept experimental sites for advanced technology, have demonstrated the "smartness" that could suppress COVID-19.

COVID-19 has highlighted the need to redefine smart cities to include the

4. Grand View Research.
5. Diamandis and Kotler, pp. 3–12.
6. United Nations.

concept of resilience. Cities must actively reduce downside risks and truly solve social issues rather than remain as demonstration test sites for new technologies that can accelerate economic growth. They must become genuinely sustainable, human-centered, transformable, and tolerant.

It is useful to compare smart cities to a smartphone. A smart city needs an "urban OS" upon which various stakeholders, including citizens, can flexibly develop and implement applications that contribute to problem-solving, with opt-in and opt-out features. What COVID-19 has illustrated is that excellence in technology and vision of the urban OS is not enough. It must also be flexible enough to address unknown issues of vulnerability that may arise in the future.

Smart Cities before COVID-19
The Evolution of the Concept of the Smart City

What is a smart city? There are no straightforward answers. "Smart" is a generic word that can mean many things. Similarly to other general terms, such as "sustainability" and "globalization," "smart" is now commonly used in the global development discourse but without precise meaning or definition.[7] It was not until the 2000s that the term "smart city" became popular, and since then it has been used in a variety of ways. In the most common early usage, "smart cities" referred to places that conserved resources, especially energy, and that put in place more efficient transport systems. They did this by using cutting-edge information and communication technologies (ICT); environmental technologies; smart grids and storage batteries that enable efficient use of renewable energy; extensive electrification of transportation systems, including electric automobile charging systems; and by promoting energy-saving home appliances and building codes and standards. Most early smart cities targeted energy and environmental issues, but few found a way to monetize the benefits. As a result, the number of smart city demonstration projects increased around the world, but without a sustainable financial model.

In the 2010s, smart cities began attracting attention again not only for environmental and energy benefits but also for the potential of autonomous driving and industrial technology represented by robots. Against the backdrop of the spread of high-speed internet, cloud computing, and the Internet of Things (IoT), there was renewed interest in data-based solutions to social issues. According to a McKinsey report, smart city solutions such as air quality monitoring; energy use optimization; and electricity, water, and waste tracking could produce

7. Townsend.

results such as 10 to 15 percent fewer GHG emissions, 30 to 130 fewer kilograms of solid waste per person per year, and 25 to 80 liters of water saved per person per day.[8]

In its new formulation, a "smart city system" can be described as a model that embodies a data-driven society with structural features embedded in four layers. The first layer is "perceptual," consisting of sensors, smartphones, cameras, and signal lamps that collect data. The second layer is the "network," which consists of the internet, IoT, and mobile communications network technologies that facilitate the real-time transfer and storage of information. The third layer, the "platform," continuously analyzes data using cloud computing. The fourth layer is the "action"—the decisions and management responses taken by policymakers and city managers.[9]

Examples of the World's Smart Cities

Smart cities are everywhere. Notable cases include Masdar City, the United Arab Emirates (UAE), a planned new city where almost all electricity can be supplied by renewable energy with zero carbon dioxide emissions; Amsterdam, the Netherlands, where smart meters will improve energy efficiency; Barcelona, Spain, which has an ecological approach that actively incorporates citizen participation; and Copenhagen, Denmark, where compact, highly convenient, and energy-efficient "human-centered smart cities" are being designed. In addition, countries such as Finland, which has a concept called "Aurora AI" with electronic administration that makes heavy use of AI, and Estonia, which advocates for a "Data Once Policy" and the digitization of administrative procedures across the country, are working on new solutions.

In China, there are more than a hundred smart cities of various sizes and forms, rooted in the Made in China 2025 national strategy. Xiong'an allows only self-driving cars on its streets. Shenzhen is now called the most innovative city globally.

Smart cities in South Korea and Taiwan have taken advantage of the fact that these countries have the highest ICT infrastructure development rate and high digital literacy. In both countries, digitization and technological innovation is advancing rapidly in public and private sectors. Singapore has already incorporated modern ICT into its city management practices.

Even in Southeast Asia, smart cities' efforts are being strategically promoted throughout the region. The ASEAN Smart City Network (ASCN) is a smart

8. McKinsey Global Institute.
9. Wu and others.

city promotion platform that was proposed at the ASEAN Summit Meeting in April 2018. It is a regional framework, through which twenty-six major cities nominated by ASEAN member countries will select priority social projects, formulate action plans, and check the projects' progress at regular ASCN meetings.[10] Among these twenty-six cities, the Bang Sue smart city in Bangkok is an advanced example in Asia of a master plan that calls for the city to deploy a fifth-generation mobile communication system (5G) and abundant sensors within the city, and analyze the collected data by making full use of AI.[11]

Within Africa, too, smart city plans are underway. They include Kigali Innovation City (Rwanda), Konza City (Kenya), Eko Atlantic City (Nigeria), the Village of ICT and Biotechnology (Côte d'Ivoire), and Hope City (Ghana). Kigali Innovation City (KIC) announced its plan at the World Economic Forum in Africa conference held in Kigali in 2016, and will cover residences, offices, universities, research institutes, and factories on a site of over sixty hectares. The total cost is over US$400 million for this flagship project aimed at environmental conservation and resource efficiency through big data management and full use of renewable energy and ICT.[12]

These examples all highlight the popularity of smart cities in Asia, Africa, and Europe, and point to the potential for rapid uptake of new models of smart city management as global experience accumulates.

The Impact of COVID-19 on Smart Cities

COVID-19 showed that although cities have an advantage of creating value through agglomeration, they also have a weakness of more rapid contact-based transmission, given high population densities. As a result of COVID-19, large-scale urban lockdowns have been happening around the world. These were adopted as a precautionary measure to slow the spread of infection worldwide, but at significant economic cost of lower output and reduced employment.

COVID-19 underlined the potential and the limitations of new technology in smart cities. In some cities in China, Taiwan, Singapore, and South Korea, contact tracing applications on mobile phones linked to citywide ICT recognition systems proved effective. The best-known and extensively applied example is China's "Health Code." However, in many other instances, including in Japan and the United States, democratic values of data privacy meant that tracing apps could not be widely implemented. Even in Barcelona, Spain, regarded by many

10. ASCN.
11. JICA and others.
12. Rwanda Development Board.

as one of the most advanced smart cities, the spread of COVID-19 had not been halted as of January 2021, and citizens are being encouraged to use old technology means of social distancing and handwashing.[13] Most smart cities have not functioned smartly against infectious diseases.

COVID-19 has also reduced budgetary allocations for smart city development. Public funds have been reallocated to public health; private foreign investment has collapsed. Thus, smart city plans in many developing countries have been delayed. In Indonesia, the plan to relocate the capital by 2024 from Jakarta to an environmentally friendly, data-driven, smart city on Kalimantan Island has been put on hold, despite its prominence as a central policy of President Joko Widodo's second term. Egypt had also planned to open a new administrative capital about fifty kilometers east of Cairo by the end of 2020, but this has been delayed to 2021. In Saudi Arabia, the plans for construction of the futuristic city "NEOM" on the Red Sea coast, in which the country had planned to invest US$500 billion—more than 70 percent of GDP—are being reviewed, as a result of the stagnation of global crude oil demand.[14] Even in Thailand, the installation of network equipment to introduce 5G into several smart cities, including Bang Sue, which began in the first half of 2020, has been delayed due to the economic slowdown caused by the pandemic.[15]

These postponements and revisions are largely due to the difficulty in raising funds for smart city projects, given economic stagnation or recession accompanying COVID-19. However, funding is not the only issue. The pandemic has also raised questions about how future smart city plans will ensure resistance to various VUCA (volatility, uncertainty, complexity, ambiguity) that can occur in the future. Policymakers everywhere are being forced to rethink their strategies as they become aware of this new challenge.

COVID-19 may yet prove to be a long-term boon for smart cities. It has created a "new normal" for remote work, distance education, and telemedicine, and underlined the necessity of adopting digital technologies as rapidly as possible.

The implications of the impact of a transition to digital life on city infrastructure and buildings is still unclear. Demand for office space could decline. Urban segregation and even out-migration could occur as people at higher income levels look for new ways of living and working outside the city in response to the pandemic. Some analysts worry about an increase in urban sprawl and inequalities across income, race, and gender.[16]

13. Info Barcelona.
14. *Nikkei Newspaper* (2020a).
15. Quoted in Leesa-Nguansuk.
16. United Nations.

However, the majority opinion is that a world where VUCA is expected to increase will be a world where smart cities will become more important. Smart city plans simply have to evolve to allow people to conduct their daily social and economic lives while managing whatever uncertainties the future may bring, be it serious infectious diseases such as COVID-19 or something else.

Infectious Disease Management in China: New Value of Smart Cities

Before the COVID-19 pandemic, EMS (energy management system) and MaaS (mobility as a service) were central to the idea of smart cities. These systems and services showcased how a data-driven society could employ high-speed internet and cloud computing, sensor technology, and smartphones to collect a large amount of citywide data. AI, equipped with algorithms in ultra-high-speed computers on the cloud, could then be used to analyze big data through machine learning to solve pressing social issues. Proponents argued that the model would create new business opportunities, attract investments, generate employment, and create a broader ecosystem of stakeholders that would increase the value of the city.

In the new vision of the future, it has become a requirement for smart cities to go beyond considerations of energy and mobility, to visualize and manage "invisible enemies" using digital technology. From this point of view, China's approach to infectious disease management offers one model for using digital technology. The "Health Code" is a database of citizens' behavior and health status collected through various channels and stored on a data platform specifically constructed by the Chinese government as part of their national strategy. By collating data with national ID numbers, China is able to see how its broad societal rules and norms are reflected in the behavior of individuals.

China locked down several cities in response to the COVID-19 pandemic and has succeeded in suppressing the spread of infection since the middle of 2020. Part of the strategy was to publicly monitor people's movements and economic activities according to the Health Code. The Health Code is a dynamic code for mobile phone apps and consists of three colors: green, red, and yellow. It is automatically checked and generated by the municipal system using information received from users' self-reports and from disease management big data. The green Health Code acts as a digital pass that allows people to travel to places where others congregate, such as public transport, communities, offices, supermarkets, and pharmacies. When a user contacts an infected person, the Health Code may turn red or yellow, and the user can be notified to quarantine immediately. The Health Code is not easy to forge, and the application screen must be presented whenever entering or using public places or transport systems.

The benefit is that it is possible to create a "safe zone" that gathers only those who have proved, by showing the green color on their screens, that they are very unlikely to be infected. These people can then continue to carry out the same social and economic activities as before.[17] The disadvantage, of course, is that citizens who are indicated as being in the yellow or red risk categories are subject to significant restrictions, leading to inconvenience and discrimination.

CCTV cameras also provide data input into the Health Code. These cameras, which have been placed in many cities in China for crime prevention, are networked by high-speed communication. They can collect personal data and collate it with other data sources by using biometric authentication technology. In addition to the heat-sensing function (thermography) on the camera side, China has introduced a technology that detects and instantly identifies individuals with a fever. In addition to the fixed CCTV cameras, drones are used to fly over an urban area and similarly detect feverish citizens. Drones are also used for unmanned spraying of disinfectants in urban areas.

The Health Code relies on noncontact detection and collating of data through new technologies, including face recognition, that are being enthusiastically supported by the Chinese government. The high-tech companies SenseTime and Megby, known for their face recognition technology, have developed and deployed noncontact temperature measuring software using AI. SenseTime is also developing and deploying a "smart AI epidemic prevention solution." It combines AI algorithms and infrared thermal technology to detect heat with an error of fewer than 0.3 degrees and can identify unmasked people with over 99 percent accuracy. Based on its experience with the Health Code, China is now aiming to standardize the concept and method of monitoring cities to prevent infectious diseases, by proposing it to technical committees in international standards bodies such as the International Standardization Organization (ISO) and the International Electrotechnical Commission (IEC). Since the related agreements of the World Trade Organization (WTO) require member countries to create domestic standards based on international standards, if ISO, IEC, and others accept China's proposals, it is more likely that future smart city development in the world will adopt the Chinese method as a standard technology for pandemic surveillance.[18] With other countries scaling back their smart city investments, China's determination to press ahead with using digital technologies for pandemic management could strengthen its competitive advantages in this sector.

17. Quoted in Xiheng.
18. *Nikkei Newspaper* (2020b).

A Human-Centered Smart City to Enhance Sustainability

The limited take-up of the Chinese-style Health Code shows it cannot be a model for smart city development in the rest of the world. We argue that the following three conditions must be met to advance a human-centered, sustainable smart city:

1. Criteria and commitment to introduce critical technologies in the public and private sectors

2. Construction and operation of a robust digital infrastructure through a public-private partnership

3. Consideration for privacy protection and seamless data sharing between the public and private sectors

The first condition requires a commitment to the use of critical technology. If technology adoption remains only a recommendation, subject to individual choice, it may not be effective unless a minimum threshold number of installations are secured. It is due to this democratic dilemma that tracking apps similar to Health Code are not widespread in Japan or the United States.

The second and third conditions call for stronger public-private cooperation. For example, democratic nations typically oppose the seamless sharing of data between the public and private sectors. In South Korea, nevertheless, there is a growing willingness to restrict personal rights and to share the whereabouts and behavior history of COVID-19-infected persons, once these are confirmed to have contracted the disease through a positive PCR test. Similarly, in Japan, the "Amendment of the Act on Prevention of Infectious Diseases and Medical Care for Patients with Infectious Diseases" and the "Act on Special Measures for Countermeasures against New Infectious Diseases" were approved by the Cabinet on January 22, 2021. The Japan Federation of Bar Associations is strongly opposed, noting that legal possibilities contained in the new acts, to impose penalties for noncompliance, display a lack of consideration for fundamental human rights.[19]

This is not the first time that conflict has arisen between surveillance-based solutions that make full use of digital technology and forcible sharing of personal information without obtaining sufficient agreement from citizens. In a data-driven society, accelerating personal data visualization and strengthening social monitoring and management are inseparable from protecting personal information.

19. Japan Federation of Bar Association.

Consider the example of Google's affiliate Sidewalk Labs (SWL) project in Toronto, Canada. In 2017, a public corporation, Waterfront Toronto, initiated a redevelopment project for the waterfront area. SWL won the tender and, in the spring of 2019, it put forward a Master Innovation and Development Plan (MIDP). Its vision for the redevelopment project, called "Sidewalk Toronto," was expected to utilize the latest sustainable technologies such as modular wooden construction, automatic garbage collection, and data utilization in each field. It was billed as one of the world's most advanced data-driven city projects.[20] The plan attracted worldwide attention, with considerable speculation as to how Google's various data-driven social problem-solving applications could be advanced in Sidewalk Toronto. However, a group of activists criticized SWL's failure to prioritize consensus-building with the public, leading a representative of the Waterfront Toronto Digital Strategy Advisory Board (DSAP) to criticize the project for too much "technology for technology," and the project was finally canceled in May 2020.[21]

There may have been other reasons for the cancellation, including the response to COVID-19, but the example shows the importance of considering the relationship between humans and technology in smart city planning. If new technologies are introduced and promoted without obtaining citizens' buy-in and agreement, the project may fail. Conversely, if citizens agree in advance to share their data and adopt the necessary technology, a smart city can provide public goods, including controlling the spread of infectious diseases, by actively developing and operating digital infrastructure.

The breakthrough in smart cities will come about by improving the architecture of the model. Returning to the original four-layer construct of the ideal smart city, laid out at the beginning of this chapter, the "network layer" and "platform layer" should be developed as public goods and operated as effectively as possible rather than as a single vendor's monopoly infrastructure. The dialogue and consensus-building with citizens should be encouraged at the level of the "perceptual layer," of what kinds of data to collect and the "action layer" of the type of decisions that policymakers are empowered to take. In the presence of VUCA, the "perceptual layer" needs to be able to evolve flexibly according to the times, and the "action layer" must become human-centered.

Architectures that realize "human-centered decisionmaking" in this way have already been tried in Barcelona, Spain, and Aizuwakamatsu, Japan. For example, in common with many other cities in Japan, Aizuwakamatsu City, Fukushima Prefecture, is suffering from a decrease in the youth population and

20. Sidewalk Toronto.
21. CURBED.

from negative population growth due to a decline in the birth rate. To overcome this urban structural issue, Aizuwakamatsu City launched a smart city plan in 2012 to make the entire city smarter.[22] The architecture design incorporates the idea of FIWARE, the next-generation internet infrastructure software developed and proven in the European Union (EU). FIWARE has adopted an open international standard API called NGSI (Next Generation Service Interfaces). There are two features: (1) linkage and use of data beyond the local system, and (2) exclusion of vendor lock-in, which consists of a group of software components called Generic Enabler (GE). The data infrastructure is an open API with high interoperability, and partnerships among industry, government, and academia are building a "human-centered architecture" that can be used for solving social issues and urban development, with the option of an opt-in method. The overall architecture is collectively referred to as the "urban Operating System" (OS).[23] Demonstration projects utilizing open APIs with high interoperability are being carried out one after another, and citizen services such as regional digital currencies and remote medical care systems have begun to be implemented. It is hard to say whether the architecture has been useful in addressing an unknown shock, like COVID-19, but there is a sense that smart cities with urban OS and open APIs, with opt-in efforts to encourage citizens' prior consent and partnerships with diverse stakeholders, will create more resilient and sustainable urban agglomerations over the medium-to-long term.

The Long Journey to a Smart City Breakthrough

Historically, public health concerns have been a significant turning point in urban policy. The plague, which was intermittently prevalent from the sixth to the eighteenth centuries, disrupted the feudal social villa system and induced growth of commerce and industry centered on urban areas. In late-nineteenth-century Paris and London, which saw massive inflows of a large working population during the Industrial Revolution, cholera spread in unsanitary and inadequate living environments because urban infrastructure development did not keep up. Ultimately, this became an opportunity for roads and water and sewage systems to be improved. The 1918 influenza pandemic (1918–20), a global pandemic that infected more than 500 million people and killed 20 to 50 million people, was the catalyst for the introduction of social distancing as one of the urban policies as a public health measure.

Given these precedents, the impact of COVID-19 is also likely to change

22. Ebihara and Nakamura.
23. Ministry of Internal Affairs and Communications.

urban policy significantly. Historians may view the year 2021 as the year when cities began to flexibly upgrade to VUCA using digital technology and human intelligence; that is, the year when breakthroughs in smart cities started to be achieved.

As Larasati points out, the development of smart cities does not rely solely on strengthening technology-driven automated procedures, but is a sophisticated model of negotiating process redesign, political and stakeholder support, and organizational and institutional changes.[24] Therefore, in any new smart city plan, it is essential to build on values and philosophies that match a region's actual conditions.

The world is learning from COVID-19 that expectations for smart cities must be raised to embrace inclusion and resilience. Smart cities are no longer limited to demonstration test sites for specific new technologies such as EMS and MaaS. Cities can have truly smart functional devices that guide people's lives in a genuinely sustainable direction. The new smart city is not just a showcase of new technology; it is a genuinely human-centered, transformable, tolerant, and resilient place to live, work, and play.

Both China's case and the case of Toronto ignored the consent of citizens in favor of the primacy of technology. The results differed; China has been successful in slowing the spread of the pandemic, but at a potential cost of discrimination and exclusion that cannot be assessed because of the absence of dialogue. The project in Toronto was canceled. By contrast, the urban OS and open API that enable citizen participation in Aizuwakamatsu City is a significant feature that gives citizens the right to opt-in; the architecture prioritizes the active will and choice of human beings over technology itself.

To create a genuinely human-centered, transformable, and resilient smart city, it is necessary to develop and strengthen the "network layer" and "platform layer" as public goods in cooperation with the public and private sectors.

The "network layer" requires a high speed, low latency, high security, large capacity communication infrastructure.[25] However, high speed communication infrastructure is often categorized as a private good, and pricing to recoup the considerable initial investment and maintenance costs can reduce citizens' access. One technology that alleviates this concern is Network Functions Virtualization (NFV). The advantages of NFV are that vendor lock-in can be avoided, investment and maintenance can be significantly reduced, and various functions can be added or changed simply by adding software. This innovative technology has been developed in India and can fundamentally change the conventional concept of communication infrastructure development, even in developing countries.

24. Larasati and others.
25. Oxford Business Group.

The "platform layer" needs to have an open API as its urban OS and to encourage a broad range of stakeholder participation, as in Aizuwakamatsu City. In addition, blockchain technology can be adopted to manage personal information while ensuring transparency and preventing falsification.

A bold metaphor for these concepts may make it easier to understand. President Zelensky of Ukraine has said, "We really want to create a country in a smartphone"—this is the idea that should be applied to future smart cities.[26] The smart city's urban OS is like Apple's iOS. The OS can be updated flexibly, various developers can create applications, and the collected data from users can be efficiently utilized. Organized like this, smart cities can provide a breakthrough in the achievement of SDG 11, "Sustainable Cities," as well as contributing to many other SDGs. Joia and Kuhl argue that smart city development in developing countries can only be considered successful if it can integrate the basic needs of all and actively contributes to several SDGs.[27] Tan and others point out that technology-enabled smart cities in developing countries can only be realized if socioeconomic, human, legal, and regulatory reforms are initiated simultaneously.

In this chapter, we have argued that to redefine smart cities in the future, it is essential to deepen the understanding of and attention to data governance and the necessary technical conditions. The international community has begun to foster dialogue through platforms such as the G20 and the World Economic Forum, based on the SDGs' perspective of "no one left behind." In 2020, the World Economic Forum selected thirty-six cities across twenty-two countries and six continents to pioneer a new global policy roadmap for smart cities. This Global Smart Cities Alliance, hosted at the forum, commits participating cities to adopt privacy protection policies, better broadband coverage, accountability for cybersecurity, increased city-data openness, and better accessibility to digital city services for disabled and elderly people.[28] There will surely be setbacks along the way, but a path toward smart cities is being created.

References

ASCN. 2018. "Concept Note—ASEAN Smart Cities Network." ASEAN Secretariat.
CURBED. 2020. "Sidewalk Labs' 'Smart' City Was Destined to Fail: The Google Company Has Abandoned Its Plan to Remake Toronto's Waterfront," www.curbed.com/2020/5/7/21250678/sidewalk-labs-toronto-smart-city-fail.
Diamandis, Peter H., and Steven Kotler. 2020. *The Future Is Faster Than You Think.* Simon & Schuster.

26. President of Ukraine Official Website.
27. Joia and Kuhl.
28. World Economic Forum.

Ebihara, Joichi, and Shoji Nakamura. 2019. *Smart City 5.0*. Tokyo: Impress.
Grand View Research. 2021. "Smart Cities Market Size, Share, and Trends Analysis
    Report by Application (Governance, Environmental Solutions, Utilities,
    Transportation, Healthcare), by Region, and Segment Forecasts, 2020–2027," May,
    www.grandviewresearch.com/industry-analysis/smart-cities-market.
Info Barcelona. 2021. "New Measures to Contain the Spread of COVID-19," April 3,
    www.barcelona.cat/infobarcelona/en/tema/information-about-covid-19/measures-for
    -the-first-stage-of-the-new-lockdown-exit-2_1009312.html.
Jacobs, Jane. 1969. *The Economy of Cities*. Vintage Press.
Japan Federation of Bar Association. 2021. "Statement by the Chairman against the
    Amendment to the Infectious Diseases Law and Special Measures Law (Kansensho-
    Hou / Tokuso-Hou no Kaisei-Houan ni Hantai-suru Kaicho-Seimei)," www
    .nichibenren.or.jp/document/statement/year/2021/210122_2.html.
JICA and others. 2020. *The Study on Development of Smart City Concept for the Bang Sue
    Area in the Kingdom of Thailand: Final Report*.
Joia, Luiz A., and Alexander Kuhl. 2019. "Smart City for Development: A Conceptual
    Model for Developing Countries." *Information and Communication Technologies for
    Development*. Strengthening Southern-Driven Cooperation as a Catalyst for ICT4D,
    edited by P. Nielsen and H. Kimaro. ICT4D 2019. IFIP Advances in Information
    and Communication Technology, vol. 552. Springer, Cham.
Larasati, Niken, and others. 2018. "Smart Sustainable City Application: Dimensions
    and Developments: Smart services for region of the foremost cultural centers of a
    developing country," 122–126. DOI: 10.1109/ICOMIS.2018.8644788.
Leesa-Nguansuk, Suchit. 2020. "NBTC: Telecom Market Value to fall 2.3%," *Bangkok
    Post*, September 11.
McKinsey Global Institute. 2018. "Smart Cities: Digital Solutions for a More Livable
    Future."
Ministry of Internal Affairs and Communications. 2016. "Smart City Aizu-area," www
    .soumu.go.jp/main_content/000452041.pdf.
Nikkei Newspaper. 2020a. "Capital Relocation, Successive Brakes Indonesia and Egypt
    (Shuto-Iten Aitsugi Brake—Indonesia and Egypt)," June 9. (Written in Japanese.)
———. 2020b. "International Standard for Smart City Government, Sense of Crisis in
    China Proposal (Smart City no Kokisai Kikaku—Seihu, Chugoku Teian ni Kiki-
    Kan," August 4. (Written in Japanese.)
Oxford Business Group. 2020. "What Is the Future for Smart Cities after COVID-19?"
    June 16, https://oxfordbusinessgroup.com/news/what-future-smart-cities-after-covid
    -19.
President of Ukraine Official Website. 2019. "I Dream about a State in a Smartphone—
    Volodymyr Zelenskij," May 23, www.president.gov.ua/en/news/ya-mriyu-pro
    -derzhavu-u-smartfoni-volodimir-zelenskij-55585.
Rwanda Development Board. 2018. "Kigali Smart City Value Proposition: Discussion
    Document." Rwanda Development Board.
Sidewalk Toronto. 2019. "Master Innovation and Development Plan Overview," https://
    storage.googleapis.com/sidewalk-toronto-ca/wp-content/uploads/2019/06/23135500
    /MIDP_Volume0.pdf.
Townsend, Anthony M. 2014. *Smart Cities*. W. W. Norton & Company.
United Nations. 2020. "Policy Brief: COVID-19 in an Urban World." www.un.org/sites
    /un2.un.org/files/sg_policy_brief_covid_urban_world_july_2020.pdf.

United Nations Department of Economic and Social Affairs (UN-DESA). 2019. *World Urbanization Prospects: The 2018 Revision.*

World Economic Forum. 2020. "In the Face of Extraordinary Challenges, 36 Pioneer Cities Chart a Course Toward a More Ethical and Responsible Future," www .weforum.org/press/2020/11/in-the-face-of-extraordinary-challenges-36-pioneer -cities-chart-a-course-towards-a-more-ethical-and-responsible-future.

Wu, Yuzhe, and others. 2018. "Smart City with Chinese Characteristics against the Background of Big Data: Idea, Action, and Risk." *Journal of Cleaner Production*, v. 173.

Xiheng, Jiang. 2020. "Health Code: What and How?" *China Daily*, April 10.

TEN

How Digital Systems Will Transform the Future of Money and Development

Tomicah Tillemann

O pen-source digital payment networks could not only revolutionize the financial sector, but also provide a foundation for whole-of-society digital transformation. The same technologies that enable frictionless, trusted financial transactions will unlock solutions to public corruption, digital identity verification, social benefits delivery, clean power markets, and even voting. Built correctly, these systems could reinvent the toolbox that government, the private sector, and civil society use to solve public problems.

The systems that societies use to carry out payments and financial transactions come with far-reaching consequences. In the same way a country's choice of transportation infrastructure affects traffic congestion, climate, public safety, and the ability to move people, a nation's choice of payments infrastructure influences economic growth, social mobility, and the ability to move assets.

If you are a member of the middle class in an advanced economy, you may

An exceptional community of thinkers, doers, builders, and problem-solvers provided insights and inspiration along the path to completing this chapter. My sincere gratitude goes to Dante Disparte, Daniel Radcliffe, Anit Mukherjee, Han Sheng Chia, Shimpei Taguchi, Paula Hunter, Lesley-Ann Vaughan, Anca Bogdana Rusu, and Xochitl Cazador for generously lending their time and genius during the journey. While I take sole responsibility for the content, praise should be directed to Ben Gregori and Jordan Sandman, whose diligent research and round-the-clock editing were indispensable to the success of the project. Would that every writing project were shepherded by such a capable team. Lastly, thanks go to my spouse, Sarah Tillemann, whose effervescent talent as an editor is eclipsed only by her superlative brilliance as a partner, friend, and enabler of every task worth doing.

think that the global financial system works reasonably well for you. You almost certainly have access to a government-insured bank account. You use financial products such as credit cards, mortgages, foreign currency exchanges, and loans to move funds, manage liquidity, and build a credit score. And you can transfer money digitally between the accounts of your family, friends, and businesses using services such as Zelle, Venmo, and PayPal.

Widespread reliance on this patchwork architecture to facilitate regular economic activity has led economists and development experts to focus on broadening access to cards, cash, and bank accounts as a means of increasing financial inclusion.[1] Policymakers and finance professionals have, in turn, pursued this goal based on the assumption that bringing more people into the existing financial system is the best way to expand access to the services it provides. However, the goal of universal financial inclusion has been stymied by inefficiencies embedded in legacy payments systems based on cards and cash.

A new generation of digital payment technology not only offers an opportunity to rethink how societies bring people into the financial system, but to reimagine the system itself. If digital payments solutions are deployed responsibly, they could catalyze a revolution in development. A growing variety of digital payment platforms are delivering groundbreaking progress in countries where they have been adopted. Many of these systems use existing technology such as mobile phones and text messaging to operate in low-capacity environments. Telecoms and government agencies are using mobile payments to leapfrog over card-based technologies and traditional financial institutions. Solutions such as M-Pesa in Kenya, BKash in Bangladesh, Bakong in Cambodia, and BHIM and NUUP in India are building a path for hundreds of millions of previously unbanked people to join the global economy. The pandemic accelerated the adoption of digital payment tools as physical banking centers closed and transactions conducted using cash increased the risk of contracting COVID-19.

Digital payment systems alone will not compensate for the effects of bad policy or revive dying industries, but they can significantly reduce levels of friction, corruption, and societal mistrust. As nations struggle to rebuild following the coronavirus pandemic, better payments architecture may prove indispensable to communities, companies, and households looking to deploy resources more efficiently. If these systems are built using open-source code and open standards, they will be able to scale quickly and at modest marginal cost to countries worldwide.[2]

The immediate upside for societies that embrace digital payments could be profound, from eliminating much of the US$30 billion spent each year on

---

1. World Bank.
2. Lerner.

remittance fees to recouping a portion of the US$3.1 trillion in government revenue lost to tax evasion.[3] In the long run, the benefits could go beyond providing hundreds of millions with access to more dynamic, equitable financial tools.[4]

Digital payment networks, particularly those based on open-source technology, could not only revolutionize the financial sector but also provide a foundation for whole-of-society digital transformation. The same technologies that enable frictionless, trusted financial transactions will unlock solutions to public corruption, digital identity verification, social benefits delivery, clean power markets, and even voting. Built correctly, these systems could reinvent the toolbox that government, the private sector, and civil society use to solve public problems.

This chapter provides an overview for policymakers, regulators, and development practitioners looking to harness the power and potential of these digital systems. It surveys the opportunities and challenges surrounding the use of payments solutions, including:

- The shortcomings of legacy systems;

- Promising cases where digital payment solutions have already been deployed at scale;

- Emerging technologies that could further alter the payments landscape;

- The risk that poor governance could undermine future progress in this space; and

- The ways digital payments infrastructure could enable societies to safely, securely validate and transact with a range of sensitive data and digital assets.

Challenges of the Status Quo

The centrality of outdated payments architecture in daily life and commerce is part of what makes old systems difficult to uproot. In contrast to horse-drawn carriages and telegrams, which long ago assumed their place as quaint relics of centuries past, outmoded payments solutions continue to serve as the foundation of many advanced and emerging economies. Change is hard under the best of circumstances, and change that requires mustering political will to unseat entrenched incumbents, overcome regulatory hurdles, and roll out national technology platforms may seem almost unattainable. As a result of these and other challenges to deploying digital payment systems, many countries simply

3. Cecchetti and Schoenholtz; Werdigier.
4. Demirgüç-Kunt.

layer newer solutions, such as plastic cards, on top of older, analog infrastructure such as cash and paper-based checking accounts. The resulting amalgams of old and new often prove slow, expensive, insecure, and prone to reinforcing economic inequities. These dynamics also make payments systems vulnerable to regulatory capture and, in many cases, the sector suffers from a profound lack of competition.

A number of critiques can be leveled against existing payments infrastructure. Among them, it is:

- *Slow.* Only a quarter of the world's countries have deployed real-time payments systems.[5] Use of instant digital transactions accelerated during the COVID-19 pandemic, but in many regions, including in the United States, only a portion of financial institutions have been able to access and adopt faster systems.[6] The costs associated with slow payments infrastructure fall disproportionately on low-income populations who live paycheck to paycheck. In the United States, the long waits required to process and clear transactions are a prime reason for the US$35 billion spent each year on check cashing, payday lending, and bank overdraft services.[7] Low-income, marginalized populations use these services at disproportionately high rates to access liquidity more quickly.[8] This phenomenon was particularly pronounced during the pandemic, when millions faced financial ruin as they waited weeks to receive paper checks with social benefits and unemployment insurance.[9]

- *Expensive.* In many advanced economies, interchange fees are approximately 2 percent of each transaction.[10] For the United States, that translates to over US$40 billion annually.[11] Like the costs of long delays in settling payments, the burdens associated with these fees fall regressively on low-income consumers.[12] These challenges can be far more acute in cash-based economies. Withdrawals from automated teller machines (ATMs) are often capped at low levels, and each transaction comes with fees equivalent to several dollars. Pulling out enough cash to accomplish even a simple task such as filling up an automobile gas tank may require multiple withdrawals

5. FIS.
6. Ibid.
7. Wilson and Wolkowitz.
8. Brown, Eftekthari, and Kurban.
9. Marbella and Miller; Iacurci.
10. Kansas City Fed.
11. *Motley Fool.*
12. Schuh, Shy, and Stavins.

from multiple ATMs, each with its own transaction costs. Similar dynamics pervade cross-border remittances, a crucial development tool used to transfer over US$500 billion per year to families worldwide.[13] Moving money internationally through financial institutions requires banks to establish trusted relationships with a series of intermediaries in order to convey funds to their intended recipient. The transfer fees charged by each intermediary total US$30 billion per year, money that never reaches the individuals and communities that remittances are intended to benefit.[14]

- *Insecure.* Cash, credit cards, and checks are vulnerable to exploitation on two fronts. First, to varying degrees these systems cannot guarantee that payee and payer make and receive payments as intended. Second, legacy systems can be co-opted and exploited by bad actors. Harvard economist Ken Rogoff has estimated that one-third of all U.S. currency in circulation is used for crimes and tax evasion.[15] Cash is so insecure that responsible regulators would likely never approve it for use today if it were suggested as a new medium of exchange.[16] Credit card fraud costs the global economy over US$27 billion annually, a number that is expected to reach US$35 billion by 2023.[17] Tens of millions of credit card users have also been subject to data breaches that increase their vulnerability to identity theft. Check fraud is an old problem, but it surged back into headlines in 2020, as governments distributed fiscal stimulus in the form of physical checks. When a final accounting is done, criminals may have stolen over US$100 billion in assistance funds intended for needy families following passage of the CARES Act.[18]

- *Prone to reinforcing existing economic inequities.* One-third of the world's population has no access to the formal financial institutions that serve as an on-ramp to the global economy.[19] Unbanked individuals often find it difficult or impossible to secure their assets and may be forced to stockpile cash at home—a risky, sometimes dangerous proposition—if they want to maintain a financial reserve. Alternatives, such as entering expensive or potentially exploitative relationships with rent-seeking middlemen, add to the already high costs of being poor. Surveys of unbanked individuals find

13. De and others.
14. Cecchetti and Schoenholtz.
15. Rogoff.
16. Polemitis.
17. *Nilson Report.*
18. Murphy and Rainey.
19. World Bank Development Research Group.

that the most frequent impediment to accessing bank accounts is cost.[20] In order to combat the fraud and abuse challenges mentioned above, cash- and card-based financial institutions are subject to regulatory requirements to "know your customer" (KYC). The accompanying compliance costs are often too high to serve poor populations profitably. Other barriers to financial access include physical distance to financial institutions, a lack of documentation to validate one's identity, and a lack of trust in available banking options.[21]

What's Working

Technologies to mitigate each of the challenges outlined above already exist. Governments, firms, and civil society organizations have deployed digital solutions that are significantly faster, more efficient, more secure, and more equitable than the systems they replace. The scope and ambition of some of these projects is sufficiently breathtaking to convince even jaded observers that change is possible.

Successful digital payment platforms come in a variety of shapes and sizes. Some are centralized systems deployed by governments. In other cases, a company with broad reach, such as a mobile carrier, may operate national payments infrastructure. As outlined below, these solutions are changing the lives of hundreds of millions of users that rely on them. In Kenya, digital payments have already lifted 2 percent of the country's population out of poverty.[22] However, even the best digital payments systems in use today come with tradeoffs.

Government-backed platforms require ongoing public investment and political support in order to function effectively. Private-sector solutions can easily morph into monopolies with attendant opportunities for rent-seeking. Centralized systems provide bad actors with a vantage point from which to conduct malevolent surveillance. And any digital platform can prove an attractive target for cybercriminals. The solutions highlighted in this section do not follow a specific formula. Rather, they reflect the expanding universe of approaches by countries adopting payment solutions that are fit for purpose in a digital age.

20. Demirgüç-Kunt.
21. Ibid
22. Jack and Suri.

Financial Inclusion in India

Aadhaar, the digital identity platform of the government of India, created the groundwork for a series of payment innovations that are providing financial access to hundreds of millions of the country's citizens. The biometric identity architecture made possible by Aadhaar serves as the foundation for the Aadhaar-Enabled Payment System (AEPS), a cash transfer mechanism that allows government agencies to utilize an electronic Know Your Customer (eKYC) services to deliver payments, along with basic banking services, to millions of Indians. The Unified Payment Interface (UPI), an open payment software that standardizes bank transfer processes, enables apps like the Bharat Interface for Money (BHIM) and BharatQR to facilitate almost 1.5 billion monthly transactions between smartphone users, customers, and businesses.[23] Even those without internet-enabled mobile phones can transfer up to ₹5,000 (approximately US$65) by entering *99#* on a regular, non-smartphone to access a protocol similar to an SMS. By supplying this core technology to a wide range of payment providers, UPI has grown rapidly to power more than half of all digital transactions in India.[24]

Accountable Public Administration in Estonia

Estonia prioritized interoperability to build a whole-of-government approach to digital payments and services. The country's digital platforms allow agencies and banks to offer a range of advanced services. Utility payments, pension contributions, and taxes all rely on common digital infrastructure to channel information between government agencies and citizens' bank accounts. At the core of the system is a digital identity and data exchange platform called X-Road, which securely moves information and assets between individuals, companies, and government agencies. The availability of a trusted digital identity solution streamlines KYC compliance for banks, and enables financial institutions to process mortgages, loans, and even requests to open new accounts entirely online. The system has powerful implications for public administration. By simply confirming the accuracy of information already stored in the system, citizens can file their taxes in under three minutes.[25] Estonia's X-Road framework also takes extensive precautions to safeguard personal data. Users see exactly who is accessing their information and what information has been accessed in order to help identify and deter any illicit use of the platform.

---

23. *Economic Times BFSI.*
24. Sharma.
25. Enterprise Estonia.

Universal QR Code Payments in Singapore

Singapore embarked on a transition from a card-and-cash-based society to a mobile-first digital economy by centering its payments infrastructure on QR (Quick Response) codes. Singapore's PayNow application uses mobile phone numbers and QR codes to facilitate peer-to-peer digital payments. The country's Government Technology Agency launched the world's first unified standard for using QR codes in digital payments between banks, merchants, consumers, and government agencies, a protocol known as Singapore Quick Response (SGQR). Customers of different banks can easily, instantly exchange funds with each other, pay bills, taxes, and purchase goods and services using just QR codes. Singaporeans rely on a variety of digital payment channels, including credit cards, Google and Apple Pay, and other QR-based payment apps, but half of all adults in Singapore have downloaded the PayNow and PayNow Corporate apps since 2017.[26] Government agencies and banks have also implemented national programs to boost adoption of the SGQR system in the wake of the COVID-19 pandemic, particularly in the food and healthcare industries.[27]

Repurposing Existing Networks in Kenya

Kenyan mobile phone providers leapfrogged the legacy banking system to create SMS-enabled mobile money services for their citizens. Instead of relying on formal financial institutions to serve as on-ramps and off-ramps for Kenyans looking to deposit and withdraw cash, the M-Pesa mobile phone–based money transfer service leverages a network of human agents located in cell phone kiosks across rural and urban areas to exchange cash for digital credits tracked by mobile network giants Vodafone and Safaricom. These agents act like independent ATMs, allowing M-Pesa users to move cash in and out of the M-Pesa system independent of banks. Many transactions traditionally completed using cash or bank payment services, like buying groceries or paying bills, can be accomplished solely with cell phones. Since its launch in 2007, nearly 96 percent of households in Kenya have gained access to mobile money services, lifting over a million people out of poverty thanks to the increased access to financial services.[28] M-Pesa does lock users into a specific mobile vendor, but it has successfully expanded to Tanzania, Mozambique, DRC, Lesotho, Ghana, Egypt, Afghanistan, and South Africa. Other mobile money services, including BKash in Bangladesh and Tigo

26. Monetary Authority of Singapore.
27. Sharwood.
28. Jack and Suri.

in Bolivia, now emulate M-Pesa's SMS-based model, taking advantage of its simplified infrastructure requirements and growing cellular network coverage.

Blockchain-Based Payments in Cambodia

Cambodia boasts a vibrant mobile money provider market, but the highly fragmented digital payment ecosystem elevates prices for financial services and restricts payments between users on different platforms. Bakong, a project by the National Bank of Cambodia, uses blockchain[29] technology to bridge banking systems so that interbank loans and retail banking transactions all occur on a unified settlement system.[30] Consumers and merchants that rely on different banks and payment apps can process transactions in real time, fostering greater adoption of mobile financial services for the unbanked and lowering the cost for new digital payment competitors. By linking payment apps and standardizing QR codes, Bakong will also enable migrant workers to securely and instantly transmit money across borders and submit payments for medical costs or utility bills for family members back home.[31]

Benefits of Digital Payment Platforms

Despite the broad range of approaches, architectures, and technologies outlined in the examples above, the benefits from successful digital payment solutions are remarkably similar across different geographies and contexts. In addition to technical advances such as reduced transaction times and lower costs, digital systems also demonstrate an impressive ability to reach and serve groups that were previously on the margins of an economy or society.

Broader Access

Over the last decade, mobile and digital payments have driven a meteoric rise in financial inclusion. An estimated 1.2 billion people have gained access to basic financial services, which helped many start-up businesses to purchase critical goods and services and build savings.[32] These benefits particularly affect rural communities previously unable to utilize financial services due to limited internet connectivity and the long distances between many rural brick and mortar banking

---

29. Tillemann.
30. Vireak.
31. Chea.
32. World Bank (2018b).

locations.[33] The gains from digital payment platforms have also aided women and migrant workers. In regions where legal and societal barriers prevented women from independently managing their finances and building wealth, digital payments have afforded women greater control of their income and assets. A study in Kenya showed that mobile money services increased savings by over 20 percent, allowed 185,000 women to transition from agricultural to business occupations, and led to a 22 percent decline in the share of women-led households living in extreme poverty.[34] Migrant workers have gained the ability to manage family finances from abroad and send digital remittances instantly, securely, and at lower cost.[35]

As with any digital solution, there is always a risk that new systems could exacerbate existing inequities. In fields such as digital identity, organizations, including ID2020, have worked to ensure that solutions work for those who lack internet connectivity. It is important for digital payments providers to take similar precautions and design their systems with marginalized individuals in mind. Governments may need to embrace a variety of different payments systems. No society should be entirely dependent on a single solution. Low competition in payment service markets enables operators to charge high prices for products that underserve their users. Whenever possible, digital platforms should give communities new options rather than restrict their freedom of choice.

Enhanced Efficiency

Digital payments are slowly eradicating the antiquated process of reconciling and settling transactions across disconnected financial institutions. Individuals who receive digital government cash transfers spend less time waiting in lines and traveling to collect benefits. Research in Niger concluded that the country's decision to administer its cash transfer program through mobile payments saved enough working hours to enable each participant in the program to feed a family of five for a day.[36] Time savings occur in more advanced economies as well. Estonia's efficiency gains from its X-Road system are equivalent to 2 percent of the country's GDP[37] and give citizens back the equivalent of an extra 844 working years[38] annually. Individuals' ability to repurpose time that was previously wasted visiting banks, government offices, and ATMs to engage in more productive economic and family activity is one of the most powerful benefits in countries where digital payments have been adopted.

33. Bughin and others.
34. Suri and Jack.
35. World Bank Development Research Group.
36. Boumnijel and others.
37. See www.ipinst.org/2016/05/information-technology-and-governance-estonia#3.
38. See https://e-estonia.com/solutions/interoperability-services/x-road/.

Reduced Transaction Costs

Mobile payments largely eliminate the need for expensive point-of-sale terminals and interchange fees paid to financial intermediaries. Just as telecom companies can transmit text messages at the marginal cost of 1/1000th of a cent, mobile payment networks drive the cost of facilitating a transaction close to zero.[39] Lower transaction costs are encouraging many countries that lack legacy payment systems to opt for digital solutions instead of card-based infrastructure. Decentralized digital interbank settlement systems such as Ripple and Corda also reduce the cost of existing financial infrastructure. In principle, the interoperability and lower transaction fees available through use of these platforms should allow banks to reduce compliance budgets and lower the cost of services for consumers. Low transaction costs can also open the door to micropayments, and the multitude of potentially revolutionary new business models they create for everyone from street vendors to journalists. An economy in which moving assets is as easy as moving information via text or e-mail could develop new market mechanisms and incentives that more accurately reward the creation of value across society.

Increased Accountability

Interoperable payments and identity verification systems can reduce waste, fraud, and abuse in public and private finance. Estonia's digital payments system allows its government to transfer funds to citizens with a high degree of confidence that the money will reach eligible, intended beneficiaries. India's digital identity and payments platforms eliminated an estimated 47 percent of leakage after it was introduced, amounting to US$9 billion of savings each year.[40] The better data that comes with the use of digital payments systems can also help governments deploy data-driven economic and social policies.

Ensuring Responsible Governance of Payments Architecture

The remarkable benefits afforded by digital payment platforms come with a caveat: their utility depends on ensuring that systems are used responsibly and safeguarded from bad actors. Along with electrical power and computer code, digital payment networks run on trust. People need to have confidence that the platforms they trust with their hard-earned funds will operate as intended. Government efforts to illicitly manipulate or surveil networks are a clear and present danger to the long-term efficacy of digital payment systems. The potential for

39. Barker.
40. *Business Today.*

cyberattacks that compromise platform availability or integrity represent another significant concern. Either risk could quickly undermine users' confidence—and the otherwise positive outcomes associated with the use of digital payments.

Effective, responsible platform governance is the best insurance against the challenges posed by bad actors. Its importance will escalate as authoritarian governments continue to develop and export payments solutions that are both highly innovative and extremely compromised.

Alipay and Tencent's WeChat Pay, the two dominant Chinese payment platforms, include tightly integrated access to everything from bill payment and bank account management to food delivery, social media, ride shares, transit tickets, insurance, digital ID, and document storage. These platforms are among the most ambitious, successful payments solutions available anywhere in the world, and the Chinese Communist Party (CCP) is encouraging their global adoption through its Digital Silk Road and Belt and Road Initiative.[41] The CCP is also piloting a Digital Yuan, which could allow party officials to surveil the transaction history of anyone who uses their digital currency and offer similar capabilities to friendly regimes across the world. Though the CCP claims to have introduced privacy protections as a feature of the Digital Yuan, party officials reserve the right to monitor for transactions they deem illegal or a threat to national security. These measures could assist efforts to limit the economic free-dom of ethnic minorities or political dissidents. In societies dependent on digital payments, a government's ability to "de-platform" users by denying them access to funds or the ability to engage in transactions could provide a penalty almost as devastating as physical incarceration.

These trends should be deeply concerning to democratic governments. The United States, in particular, has exercised significant influence over the global financial system through SWIFT—the Society for Worldwide Interbank Finan-cial Telecommunication—an international settlement mechanism that facilitates dollar-denominated payments between countries via U.S. banks. The United States has used SWIFT to freeze international payments by individuals and organizations that finance terrorism, engage in criminal behavior, and violate international laws. SWIFT maintains strict privacy policies and is designed to extend democratic values of transparency, accountability, and the rule of law through international financial markets.[42] If innovative systems developed by authoritarian governments outcompete aging, vulnerable financial structures like SWIFT, it could have profound implications for the global system. Going forward, a country's choice of digital payment systems and digital infrastructure

41. Olsen.
42. SWIFT.

may be as important to shaping its geopolitical orientation as membership in NATO or the Warsaw Pact was a generation earlier.

The responsible governance of digital payment architecture is too important to be left to governments alone. Ideally, multi-stakeholder models with oversight from civil society, academia, the private sector, and other independent institutions could help safeguard the privacy and security of platform users. Under any circumstance, citizens and democratic governments should be wary of the serious dangers posed by digital payment systems that lack adequate oversight, privacy protections, and accountability mechanisms.

The Frontiers of Digital Payment Architecture

Despite real governance concerns, existing digital payment technologies are delivering immense benefits. The potential reach and impact of the revolution in payments technology is poised to accelerate as new technologies nearing deployment begin to come online. These innovations could empower consumers to design their own financial tools, redefine the concept of money with programmable currency, and allow payments to cross borders seamlessly. As these technologies begin to take hold, they will reshape the concept of the global financial system along with initiatives aimed at financial inclusion.

Mojaloop: A Digital Payment System as a Digital Public Good

Virtually all payment systems are designed and controlled by governments, companies, or consortia. Thanks to a powerful new category of technology solution—digital public goods—that could soon change. Digital public goods are open-source software platforms with the potential to transform the "walled gardens" of proprietary payment systems into open ecosystems that are created and maintained for societal benefit. Mojaloop is an open-source software platform that bridges divides between siloed digital payment providers. Mobile networks such as Orange and MTN are using Mojaloop to connect 100 million registered mobile money accounts into an interoperable network. The government of Tanzania is leveraging Mojaloop to break down data silos between financial providers and reduce transaction costs among businesses and individuals.[43] Open-source development can improve transparency and security of critical systems while providing organizations of all sizes with access to high-quality, interoperable digital payment systems at extremely low cost.[44]

43. Dominguez; Hunter.
44. Lerner and others.

Direct Cross-Border Payments with Stablecoins

Historically, national borders have presented an exceptionally expensive barrier to financial transactions. Stablecoins, digital currencies that provide the benefits of instant processing and finality of transactions while ensuring the stability of a government-backed currency, may erode the costs of international transfers to the point of irrelevance. Instead of relying on expensive networks of intermediary banks, stablecoins take advantage of blockchain technology to create decentralized digital accounting systems. Stablecoins are pegged to fiat currencies and designed to avoid the price fluctuations that affect cryptocurrencies with market-based valuations, such as Bitcoin. The result is a stable currency that can be transmitted across continents without intermediaries and associated costs. Numerous stablecoins are preparing for launch or already in circulation. For development actors, two of the most significant are USDC (US Dollar Coin) and Diem.[45] Several other blockchains are being used to anchor stablecoins, including Stellar, Solana, and Celo.

USDC is a stablecoin developed by Circle, a fintech company based in Boston, and administered through the Centre consortium. As of mid-year 2021, there is over US$25 billion of USDC in circulation, and it is rapidly gaining traction as a regulated solution for applications that rely on a stable digital currency. Facebook incubated Diem, previously called Libra, before spinning out the project as a nominally independent social impact organization with multi-stakeholder governance. The engineering heft and global reach of the project's progenitor organization provides Diem with a big head start as it works to become the default digital currency for low-cost, instantaneous cross-border exchange. However, the platform has faced significant regulatory scrutiny along the way, largely as a consequence of its Facebook roots. Stellar is a multipurpose blockchain that allows users and institutions with different stablecoins (such as a digital dollar or a digital euro) to seamlessly transact without intermediaries, creating a global network of interoperable financial systems.[46] Celo and Solana are high performance open-source networks that allow users to buy and sell stablecoins by equipping developers with tools to build decentralized financial applications.[47] Solutions on the Celo platform include lending tools for refugees, integration with M-Pesa, and universal basic income systems for vulnerable communities.[48]

---

45. This chapter was originally drafted while the author was an employee at New America, a nonprofit organization. As of July 2021, the author became a partner at Andreessen Horowitz, which invests actively in this domain, including in Diem, Celo, and Solana, all of which are mentioned in this chapter.

46. Stellar Development Foundation.

47. Slavich.

48. See examples at Celo DApp Library (https://docs.celo.org/developer-guide/celo-dapp-gallery).

Empowering Government Economic Policy with Central Bank Digital Currencies

The advent of blockchain technology has pushed central banks to reimagine how they manage national currencies in the digital era. Central bank digital currencies (CBDCs) could equip national currencies with new properties and improve how central banks, policymakers, and financial regulators manage money supplies and economic policy. Programmable digital currency could give governments more control over how consumers use social benefits or stimulus payments. Policymakers could program expiration dates for using cash transfers to help spur growth during slowdowns or limit the use of funds to small businesses or vulnerable industries.[49] Nearly 80 percent of the world's central banks are exploring CBDCs at either the retail or wholesale levels, with Sweden's Riksbank, the People's Bank of China, and the European Central Bank among the growing number already pursuing efforts to operationalize CBDCs.[50] Multilateral institutions such as the IMF, World Bank, and G20 are actively assessing how CBDCs could transform governments' role in finance.[51] CBDCs will need to be managed responsibly in order to realize their potential. In the absence of effective governance, they could merely port the problems of analog currencies to the digital realm.

Digital Payment Platforms and Data Stewardship

In the same way nuclear energy can power a city or destroy it, and steel can be used to build hospitals or machetes, digital payments can advance human dignity or oppress and surveil entire populations. On their own, digital payment platforms are neutral. Against this backdrop, a new opportunity is emerging for societies to adopt data models that grant users more control over their payments data.

The world's governments currently rely on two models that govern financial data. Both are vulnerable to abuse and fail to ensure individuals have control over their information. Payments systems in India and China centralize control of transaction data in government agencies that are vulnerable to privacy breaches and manipulation for political purposes. Western democracies allow private firms to package and sell payment data to advertisers who then try to influence individual behavior. In a 2015 study, MIT researchers were able to identify individuals using credit card metadata with a 90 percent success rate if they knew

49. Yu.
50. Press Trust of India; Bharathan; European Central Bank.
51. Financial Stability Board.

the details of just four individual purchases.[52] As governments begin to leverage digital platforms to power their institutions, they should rethink data ownership and data protection rules to help citizens own and control their personal data.

Placing users at the center of public data architecture could give individuals more autonomy over how private firms, governments, and researchers use their transaction history. User-centered data models could also help individuals control and monetize the value of their financial data, maintain higher degrees of privacy, and prevent government overreach and use of personal data without individuals' consent.

From Digital Payments to Digital Assets

Estonia, India, and a growing list of other countries are demonstrating the vast potential that exists when societies link digital payment platforms and digital identity verification. These two foundational pieces of digital infrastructure, along with mechanisms for responsible data management, can unlock a multitude of next-generation tools to power more productive societies and effective institutions.

The technologies that support digital payments and digital identity allow users to securely verify and transfer not only currency, but any unique, valuable data. The digital payments systems that provide data rails for secure, online financial transactions could be repurposed to exchange digital votes, licenses, educational credentials, carbon credits, and public benefit vouchers, all while maintaining a high degree of confidence that these assets could not be duplicated, stolen, or altered.

Societies with the capacity to move digital assets easily between trusted actors will have massive advantages in solving some of the greatest challenges of the twenty-first century. Interoperable digital payments and identity infrastructure could:

- *Help public officials and civil society organizations reduce waste and combat corruption.* Digital infrastructure can help manage procurement processes, prevent misappropriation of public funds, and provide new, more efficient methods to collect taxes. Bringing accountability to public revenue management could help governments recover trillions of dollars in public assets currently lost to waste, tax evasion, and corruption.[53]

- *Support a new class of secure public registries.* Governments use registries to establish ownership of property and companies. Creating digital land titles

52. De Montjoye, Radaelli, Singh, and Pentland.
53. UN News.

could unlock the economic potential of the US$9.3 trillion in global land assets that are currently unsecured due to stolen or missing titles.[54] They could also facilitate digital credentials to verify vaccination records, educational credentials, and other licenses.

- *Create trusted digital voting systems.* Digital voter registration and voting systems could mitigate threats to election integrity and support more efficient, secure democratic processes. Voting applications could verify that votes are cast by the intended citizen and transmit votes securely for tabulation.

- *Issue public benefits.* Next-generation benefits distribution could remove cumbersome identification barriers that prevent otherwise eligible recipients from accessing public benefits. New systems could also include features that target assistance to better aid specific communities and businesses while ensuring that public assistance is not stolen or diverted to ineligible recipients.

A Digital Decade for the Sustainable Development Goals

As researchers map ongoing efforts to achieve the Global Goals, one point has become clear: deploying more effective digital platforms may be the only path to achieving the Sustainable Development Goals by 2030. Particularly in light of the COVID-19 pandemic, access to trusted digital systems will be essential to helping societies and institutions rebuild. Among governments responding effectively to the pandemic, virtually all rely on world-class digital systems that enable the frictionless movement of resources and data.

In September 2020, on the margins of the UN General Assembly, a group of key development stakeholders from around the world came together to launch a #DigitalDecade focused on developing open-source solutions to power more effective public institutions.[55] The prime minister of Norway, a president of the Bill & Melinda Gates Foundation, and leaders from across government, civil society, and the private sector all committed to working together to develop a new generation of digital infrastructure. New America's Digital Impact and Governance Initiative has been fortunate to be at the forefront of this work.

From Mesopotamian canals and Roman roads to transcontinental highways and the internet, infrastructure has long provided a catalyst for transforming the landscape of human development. Digital platforms, including digital payment platforms, are the transformational infrastructure of our time. As with any piece

54. Arsenault.
55. New America Foundation.

of monumental infrastructure, these platforms come with risks and the danger
that they could be misused. But given the stakes for society and humanity, it is
time to start building. For countries that do so responsibly and judiciously, the
benefits will be immeasurable.

References

Arsenault, Chris. 2016. "Property Rights for World's Poor Could Unlock Trillions in
    'Dead Capital': Economist." www.reuters.com/article/us-global-landrights-desoto
    -idUSKCN10C1C1.
Barker, Eric. 2012. "How Much Does It *Really* Cost to Send a Text Message?" *Business
    Insider*. November 12.
Bharathan, Vipin. 2020. "Central Bank Digital Currency: The First Nationwide CBDC
    in the World Has Been Launched by the Bahamas." *Forbes*. October 21.
Boumnijel, Rachid, and others. 2013. "How Do Electronic Transfers Compare?
    Evidence from a Mobile Money Cash Transfer Experiment in Niger." Working
    Paper. Tufts University. sites.tufts.edu/jennyaker/files/2010/02/Zap-it-to-
    Me_12sept2013_No-Appendices.pdf.
Brown, Nyanya, Bahreh Eftekthari, and Haydar Kurban. 2019. "The Impacts of Payday
    Loan Use on Financial Well-Being of the OASDI and SSI Beneficiaries." https://
    mrdrc.isr.umich.edu/publications/conference/pdf/2019RDRC%20P3%20Kurban
    .pdf.
Bughin, Jacques, and others. 2019. "Digital Identification: A Key to Inclusive Growth."
    McKinsey Global Institute. www.mckinsey.com/~/media/mckinsey/featured%
    20insights/innovation/the%20value%20of%20digital%20id%20for%20the%
    20global%20economy%20and%20society/mgi-digital-identification-a-key-to
    -inclusive-growth.ashx.
Business Today. 2017. "Aadhaar Helped Indian Government Save US$9 Billion, Says
    Nandan Nilekani." October 13.
Cecchetti, Stephen, and Kim Schoenholtz. 2018. "The Stubbornly High Costs of
    Remittances." https://voxeu.org/article/stubbornly-high-cost-remittances.
Chea, Serey. 2020. "Cambodia Edges toward Digital Payments." www.omfif.org/2020/
    06/cambodia-edges-towards-digital-payments/.
De Montjoye, Y.-A., L. Radaelli, V. K. Singh, and A. Pentland. 2015. "Unique in the
    Shopping Mall: On the Reidentifiability of Credit Card Metadata." *Science*, v. 347,
    no. 6221.
De, Supriyo, and others. 2020. "Migration and Development Brief 33: Phase II: Covid-
    19 Crisis through a Migration Lens." www.knomad.org/sites/default/files/2020-11/
    Migration%20%26%20Development_Brief%2033.pdf.
Demirgüç-Kunt, Asli, and others. 2018. "The Global Findex Database 2017: Measuring
    Financial Inclusion and the Fintech Revolution." Washington, D.C.: World Bank.
Dominguez, Juan. 2019. "Mowali Tackling Payment Interoperability in Africa." www
    .sofrecom.com/publications/mowali-tackling-payment-interoperability-in-africa.
Economic Times BFSI. 2020. "UPI Transactions Reach Their Peak in July with US$1.5
    Billion."

Enterprise Estonia. "Business and Finance: E-Tax." https://e-estonia.com/solutions/business-and-finance/e-tax/.

European Central Bank. 2020. "Report on a Digital Euro." www.ecb.europa.eu/pub/pdf/other/Report_on_a_digital_euro~4d7268b458.en.pdf.

Financial Stability Board. 2020. "Regulation, Supervision, and Oversight of "Global Stablecoin" Arrangements: Final Report and High-Level Recommendations." www.fsb.org/2020/10/regulation-supervision-and-oversight-of-global-stablecoin -arrangements/.

FIS. 2020. "Flavors of Fast 2020," 7th ed. www.fisglobal.com/en/flavors-of-fast.

Hunter, Paula. 2020. "The Blueprint for Financial Inclusion—Mojaloop's Vision for Solving the Unbanked Problem." https://thepaypers.com/interviews/the -blueprint-for-financial-inclusion-mojaloops-vision-for-solving-the-unbanked -problem—1245814.

Iacurci, Greg. 2020. "The 'Black Hole' of Unemployment Benefits: Six Months into the Pandemic, Some Are Still Waiting for Aid." CNBC. September 27.

Kansas City Fed. 2018. "Credit and Debit Card Interchange Fees in Various Countries." www.kansascityfed.org/~/media/files/publicat/psr/dataset/intl_if_ august2018.pdf.

Lerner, Mark, and others. 2020. "Building and Reusing Open-Source Tools for Government." www.newamerica.org/digital-impact-governance-initiative/reports/building-and-reusing-open-source-tools-government/.

Marbella, Jean, and Hallie Miller. 2020. "Down to Their Last Dollars, Living off Family and Friends, These Marylanders Are Still Waiting for Unemployment Payments." *Baltimore Sun*, October 15.

Monetary Authority of Singapore. 2020. "MAS Urges Use of Digital Finance and E-Payments to Support COVID-19 Safe Distancing Measures." www.mas.gov.sg /news/media-releases/2020/mas-urges-use-of-digital-finance-and-e-payments-to -support-covid-19-safe-distancing-measures.

Motley Fool. 2017. "This Is How Credit Card Companies Hauled in US$163 Billion in 2016." NASDAQ. April 13.

Murphy, Katy, and Rebecca Rainey. 2020. "'Too Sweet of a Pie': Cybercriminals Steal US$8B in COVID Relief Funds." Politico, October 12. www.politico.com/news/ 2020/10/12/unemployment-fraud-coronavirus-428514.

New America Foundation. 2020. "[ONLINE]—Launching a #DigitalDecade to Strengthen Public Institutions." www.newamerica.org/digital-impact-governance -initiative/events/un-general-assembly-2020/.

Nilson Report. 2019. "Card Fraud Losses Reach US$27.85 Billion." https://nilsonreport .com/mention/407/1link/#.

Olsen, Sam. 2020. "China Is Winning the War for Global Tech Dominance." *The Hill*. October 4.

Peng, Chan Wai. 2019. "Singapore's Public Healthcare Agencies to Adopt SGQR Payments by End-2020." *Business Times.* November 11.

Polemitis, Antonis. 2014. "How Cash Would Be Seen by the Media if Invented Today." Coindesk, February 23. www.coindesk.com/cash-invented-seen-media-today.

Press Trust of India. 2020. "China's Official Digital Currency 'DC/EP' Begins Testing." *The Week*. April 20.

Rogoff, Kenneth. 2016. "The Curse of Cash." Princeton University Press.

Schuh, Scott, Oz Shy, and Joanna Stavins. 2010. "Who Gains and Who Loses from Credit Card Payments? Theory and Calibrations." Federal Reserve Bank of Boston.

Sharma, Niharika. 2019. "UPI Now Fulfills over Half of All Digital Payments in India." *Quartz India.* November 6.

Sharwood, Simon. 2020. "Singapore to Accelerate Digitalization of COVID-Kicked Economy," *Register.* July 1.

Slavich, Vanessa. 2019. "An Introductory Guide to Celo." https://medium.com/celoorg/an-introductory-guide-to-celo-b185c62d3067.

Stellar Development Foundation. 2020. "Stablecoins: The Future of Digital Money." www.stellar.org/blog/stablecoins-the-future-of-digital-money.

Suri, Tavneet, and William Jack. 2016. "The Long-Run Poverty and Gender Impacts of Mobile Money." *Science,* v. 354, no. 6317.

SWIFT. "SWIFT and Data." www.swift.com/about-us/swift-and-data.

Tillemann, Tomicah, and others. 2019. *The Blockchain Blueprint for Social Innovation.* www.newamerica.org/digital-impact-governance-initiative/blockchain-trust-accelerator/reports/blueprint-blockchain-and-social-innovation/.

UN News. 2018. "The Costs of Corruption: Values, Economic Development under Assault, Trillions Lost, Says Guterres." https://news.un.org/en/story/2018/12/1027971.

Vireak, Thou. 2020. "NBC Launched Bakong Inter-Bank Platform." *Phnom Penh Post.* October 28.

Werdigier, Julia. 2011. "Tax Evasion Costs Governments US$3.1 Trillion Annually, Report Says." *New York Times,* November 28.

Wilson, Eric, and Eva Wolkowitz. 2017. "2017 Financially Underserved Market Size Study." https://finhealthnetwork.org/research/2017-financially-underserved-market-size-study/.

World Bank Development Research Group. 2014. "The Opportunities of Digitizing Payments." https://btca-production-site.s3.amazonaws.com/documents/180/english_attachments/The_Opportunities_of_Digitizing_Payments.pdf.

World Bank. 2018. "Financial Inclusion on the Rise, but Gaps Remain, Global Findex Database Shows." www.worldbank.org/en/news/press-release/2018/04/19/financial-inclusion-on-the-rise-but-gaps-remain-global-findex-database-shows.

———. 2018b. "Financial Inclusion Overview." www.worldbank.org/en/topic/financialinclusion/overview.

Yu, Geoffrey. 2020. "China and the Dawn of Digital Currency." www.bnymellon.com/latam/en/insights/aerial-view-magazine/china-and-the-dawn-of-digital-currency.html.

ELEVEN

A Short Story of Transmediary Platforms

Bright Simons

Winston Soko[1] rose from his desk, gently closed his laptop, and paced around his modest but elegantly decorated office thinking about the mini-crisis brewing in Kasungu.

NASFAM, the Malawi smallholders' cooperative, had called him that morning, lamenting delays in a long-awaited digital seed certification program, which they blamed for a severe crop failure in the farmlands adjoining the central regional town.

Winston's organization, Praxis, had pitched a vision to many Malawian agricultural stakeholders more than two years ago, at the Seeds Traders Association of Malawi (STAMM) annual congress. It was a powerful vision. An integrated solution that would connect all the key actors in the Malawian agricultural ecosystem and bring unprecedented transparency, efficiency, and, ultimately, productivity into the cluster of industries defining the agricultural sector and its public sector support system in the Southern African country.

In the first incarnation of the strategy, Praxis was to be a central hub for data exchange, standards development, quality assurance, capacity building, and trade facilitation. Indeed, a veritable one-stop shop backed by a unified technology platform for the sector as a whole.

But being the hub also meant being the intermediary. In a world of digital platforms, such a model seemed fairly ordinary, but it also meant that everyone stayed where they were while the "hub" had to run around trying to bridge the

---

1. Names of individuals and organizations have been changed for prudential reasons, except for "Agrotrack," which is the real name of the platform initiative.

gaps. This was not a very hubby thing; hubs are expected to sit in the center while minions orbit. Delays, given the expectations, would inevitably be perceived as the hub's fault.

The jewel in the central hub's crown would be the seed certification protocol. This had many ingredients: streamlined quality testing, "agricultural extension support" to both commercial seed growers and the farmers who bought their seed, an independent phytosanitary inspection regime, export promotion capacity building, horticultural skills development, agroforestry and environmental safeguarding measures, and a host of other elements. These elements were perceived to be intertwined by local development specialists, with whose help Praxis had conceived the concept as crucial to truly solving the conjoined problems of food security, rural poverty, malnutrition, deforestation, and land degradation. The functions were to be streamlined and enriched by digitization atop the common tech platform.

With the Sustainable Development Goals (SDGs) serving as the backdrop for all these activities, isolated interventions had no place in the strategy. The cardinal principle of the Rio+20 framework, the animating philosophy of many SDG implementing mechanisms, is simple: "None of the goals are standalone."

If bad seeds lead to bad harvests, inevitably it will drive farmers to use too much pesticide, which will poison groundwater. More exposure to toxic chemicals would certainly mean sicker farmers and thus lower productivity, but its lingering and residual impacts, including congenital and developmental problems in the unborn, infants, and toddlers, would have severe adverse impacts on education and, obviously, community health. Solutions to social problems must exhibit *connectedness*.

In the first year of trying to roll out Zambiri—the name given to the "connected hub" initiative (based on a word from the Nyanja language popular in Malawi and loosely translated as "abundance")—Praxis had frequently found itself paddling against the current. Occasionally, the tide would turn, and momentum seemed imminent, only for something to pop out from the woodwork and derail carefully laid plans. Typically, this would be some "stakeholder" claiming that some other initiative already covered some aspect of what Zambiri was meant to do. The said initiative would have been missed during Zambiri's mapping of the ecosystem because it would more likely exist in the covers of deskbound files in some departmental backwater in Lilongwe or Blantyre than concretely on the ground in the provinces. Yet someone would keep resurrecting it as a reason why Zambiri had to steer clear of some crucial area.

As Winston had learned very quickly when he first got into this line of business, development practice "problems" were rarely fallow fields, sitting idly, waiting to be tilled by solutions into success stories. They were very often prized farmland "owned" by "stakeholders" who rarely gave them up without collecting serious rent or the promise of rent. The notion of problems as assets rather than liabilities was a mind-warping and completely transformative insight for Winston in his professional intellectual development.

All that said, nine months earlier, the seed certification problem had almost been solved. It was a seeming low-hanging fruit that could prove the overall Zambiri concept and thus build credibility to be expended in driving through other, more complex initiatives. It was, as Winston's ever-enthusiastic program director had called it, the *golden wedge* to get Zambiri through the door. Best of all, in Malawi, the utility of seed certification was far from esoteric.

Fake Seeds as a Major Food Security Factor

Initial estimates suggested 25 percent of seed packets sold in Malawi were either outrightly fake (with falsified packaging and/or content) or of very poor quality. Poor quality seeds were, in turn, blamed for yield loss of at least 30 percent. This translated to a million farmers suffering a 40 percent loss of income through

Box 11-1. Glossary

The following definitions of key concepts and terms are used frequently in this chapter.

Ecosystem: The largest unit of a market or productive social network bound by a discernible set of relationship rules guiding the collective generation of socioeconomic value.

Intermediation: An opportunity-seeking or problem-solving model based on the entrepreneur/intervener creating value for a critical mass of actors in a network by bridging nodes in the network at a lower transaction cost than the next readily available alternative. The entrepreneur/intervener is known as an intermediary.

Nodes: The smallest unit in an ecosystem capable of making a discernible contribution to the aggregate value creation. In a supply chain, for instance, the nodes are often companies involved in the production, distribution, and logistics management needed to move a product from one point to another in an economically viable way.

Systems Entrepreneurship: A concept of entrepreneurial action based on the idea that ecosystems have nexus points for directed intervention with the potential to maximize the social benefit content of value generated at multiple levels, thereby helping address interconnected social problems.

Transmediation: A method of intervening in an ecosystem to solve interconnected problems by reducing the risk for various nodes in reconfiguring their identities to optimize their contribution to overall value creation while maintaining structural integrity of the ecosystem.

diminished productivity as a result of poor harvests.[2] Fix this, and Praxis would prove that Zambiri was not just the usual "workshop talk."

Six months earlier, as he stopped pacing to relax in his office chair, Winston thought wistfully that a massive breakthrough seemed to be on the horizon. The Seed Services Unit (SSU), the nation's premier agricultural regulatory agency, had agreed to partner on the Seed Certification Program (SCP), Zambiri's initial flagship. Discussions commenced on how to embed the Zambiri-SCP into the SSU's inspectorate and validation processes while maintaining a link to the other elements of the initiative, some of which had required—or, more accurately, would require—other sponsoring stakeholders.

As conversations proceeded, the design of the Zambiri SCP technology platform (Zamstep) became a bit of a sticking point. Certain SSU roles seemed natural, given the organization's statutory powers and legal mandate, but upon closer inspection, the SSU's operational setup revealed serious incompatibility.

One fascinating example was the logistical role envisaged for the SSU. It was, according to the blueprint, to become the central repository of unique identifiers for seed packets sold by the seed marketers. Zamstep's ledger mechanism made SSU an inventory manager for the unique serial identifiers affixed as physical tags to each seed packet.

Farmers were expected to use these identifiers to confirm the certification status of a packet of seeds they buy at an agrovet—the shops selling agricultural and veterinary inputs. They would do so via the simple but powerful instantaneous messaging tool known as USSD, available on virtually all phones in the world today.

The idea was extremely straightforward: seeds that undergo the proper certification process got the tags; those that did not must do without and forgo the brand advantage. Farmers, with just a basic feature phone, could validate the tags prior to purchase, preventing fraudsters from attaching false tags on uncertified seed. Now that farmers could easily verify, right there in the shop, which seed packet had gone through the rigorous certification process and thus had the endorsement of the government and the mainstream industry, brands would have even more of an incentive to maintain their compliance with the certification system. It was that simple.

This technology would equip even the poorest farmers who had even the most elementary phones to partake in a degree of transparency across the seed sector that was previously unimaginable. If only SSU could also become a large-scale inventory manager for the physical tags and dedicate bandwidth to distributing them to seed packing companies. This would be in addition, of course, to its

---

2. The data in this section draws on unpublished research conducted through surveys, interviews, and sampling activities carried out by various Agrotrack partners between 2019 and 2020.

ongoing work of inspecting nurseries of seed growers, testing sample batches of seeds at packing units, and providing training to various actors in the seed supply chain.

Furthermore, SSU would also have to invest in a range of security enhancements to its operations to prevent undeserving seed companies from getting access to the Zamstep tags. Suffice it to say, the devil was in the details. New twists and turns kept popping up. Simple things quickly unfurled into complex subroutines and multiplying project task lists. Synchronization across the different Zambiri subcomponents within the SCP and allied programs began to look next to impossible.

Praxis's SCP project committee was on the verge of despair until six weeks ago, when another breakthrough suddenly erupted into view. Through a chance encounter, Winston's colleague Doreen Banda had been introduced to the organization through a program called AgroTrack, which was already active in East and Southern Africa and which, to all intents and purposes, had solved very similar problems in other countries in fairly similar contexts. Due diligence had ensued at breakneck pace. The insights garnered from a slew of intense engagements had led to major revisions of the original Zamstep strategy. A trial run of the new model had been quickly designed, and early indications were that it could take off in just two months' time.

Winston stared from his office chair at the purring blades of a cream-and-gold-bladed fan. He then made for the small refrigerator in his executive unit in the Praxis head office. He grabbed a can of Grapetiser, pulled the stopper, gingerly set it to his lips while taking in the sprawling abstract shapes of the faux Dali painting on the wall. A faint smile formed around the edges of his lips. The pieces in the collage were beginning to finally take shape. Previous failures were cast in clear context like Florentine arches against a Tuscan landscape, giving depth to the subject matter. This time, he said to himself, things would be different.

Creating Ecosystemic Change through Technology

The story of Zamstep's ups and downs mirrors that of many technology systems introduced as a wedge to pry open possibilities for building ecosystemic[3] change. Because social problems are always interconnected, naïve solutions to one problem often exacerbate another.

3. While we offer alternative perspectives on the notion of "ecosystems" to press further points down the script, the simple definition given by Guerrero and others suffices at this stage of the discussion: "The interconnectedness of organizations working together in innovative ways to act entrepreneurially through collaborative efforts . . . often termed ecosystems."

Box 11-2. Some Key Concepts

At the conceptual heart of this chapter is the literature on "systems entrepreneurship" and business and technology "ecosystems," often referenced as the "Dartmouth School." The "leverage points" framework popularized by Donella Meadows is central to this. Its starting point is a claim that many discrete social problems, from SME financial inclusion to lack of trust in agro-supply chains, can increasingly only be tackled by interconnected *systems-shifting technology platforms*, an idea advanced by Dartmouth University's Ron Adner. These platforms are developed through a type of systems entrepreneurship called *transmediation*. We refer to these platforms as *transmediation platforms*, and profile an exemplar.

"Systems entrepreneurship" itself is not very familiar to the general public. But at the elite practitioner level, it is gaining rapid prominence. Since 2019, for example, the World Economic Forum has heralded a transition of focus from "social entrepreneurship" to "systems entrepreneurship," suggesting a degree of mainstreaming.

Emphasis has evolved beyond the measurement of social returns in business models to determine if a particular entrepreneurial mission is driven primarily by "purpose" rather than "profit." The "social enterprise" world must confront the reality of "single enterprise models" lacking the leverage to deal with the multifaceted nature of virtually all social problems. Solutions that ignore this reality generate negative externalities that create new problems at a systems level.

The far-reaching work of Julie Battilana adds the crucial dimension of "power" to any process of systems-shifting, which, as a social phenomenon, is best viewed through an ecosystemic lens, too.

[1]The works cited in this box are listed in the references section at the end of the chapter.

Yet most problem-solving tools are best presented as targeting a discrete problem at a discrete site to have any chance of adoption. Unless the tool can evolve well to address the gaps and externalities caused by the connections between the site of intervention and other systems in the neighborhood, failure is inevitable. Choosing the right site to embed the wedge creates, in the language of this growing area of "systems entrepreneurship,"[4] the essence of *leverage*.

Many entrepreneurs approach such systems through intermediation. Usually, the idea is to bridge some gap that will, in turn, close a loop to maximize some synergy across disparate actors whose resources, capabilities, interests, focuses, and directions are seen as likely to achieve a resonating amplitude *if only they could all be connected* via some hub.

4. As highlighted in the sidebar, the ideas and arguments flowing through this chapter are steeped in current debates and commentaries on the concept of "systems entrepreneurship." The World Economic Forum's recent decision to signal a transition of focus from "social entrepreneurship" to this newish approach implies a growing mainstreaming of system entrepreneurship's core ideas.

For example, the vast majority of financial inclusion innovations rest on this principle of "connecting nodes" in a well-defined system as a means of reducing transaction inefficiencies.[5] Most mHealth solutions seek to connect underserved communities with a surplus of capability elsewhere in the communal ecosystem. And many agritech solutions base their value proposition on connecting farmers directly with higher-margin buyers.

While intermediation is indeed a very potent way of amassing the capacity to induce positive change, the new SDG-driven emphasis on solving connected problems in a connected manner has shed light on many limitations of the inter-mediation model.[6]

Intermediation tends to be highly potent where the nodes that must be connected are stable, self-motivated, specialized, clearly incentivized, and the medium of exchange very clearly encapsulates the value created as a result of the exchange. Those who build the hubs and make them acceptable to multiple nodes can often amass vast power to enforce the norms needed to preserve the essential stability of pricing and divisions of labor. And norm-setting power is a critical success factor in all ecosystemic solutions.

Unfortunately, in many ecosystems these stable preconfigurations do not exist to be exploited by technology solutions. A taxi industry with defined roles such as riders and drivers and fee rates based on seasonality, distance, and time pro-vides a good enough blueprint for an Uber-style ride-sharing culture to emerge in many diverse national contexts. Becoming a hub for trust-forming practices in the agricultural supply chain is, sadly, not as precedent-bound.[7] The specialisms on which stable hub-and-spoke development models thrive often look good on paper but are poorly manifested in practice. "Connecting the nodes" in many interconnected development contexts thus involves considerable "role discovery."

---

5. See, for instance: *Nicholls, Paton*, and Emerson (2017). To date, the assumption has been that this will be best achieved by finding new ways for social enterprises to align with conven-tional capital markets. This normative view of social investment requires, first, that any potential investees adapt their organizational strategy to approximate a conventional for-profit business and, second, that new intermediary institutions be developed that can "dock" such social businesses with mainstream sources of capital. This approach has achieved some notable successes to date, but is constrained by the pool of potential social or environmental projects that can generate conventional financial returns.

6. For an interesting discussion on social entrepreneurial intermediation limitations, see *Nich-olls, Paton*, and Emerson (2017).

7. Some of these issues are amply raised in Guerrero and others, especially where they attempt a theorizing of "the role of intermediaries in the configuration of the entrepreneurial identities of Mexican SPOs and BMIs, as well as several externalities generated during the process of capturing the social and economic value, especially when social innovations are focused on solving societal, economic, and ecological social problems."

Enter the Transmediaries

Winston sat down over a nice *chambo*, the fabulous local fish barbecue, with the chaps from the Agrotrack initiative, the group that had solved problems similar to Zambiri's and Zamstep's in a couple of other countries. His first question was about the two phrases that has stood out in the initial flurry of e-mails: "shifting the nodes" and "priming identities." They sounded a bit too exotic for the context at hand: reinfusing life into Zamstep and, by extension, Zambiri.

The leader of the Agrotrack delegation, which had flown in from Zambia, had a clear view of what had to be done. Agrotrack was deeply embedded in COMESA's strategy for getting regional agro value chains to blend seamlessly into each other. Its representatives displayed a missionary zeal about the approach to technology needed to make this daunting task feasible. The two visitors called themselves "transmediaries" and spent a good twenty minutes diagnosing the flaws of any hypothetical "non-transmediary" approach to solving the problem of agricultural supply chain optimization using technology as the principal catalyst.

What stuck with Winston were their testimonials and mini–case studies. The twists in technology innovation used in making Agrotrack viable in Kenya and Tanzania as an enabler of a digital approach to certification resonated with Winston's own experience in Malawi.

First, Agrotrack had been built in agile fashion within seed certification agencies' internal operations in a kind of inside-out process. This was described as "seductive insurgency." A whole host of functions within these agencies had been turned upside down by internal insurgents simply displacing a bunch of hallowed cultural practices from within.

Second, Agrotrack actors had embedded deep into the seed association's rather lean coordination function until their mission had become indistinguishable from the search for deeper relevance of the association, especially in relation to its bigger members.

Lastly, rather than focusing exclusively on a hypothetically universal problem for the actors in the ecosystem, it prioritized the "problem formation" process itself by not taking for granted the ecosystem's need to justify its existence. The choice of how to approach this existential justification eventually gets settled in favor of eliminating problems through the alignment of internal expectations, unresolved differences, and incomplete understandings of the roles and functions of the different actors. "Problem formation" means unpacking the elements of an observed malfunctioning at a system level and reinterpreting it as failures in the configuration of current relationships.

The inevitable direction of such a "solution discovery from system redesign" approach is the rebalancing of certain taken-for-granted identities and positions within the ecosystem. And all these discoveries and findings had been encoded into Agrotrack's design, culminating in what its proponents called a "Social Systems Transmediation Platform."

From a practical point of view, it was clear to Winston that rather than technology being some commoditized slave in the service of meeting SDGs 1 and 2 (poverty reduction and zero hunger) and elements of the other connected goals in Malawi, he had to understand in a much deeper way how to alter the way the principal actors saw their roles using the technology as a conductor.

The deal to wrap Agrotrack's methods around Zamsteps' objectives of modernizing the seed certification system in Malawi was sealed at that lunch. As the gingery zest of the sizzling fish dulled between the gritty bites of *nsima* and *ndiwo,* Winston and the two Agrotrack emissaries plotted the roadmap and accompanying narrative for Agrotrack's entry into Malawi.

Agrotrack: A Transmediary Solution

Three chief functions were expected of Agrotrack, at least in phase one:

- regulatory procedures transformation (reg-tech)
- supply chain business process automation (ex-ERP)
- citizen engagement, outreach, education, and behavior change (civic-tech)

The first domain was for government, the second for industry, and the third for general public or consumer base. Reg-tech, extended enterprise technology, and consumer-facing technology for these three domains have not traditionally been fused in this manner.

The notions of "digital transformation" of enterprise and government brought in their wake a whole raft of "glue-ware" that served to interlink technology domains.

In the past, industry software for managing things like inventory, quality control in manufacturing, financial audit trails, and the like rarely had reason to talk to government solutions for social security processing, tax administration, or environmental permits assessment. Much less to social media graph apps, ride-sharing services, daily calendar schedulers, or the other apps beloved by the modern consumer. Each domain of technology related to the other as nonoverlapping magisteria.

But the mantra of "digital transformation" has impelled institutions to "think different" in the world of bits and bytes. The internet, and the cloud computing logic it has imposed, means that interfaces can be highly personalized, to a point where strict demarcations of whatever system in the backend is powering the ultimate functionality become redundant.

To illustrate, if an individual wants a quick deal on a flight, she does not mind seeing the ad for the ticket shown to her while browsing a virtual Milanese hotel catalog. If she clicks on that alluring "get the deal now" banner ad, she should not get the slightest hint that there is some API calling some giant airline distribution system. Increasingly, that distribution system is also sending some notifications to some government anti-terrorism scanner, whether it knows it or not. As the problems that technology aims to solve weave more and more into each other, so do the technology solutions themselves. This is the brave new world of hyper-integration.[8]

Agrotrack respected these trends, even if being social innovation–oriented meant that its ethos had to take into account the balance of interests and how it favors the underdog—in this case, the farmer. But the essence of highly customizable interfaces obscuring great backend complexity to accommodate the considerable divergence in use cases at industry, government, and business levels was par for the course. The concept of the "super-app" no longer means only that what were once considered standalone apps now appear as mere features in some app. It also refers to the interface agility that is dissolving the boundaries of technology use across government, industry, and the masses.

As an African hyper-integrated solution, however, Agrotrack causes a number of second-order complexities. Many industry players in Malawi and elsewhere in the region needed the solution to offer specific new procedures rather than accommodate existing procedures, since there were barely any coherent ones in many small- and medium-size operations. The government needed functions that streamlined longstanding administrative ambiguities. And consumers still needed a human touch even though "convenience" theory would suggest otherwise. Herein lay the great prospects for full-on transmediation.

The scenarios harked to various discussions in the "technology for social good" literature that Winston was familiar with. One group of scholars had summarized the new complexity as "digital ecodynamics."[9]

When Winston eventually saw how vividly agile technology interfaces could define the culture at government and corporate levels and thereby recast relationships long considered stagnant, he was stunned. A well-known schematic from the literature grouped sustainable supply chain platforms into three categories: alterationist, redistributor, and capability builder.[10] Agrotrack showed how easily these categories could weave into each other.

Winston watched in awe as hidebound bureaucratic structures melted, or at

8. Simons.
9. Ahuja.
10. Schroder, Prockl, and Constantiou.

least mellowed, in the face of clever technical routines that exposed many buried protocols, as people suddenly began asserting certain privileges or quickly discarded burdensome paper mandates, and as more and more functionaries started embracing realistic roles.

As someone familiar with the academic canon on ecosystems and platforms, he could track the making of interesting new theory here. A Dartmouth scholar called Ron Adner, for instance, had once defined ecosystem as an "Alignment structure of the multilateral set of partners that need to interact in order for a focal value proposition to materialize."[11]

Adner's key insight was that disparate actors must recognize a common value proposition (which he calls the "productive level of analysis for ecosystems in [business] strategy") but strictly on the back of shared acceptances of each other's identities (encompassing roles, specializations, positioning). Stability of identities was crucial to alignment, and thus trust and a key prerequisite for ecosystem bonding and success.[12] Winston's Agrotrack experience suggested, however, that identities could be highly malleable in the presence of mimetic technologies that expanded the range and scope of an actor's capabilities through a meta-agent's constant mediation and remediation of the process of defining value propositions.

Praxis finally concluded that they needed to second the staff to manage the once intimidating inventory function at the regulatory agency. But the design of the process flow, blending as it did consumer-tech and enterprise, only needed a few young graduates from the University of Malawi. Winston's rejection of hallowed academic dogma was complete. He finally understood what "shifting the nodes" and "priming identities" meant.

The implicit goalpost for Zamstep—or any seed certification modernization program in Africa, for that matter—had been the attainment of "tamper--proofing." When a checklist has been developed for assuring the quality of production processes and thus ultimately of the seeds themselves, how does one confirm if the regulatory regime, as staffed by agents of the regulatory system, steeped in a particular bureaucratic tradition, actually enforces that checklist? How does one prevent circumvention *within* the system?

Even if the checklist is properly enforced, and the seeds the system delivers to the farmer is properly quality-assured, one must further ensure that the higher level of quality does not come at a higher price, thereby distorting the incentives for poorer farmers to use certified seed in the first place. How is the farmer supposed to know this method of verification anyway? And what role does the

11. Adner.
12. See also Skalen and others on "the failure of co-creation."

retailer have in ensuring last-mile availability of certified seed and awareness of the farmer?

A connected solution in a hyper-integrated context is one that elegantly makes one goal in a subsystem the input or motivation for another, and the emergence of whole subsystems the output of some incentive.

Agrotrack's target was to make system circumvention self-defeating by reordering certain assumptions embedded in the legacy ecosystem. For instance, the regulatory seed inspector's role as signatory to compliance formalities had long been one with no consequence beyond the specific, time-bound, relationship with the seed grower. They performed an audit and wielded their signature in momentary power. But both their significance and their privilege were transient, and thus incapable of inspiring durable compliant behavior.

In the new Agrotrack model, the inspector's records were indelibly linked to a batch, traceable to the level of the seed packet, and were callable whenever a complaint came from a farmer. Farmers' ability to give instant feedback through automated surveys and self-initiated engagements constituted a kind of democratizing co-creation power in the system design process.[13]

The complaints unit now had a direct basis and scope of engagement with specific inspectors. The result was a triangle of accountability involving a champion of farmer interests, an extension officer whose job was to bring the seed grower's capacity up to the mark, and an inspector whose duty was to confirm that a particular batch of seed was fit for the market.

The farmers' cooperatives would now have a basis and scope of engagement with the seed growers' association that could be informed by aggregate data as opposed to scattered word-of-mouth claims from disgruntled farmers strewn across rural Malawi.

It was apparent to Winston, as he waltzed through the different Agrotrack training sessions and live demonstrations ahead of the new system's phase one deployment, that several permutations of behavioral algorithms at institutional and human levels were possible. And this was what was powerful about this model of societal technology design. The transparency and accountability enabled by the technology was modular. Its design, according to the node-shifting philosophy shared with him more than a month ago, had ensured this result rather vividly.

By generating new sources of agency, almost on the fly, Agrotrack as a transmediary platform was playing the role of meta-agency and creating a canvas for co-creation of the value proposition—quality, genuine seed—practically and not just on paper.[14]

---

13. Hein, Weking, Schreieck, and others
14. Similar dynamics are described in van den Berg and Verster.

The Burden of Transmediation

When the most penetrating insight came, though, Winston was not fully braced for it. His epiphany was that the right role for an organization like Praxis, facilitating the introduction of such an innovation into virgin context, was not just to shift the nodes in the ecosystem. More fundamentally, it was to *juggle the nodes* and to reconfigure the relationships into more agile patterns that can evolve with the changing conditions.

Winston hesitated, because the revelation also seemed to scream: BURN-OUT! Agrotrack's improvement over the original Zambiri SCP was not really about doing less work and becoming less central, it was about doing more work turning all these nodes into nano-hubs in their own right. The thought almost made him shiver in its implications for workloads. But there was, underneath it, an exhilaration as well. Winston found the challenge stimulating. Doreen must have guessed what he was thinking, because she chose precisely that moment to bring up the issue of how to onboard the seed traders' association.

One thing obvious from the start was how the same ubiquity that such a multipronged technology strategy would give its promoters could also generate serious resentment. It is easy for ubiquity to be misinterpreted as a power grab. Addressing that risk required what Doreen would start calling "refractory attribution." This was a fancy way of saying that, at any given moment, perceptions of who exactly was promoting Agrotrack needed to become more diffuse. Farmers needed to see more of the hand of government. But retailers should "feel" the seed associations more. While the seed growers experienced more of Praxis's intense engagement, the system could no longer be seen as "that Praxis project." Credit had to be almost deflected from Praxis and other core partners to supernodes at strategic points and the formation of node clusters with some degree of autonomy strongly encouraged. Those supernodes could be religious welfare associations, NGOs, civil society groups (CSOs), and aid agencies.

The more diffuse the promotional effort, the more transmediary Praxis could become in driving far bigger institutions toward the desired outcomes without butting against the backlash of power dynamics. But that meant the technology platform, Agrotrack itself, had to allow user communities to customize modules in ways that heightened ownership.

After a rich and at times rowdy debate between Winston and Doreen over some *mawewu*, the refreshing local maize drink, supplemented later on with a Philly-style cheeseburger at a joint in the newly refurbished Chirichiri mall, the two schemers felt knowledgeable enough to start creating a matrix to distinguish the role Praxis had tried to play in the rollout of the original Zambiri digital seed platform versus their new situation as strategists of Agrotrack's instillment into Malawian agriculture. They were treating the platform as a "sensemaking device," in the words of one group of scholars, for better definition of available partnership models.[15]

Table 11-1 below provides the highlights of the distinctions they mapped out at the end of the exercise.

Some Sustainability and Scalability Issues with Transmediary Technologies

Much as the technology design innovations at the core of Agrotrack were helping drive implementation in weeks rather than years, there were lingering issues of scalability and sustainability. A significant proportion of the smooth deployment could also be traced to the experience of the Agrotrack team across a number of different contexts.

Unlike the original Zambiri strategy, Agrotrack deemphasized subscriptions and tied its revenue model to event-driven transactions. The enterprise attracted some fees by giving seed growers specific identifiers for embossing seed packets, and also through the secure retail channel for commercial seed growers.

Winston pondered the justification that had been provided by the Agrotrack regional lead, who sits in Nairobi, when he called her earlier in the day to discuss the issue of tying revenue to transactions rather than subscriptions. He was persuaded by the transparency-driven rationale that people should pay directly for the value created by new efficiencies and cost-cutting activities. But he kept wondering if there were also some cultural constraints to address. Agrotrack's continuing survival and growth provided assurance that they were on a good path, but one could always ask if they should have been expanding faster. One of Agrotrack's strategic priorities had always been to achieve regional harmonization of seed quality assurance standards across the COMESA area. This was a major issue in a region where food security is a longstanding major risk factor. As COMESA specialists have consistently emphasized, "The population in the COMESA countries is increasing at 2.3 percent while food production is growing at 2 percent, a situation that has brought about food insecurity to 130 million of the 600 million people in the region."[16]The urgency of the food security situation has often prompted COMESA to seek radically innovative approaches. COMESA's subregional SDG framework was typical in recognizing that the goals of famine prevention, improved nutrition, and the reduction of the alarmingly high poverty rates among farmers are all heavily intertwined, requiring multifaceted solutions.

15. Selsky and Parker.
16. COMESA (2018).

Table 11-1. Comparing Intermediation and Transmediation Platforms

	Intermediation Platforms	Transmediation Platforms
	Connect established value nodes in ways that increase the bargaining power of their owners and controllers.	Create relationships, which then define the nodes and create value by configuring relationships—which, in turn, enable new nodes to emerge.
Nature of networks	A classic example of this example would be a price discovery app for rural farmers to connect directly with urban produce buyers like restaurants. Solutions like these, by connecting multisided markets of producers and consumers or by connecting formal civic institutions to the informal desires of citizens, try to remove transaction costs. But they rarely shift roles and identities of key actors.	A classic example of this process is seen in "ethical label" platforms, which allow new nodes of value to emerge constantly as consumer feedback shapes the relationships among certifiers, supermarkets, labor, and producers.
Core value proposition	Exploit gaps for arbitrage.	Increase points of synergy.
Approach to information	Strengthen position in knowledge networks by taking advantage of uncertainty	Invent new forms of transparency to redesign the underlying trust models.
Allocation of credit	Platforms are relatively inflexible about the allocation of credentials and try to consolidate "credit for attainment" as another zero-sum resource. "Credit" in this sense refers to the social capital that accrues from being the hub that everyone recognizes as indispensable. Because power is maintained by everyone knowing about the indispensability of the intermediary, sharing credit for progress with other stakeholders tend to be much harder.	Platforms are designed to distribute credit for outcomes as flexibly as possible, in order to sustain buy-in. They facilitate secondary and tertiary branding sub-narratives (beyond the usual emphasis on "founders" and "visionaries" who birthed the solution) and may, in fact, support a plethora of branding or sub-branding initiatives around narratives beyond the "founding myths" so common with conventional solution bringers.
Approach to growth	Growth aims to expand global reach by being deployed in a pretty much identical fashion everywhere.	Growth aims to be compatible across jurisdictions, in a way that can adapt the process considerably from place to place without compromising the essence.

However, COMESA's core challenge was to create a "regional infrastructure for food security" that facilitates trade, the sharing of best practices, and the pooling of investment resources to address large-scale problems that afflict the region as a whole, such as climate change.

A lucid example of thinking along such lines can be found in the context of "post-harvest losses." By one estimate, 60 percent of the region's food kept in traditional granary storage was lost or spoiled within ninety days of harvest.[17] While the construction of modern granaries, particularly through the integration of metal silos across farming zones, would no doubt considerably reduce food losses, a simple opening of trade corridors would achieve similar success at less than 15 percent of the comparative investment. Richer COMESA countries could serve as both off-takers and consolidated storage sites for the entire region in the immediate post-harvest period.

Facilitating trade by removing technical barriers and harmonizing policies and regulations has thus emerged as one of the most critical priorities in the COMESA food security agenda. This was one of the many SDG contexts where national solutions are considerably suboptimal in comparison with multilateral arrangements. Regional harmonization of standards trade could dramatically bolster the capacity of the region as a whole to respond to seasonal food crises.

But "food security," hugely important as it is, remains only one of a number of vital opportunities presented by regulatory harmonization. As COMESA's anchor strategy in the standards uniformity agenda observes:

> [COMESA] recognized the importance of standardization and quality assurance in the promotion of health, the enhancement of the standard of living, the rationalization and reduction of unnecessary variety of products, the facilitation of interchangeability of products, the promotion of trade, consumer protection, the creation of savings in government purchasing, improved productivity, the facilitation of information exchange, as well as in the protection of life, property, and the environment."[18]

Agrotrack was therefore strongly positioned as a mere starting point in the journey to embed its logic more deeply into COMESA's intergovernmental agro-nervous system. The food security efforts could help Agrotrack understand what makes COMESA tick, and over time greatly enhance its responsiveness in a broad number of other SDG-related areas, using interconnected innovations that span technology, change management, and operational philosophy.

Transforming the COMESA Seed Harmonization Implementation Plan

17. Costa.
18. COMESA (2014).

(COMSHIP) from mere documents into a living, breathing, systems-changing organism capable of migrating into multiple national agricultural regulatory structures would amount to an enormous victory for Agrotrack. It would foster stronger trust with COMESA, thereby opening the door to collaboration in the health and governance sectors, in truly transmediary fashion. But it would also require considerable resources.

The capacity to support customized narratives was clearly critical in the context of cross-country adoption of technology. Traditional one-size-fits-all approaches to traditional digital platforms are not suited to complex multi-jurisdictional challenges.

Getting to such a stage with COMESA would obviously represent a major step-change for the Agrotrack expansion strategy. The initiative would then be able to ride on the back of intentional synergies as it scales across national borders, benefiting as it would from ready-made channels to transmit best practices without the need to build legitimacy from scratch at the institutional level.

Of equal criticality would be the ready-made frameworks for engaging with local regulatory authorities in each market, a barrier that no techno-innovative system had yet scaled within the region.

From what he had seen, Winston was convinced that only the Transmediation Platform approach and strategy was agile enough to break down the institutional inertia holding back regulators from pursuing technology-driven reform. The COMESA partnership would also bring "social proof" of the concepts in a manner that speeds up adoption of the underlying approaches.

It seemed quite clear to Winston that the massive barriers at the national level in creating connected solutions across complex ecosystems are only multiplied when a cross-border element is added.

If Transmediation Platform solutions are compelling at the national level, they should be even more critical when seeking to develop multilateral responses to problems that are not optimally addressable at the national level.

In the messy multilateralism of the anarchic interstate system, the old issue of power and its role in shaping norms, behavior, and expectations of technology attains a grander and more overbearing posture. But that was all the more reason why one needs transmediation, because national borders are even more difficult to bridge using traditional intermediation techniques.

Transmediation Platforms Are about "Power Representations"

That evening over some *mawewu*, as Winston caught up with Doreen, they decided to try their hand at crafting a general typology of power in technology ecosystems and how they intersect with the different modes of social change.

Doreen postulated that the different postures one could adopt as a technology changemaker in any context broke down into two broad categories: traditional and radical. There was nothing revolutionary there. But she clustered into segments the different platforms such a changemaker might create. Within the traditional bucket, she included commercial apps, commercial platforms, and mass collaboration platforms. In the radical bucket, she included social purpose platforms, social systems intermediation platforms, and social systems transmediation platforms. Her approach made Winston pause to reflect.

As the world around those who care about sustainability, social transformation, and social good continues to change rapidly, the "social" element in changemaking has had to be projected more and more forcefully. The focus needs to shift from intermediary-driven attempts to induce connectedness in ecosystemic solutions to transmediation approaches such as Agrotrack, which emphasize flexibility in identities and continuous discovery of the value propositions binding the ecosystem together.

Conclusion: Reflections of a Transmediary Entrepreneur

After yet another helpful exchange with Doreen, Winston contemplated his situation for a long, drawn-out moment. Transmediation Platforms, he no longer had any doubts, represented a step-change in the progression of the much touted and loosely manifested "technology for social good" concept.

Figure 11-1. The Extent to Which an App Is Dedicated to Social Problems Whose Solutions Only Become Viable When Deployed at Scale

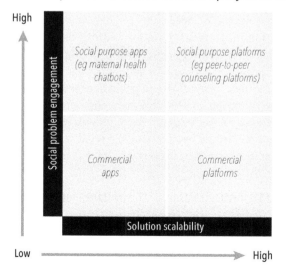

Figure 11-2. The Degree to Which a Platform Interconnects with Other Tools to Cover Interrelated Social Problems

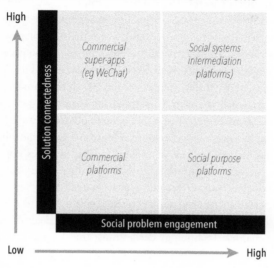

Figure 11-3. The Extent to Which a Platform Allows for Diverse Stakeholders to Collaborate on Solutions to Social Problems at Multiple Levels

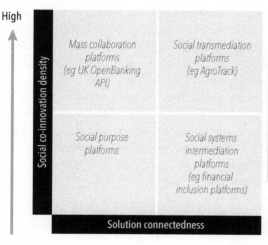

Note: "Connectedness" refers to the ability of a technical solution to address related externalities, even as it targets a particular problem, often by interoperating with other solutions or generating submodules that tackle the externalities created by adjacent solutions with reasonable cost.

Over the years, he realized, a radical truth has been emerging about the world of digital platforms in general, but theorists and practitioners have yet to fully appreciate the starkness thereof: the days of seamless growth and colonization of domains by traditional mega-platforms like Facebook and Amazon are over. More and more, the "paths for growth and to dominance" of new digital platforms lie across highly regulated, fragmented, contested, politically sensitive, human rights–sensitive terrains such as health systems, educational reform, democracy rebirth, energy shifts, and, of course, SDGs attainment.

There is only so much innovation in financial wizardry, social conversation priming, and entertainment streaming that a mega-platform can knead and bake into giant monopoly towers in cyberspace. Hoarding data, consolidating algorithmic power, appropriating ecosystem value, and so on does not reward with scale as easily in the vast, still non-platformed terrains named above as it did in the financial, media, and commerce domains of yesteryear.

Growth and scale in this new world require a willingness to see stakeholders asserting power in their participation in the kind of connected solution-building described in this chapter. Technology design must thus be polycentric in character. Transmediation Platforms are congenitally polycentric for this very reason.

Winston reclined in his seat and allowed his mind to wonder a bit, surveying the intellectual journey that had brought him to the point of reassessing his entire philosophy of how to utilize the techno-innovation systems he had long decided were indispensable in the quest to address deep, long-festering, cankers in society.

The problem, as he saw it, was that the mainstream of development practice was yet to come to terms with this impending age of Transmediation Platforms and the critical place they occupied in the unfolding era of hyper-integrated technology systems. Too few people have recognized their need for such platforms in the quest to break down the interconnected barriers confronting SDG attainment in many parts of the developing world.

But as he drifted in and out of deep reflection, the prospects of Agrotrack in Malawi kept rising from the fog as belonging to the raft of showcase examples that could perhaps compel the development industry to take a good, hard look at this transmediary phenomenon whose power was becoming increasingly obvious to him. "Change is in the air," Winston thought, as he reclined in his office chair and drifted off to a dreamland of possibilities.

Epilogue

Alice Nyasulu unfurled her FlexScreen and activated the presentation on her smartwatch. "AgroTrack: a Decade of Change in COMESA" popped up like a neon banner and shrunk discreetly as the rest of the 3D display unbundled. She scanned the main blocks of animations, which showed how secure and transparent digital seed certification evolved into an information market for new forms of insurance, invoice discounting, warehouse warranties, and, ultimately, a revolution in cooperative organic farming and communal agro-processing. The acceleration of a regional agro-exchange better positioned COMESA to harness the African continental free trade area opportunity more thoroughly than anyone could have imagined a decade ago.

On the eve of the big SDGs reckoning summit in Nairobi, Alice was filled with pride and passion, instead of apprehension, as she prepared to deliver the blockbuster curtain-raiser talk of the ceremony. Just two days earlier, the situational report had delivered the good news that the COMESA region had not only made the fastest progress in meeting several connected SDGs, but it had done so largely as a result of local rather than foreign aid-driven interventions.

Alice took a deep breath as she glanced over the last but one anime-slate in her turbo deck—the one announcing a slew of Transmediation Platforms to launch in the next decade.

References

Adner, R., and R. Kapoor. 2010. "Value Creation in Innovation Ecosystems: How the Structure of Technological Interdependence Affects Firm Performance in New Technology Generations," *Strategic Management Journal*, v. 31, no. 3.

Adner, R. 2017. "Ecosystem as Structure: An Actionable Construct for Strategy," *Journal of Management*, v. 43, no. 1.

Ahuja, S., and Y. E. Chan. 2016. "Digital Innovation: A Frugal Ecosystem Perspective." Thirty-Seventh International Conference on Information Systems, Dublin.

Battilana, J., and T. Casciaro. 2021. *Power for All: How It Really Works and Why It's Everyone's Business*. New York: Simon & Schuster.

Battilana, J., B. Leca, and E. Boxenbaum. 2009. "How Actors Change Institutions: Towards a Theory of Institutional Entrepreneurship," *Academy of Management Annals*, v. 3, no. 1.

COMESA. 2014. COMSHIP Concept Note, High-Level Summit of Ministers.

———. 2018. "Seven COMESA States Have Harmonized Seed Regulations." Public Announcement, December 14.

Costa, S. J. 2014. "Reducing Food Losses in Sub-Saharan Africa: Improving Post-Harvest Management and Storage Technologies of Smallholder Farmers." UN World Food Program.

Guerrero, M., C. A. Santamaría-Velasco, and R. Mahto. 2020. "Intermediaries and Social Entrepreneurship Identity: Implications for Business Model Innovation," *International Journal of Entrepreneurial Behavior & Research*, v. 27, no. 2.

Hein, A., J. Weking, M. Schreieck, and others. 2019. "Value Co-Creation Practices in Business-to-Business Platform Ecosystems," *Electron Markets*, v. 29.

Meadows, D. 1999. *Leverage Points: Places to Intervene in a System.* Hartland, Vt.:
    Sustainability Institute.

————. 2009. *Thinking in Systems: A Primer.* London: Earthscan.

Nicholls, A., and Paton, R. 2009. "Emerging Resource Flows for Social
    Entrepreneurship; Theorizing Social Investment." British Academy of Management
    Annual Conference, September 15–17.

Nicholls, A., *Paton*, R., and Emerson, J. (eds.). 2017. "Creating Economic Space for
    Social Entrepreneurship," in *Social Finance.* Oxford University Press.

Schlaile, M. P., S. Urmetzer, M. B. Ehrenberger, and others. 2020. Systems
    Entrepreneurship: A Conceptual Substantiation of a Novel Entrepreneurial
    "Species." *Sustainability Science,* v. 16, no. 3, 781–794.

Schroder, A., G. Prockl, and I. Constantiou. 2021. "How Digital Platforms with a
    Social Purpose Trigger Change towards Sustainable Supply Chains." Proceedings of
    the 54th Hawaii International Conference on System Sciences.

Selsky, J. W., and B. Parker, 2010. "Platforms for Cross-Sector Social Partnerships:
    Prospective Sensemaking Devices for Social Benefit," *Journal of Business Ethics*, v.
    94.

Simons, B. 2019. "A Farewell to Disruption in a Post-Platform World," Center for
    Global Development.

Skålén, P., S. Pace, and B. Cova. 2015. "Firm-Brand Community Value Co-Creation as
    Alignment of Practices," *European Journal of Marketing*, v. 49, no. 3/4.

van den Berg, C., and B. Verster. 2020. "Co-Creating Social, Digital Innovation to
    Recognize Agency in Communities: A Learning Intervention: Research in Progress."
    Conference of the South African Institute of Computer Scientists and Information
    Technologists.

World Economic Forum. 2018. "Beyond Organizational Scale: How Social
    Entrepreneurs Create Systems Change." WEF Report.

————. 2019. "From Social Entrepreneurship to Systems Entrepreneurship: How to
    Create Lasting Change."

TWELVE

Unleashing Meaningful Breakthroughs

Ann Mei Chang

A s Bitcoin prices spiked and speculation in cryptocurrencies reached new heights in 2017, the blockchain (the distributed ledger technology underlying Bitcoin) was riding its own hype cycle that permeated the far reaches of tackling global poverty. The World Bank established a Blockchain Lab; fifteen United Nations entities had blockchain initiatives; the U.S. Agency for International Development (USAID) published a primer; and it seemed as if just about every international NGO was looking for a way to join the party. The breathtaking possibilities seemed endless—whether supporting financial inclusion, improving access to energy, tracing supply chains, protecting the environment, providing legal identity, or improving aid effectiveness.

By 2018, the luster had already begun to wear off. A survey of forty-three widely publicized blockchain-based development pilots "found a proliferation of press releases, white papers, and persuasively written articles," but "no documentation or evidence of the results blockchain was purported to have achieved in these claims."[1] All too many organizations sought to incorporate blockchain into their projects to appear on the cutting edge. Yet, more often than not, they got bogged down with a still nascent technology that introduced unnecessary complexity when a simple database would do.

The lesson? Adopting technology for technology's sake can be a dangerous trap. At the same time, many of the breakthroughs that are desperately needed to reach the Sustainable Development Goals (SDGs) may, in fact, be enabled by frontier technologies. But if we are to realize that promise, we must employ

1. Burg, Murphy, and Pétraud.

proven design methodologies, consider older technological advances that have yet to reach billions who could benefit, and vastly increase financing for both the smart risk-taking and shared technology platforms that hold the potential to accelerate progress. The breakthrough we most need is a new approach to innovation, not yet another new technology.

Breaking through with Better Design

The tendency to herd toward frontier technologies is not new. As mobile phones proliferated across Africa earlier this century, so did the enthusiasm to harness these devices to improve health, education, agriculture, and beyond. In Uganda alone, dozens of mobile health (mHealth) pilots were deployed; for the most part, without regard to duplication of effort, integration with government systems, or a pathway to scale. The situation became such a drain on the health ministry that it took the unprecedented step of issuing a moratorium on further mHealth projects in 2012, so they could institute consistent policies and ensure better coordination.[2] Sadly, the global development landscape is littered with flashy tech solutions that never lived up to their promise. In a well-known example, Nicholas Negroponte's heralded One-Laptop-per-Child initiative garnered a lot of press when it launched in 2005, but never delivered on its goal to transform education and lift millions out of poverty. Costs were too high, elements of the design were impractical, tech support was nonexistent, and the practicalities of training teachers and incorporating devices into the classroom were ignored.[3]

It's tempting to believe these well documented examples are outliers, but the tendency toward the shiny and new versus the boring and pragmatic remains commonplace today. To quote Kentaro Toyamo, "Technology is never the main driver of social progress. Technology is only an amplifier of human conditions." After a decade of designing technologies for humanitarian causes, Toyama found that no technology, however dazzling, could drive social change on its own.[4] Many other luminaries in the technology for development arena, such as Tim Unwin, have drawn similar conclusions.[5] In other words, before we plow ahead and conclude that "there's an app for that," we must take the time to understand the context and concerns of the affected communities. Frontier technologies can only realize their potential if we stay grounded in real problems, have the humility to recognize and validate uncertainties, and design for the scale that will be needed from the start.

2. McCann.
3. Wooster.
4. Toyama.
5. Unwin.

An important mantra among entrepreneurs is to "fall in love with the problem, not the solution." Alas, given the pressures on global development practitioners to differentiate themselves and their organizations, there's been a tendency to look for quick wins that give the *perception* of being on the cutting edge rather than invest in the painstaking work of listening to affected communities, questioning assumptions, and continually learning and adapting to find a solution that works. Not surprisingly, this rarely results in meaningful impact that can be both scaled and sustained.

To address this and other predictable and preventable mistakes that have caused digitally enabled programs to fail over and over again, a community-driven effort codified learnings over the years to create the Principles for Digital Development in 2014.[6] These nine living guidelines have now been endorsed by over two hundred global development organizations and capture best practices for using information and communication technologies (ICT) in development projects, based on the practical experiences and learnings of hundreds of development practitioners. In 2015, the International Development Innovation Alliance (IDIA, a collaboration among leading global development donors and agencies) committed to six principles for innovation along similar lines.[7] They were later expanded to eight in 2018 and endorsed by the G7 as the Whistler Principles to Accelerate Innovation for Development Impact. These sets of principles represent an important start and articulate a consistent view on the best practices for innovation: user-centered design, the importance of understanding context, smart risk-taking, fast iteration, building for scale and sustainability, and collaboration. Unfortunately, when it comes to action, the sector still falls far short of its rhetoric.

If we are truly committed to accelerating progress toward the SDGs, we must start, first, by understanding the realities of the participants, communities, and ecosystems that will be affected, so that any solution is designed appropriately for the context. Second, it's important to approach any intervention with deep humility, be explicit about the risks, and validate our assumptions. Third, the most basic technologies can simplify data collection and enable us to more quickly learn, iterate, and adapt. Finally, initiatives should not start and end with a pilot. To move the needle meaningfully on the SDGs, we must design for scale and sustainability from the start.

6. Principles for Digital Development.
7. The International Development Innovation Alliance.

Understand Context

Perhaps the biggest source of failure for technology-based solutions in global development is simply a lack of understanding and appreciation for the local context—whether that be individual capacity, social norms, or community dynamics. Witness the innumerable attempts to set up computer labs that fall into disrepair, smartphone apps designed for people who do not have smartphones, and lauded inventions like the PlayPump (a children's merry-go-round that pumps water)[8] and Soccket (a soccer ball that generates electricity)[9] that were impractical and quickly fell into disuse.

To make matters worse, digital solutions may only serve to further marginalize millions of women. With the mobile internet usage gender gap at approximately 30 percent in developing countries, well-meaning digital resources can be out of reach and risk further entrenching existing inequities. Even efforts deliberately targeted at bringing women online have largely failed. Digital skills training can only go so far when areas in the Sahel and northern India ban women from using mobile phones outright. And for women living on under a dollar a day, initiatives to promote digital activism can seem disconnected from their realities.[10]

These and so many other instances where heady promises crashed into disappointing reality should serve as an important caution when deploying technology that will directly touch individuals and communities (in contrast to a disaster prediction system that is used by experts). Here, we must start with a deep understanding and appreciation of the context and underlying drivers of the problem we aim to address—through ethnographic research, social science, and a lot of listening. The first of the Principles for Digital Development, "design with the user" and human-centered design approaches, offer valuable guidance for cocreating with intended customers throughout the project lifecycle to ensure any technology is introduced in a way that truly enhances lives.

Test Assumptions

Even when the initial design is strongly rooted in the local culture and context, there is inherent uncertainty in any new intervention. This is where a healthy dose of humility is needed. One of the wonderful aspects of mission-driven work is the collegial and supportive environment, built on a sense of shared purpose. The downside is that mutual encouragement can quickly devolve into groupthink.

8. Stellar.
9. Starr.
10. Sterling.

Who has the heart to shoot down the plans of an enthusiastic coworker who has been working long hours and making financial sacrifices for the cause? Thus, it can take an intentional effort to take a step back, play devil's advocate, and ask the tough questions about what might go wrong. But doing so is necessary to surface risks, create a proactive learning agenda, and target lightweight experiments for validation before a larger investment is made.

The real needs of real people must come before any frontier technology, however exciting. Once we have gained a deep understanding of the problems and have identified a successful approach to drive change, technological advances hold unrivaled potential to reduce costs, increase reach, and improve targeting and analysis. For example, before investing in a digital agriculture solution, we might start by validating the key elements with an in-person service to confirm that recommended farming techniques are adopted, loans are repaid, and farm yields are increased. Based on these learnings, technologies such as mobile money and video tutorials could enable us to affordably reach a far wider audience with the proven practices. In contrast, many mobile-enabled agriculture apps have been launched with much hoopla, only to fall far short of the hoped-for adoption and impact.[11] Similarly, before driving massive publicity and investing large sums, a prototype PlayPump could have been placed in a village to observe whether children's natural play patterns would turn the roundabout enough cycles each day to generate the energy needed to pump a sufficient quantity of water for a village.

How we measure success matters. Most global development programs tend to focus on activities performed, such as the number of people reached, then hold implementers accountable for delivering to those numbers. In reality, providing digital skills training for a thousand women is not particularly meaningful if at the end they still cannot afford a data plan or are prohibited from accessing the internet at home. Instead, when testing new solutions, unit-level metrics (such as the adoption rate, engagement rate, retention rate, success rate, and unit costs) are a far more meaningful indicator of success. If we are using cryptocurrency to try and make cash transfers more secure, it matters less how many people received a deposit and matters more what percentage of them were able to easily access and use those funds. For more mature interventions, shifting measurements to focus on outcomes rather than activity better aligns the interests of all parties toward delivering more cost-effective results.

11. Emeana, Trenchard, and Dehnen-Schmutz.

Accelerate Progress

While digital development initiatives typically focus on how technology can be directly applied to improve lives, the potential to drive faster feedback loops for interventions of all stripes may, in aggregate, have an even more profound impact. Mobile-enabled digital tools can facilitate a near real-time two-way stream of communication to provide visibility into how a service is being received by those who use it, track operational data, and gather indicators of effectiveness. This data, in turn, can unleash the possibility for the rapid adaptation and improvement needed to amplify impact by responding to user needs, addressing service inefficiencies or disruptions, and continually optimizing to increase effectiveness.

In simplest form, pure Short Message Service (SMS) or Interactive Voice Response (IVR) systems can create a direct line to the people we aim to serve. Feedback can be solicited immediately to assess customer satisfaction, or even years later, as Harambee Youth Accelerator in South Africa does to keep their fingers on the pulse of the employment trajectory for their participating youth long after their direct engagement. Feedback systems can also be used to track broader trends, such as with UNICEF's U-Report, which surfaces the voices of over 10 million young people in sixty-eight countries to give policymakers insight into their opinions, concerns, and attitudes.[12] In Uganda, a study found that over half of U-Reporters interviewed saw at least some changes made in their district as a result.[13] Multiple platforms have emerged to facilitate such direct community engagement, including UNICEF's RapidPro (which powers U-Report), Ushahidi (based on open source software developed in Kenya), FrontlineSMS, CommCare, and Premise (which crowdsources data from a network of hundreds of thousands of people around the world).

More sophisticated smartphone apps, particularly in the hands of intermediaries such as agricultural extension workers, community health workers, or teachers, can both increase productivity and accelerate feedback. For example, the Smart Health app, developed by Living Goods and Medic Mobile, includes a clinical decision support system to help community health workers make consistent and accurate diagnoses and develop treatment plans. At the same time, patient health data is captured in digital form (enabling real-time monitoring of health worker performance) and integrated with government systems (providing immediate visibility into any concerning trends).

Given the constraints arising from lockdowns imposed during COVID-19, many development organizations were forced to rapidly transition from in-person and often paper-based monitoring to some form of digital data collection.

12. Rehman.
13. Peixoto and Sifry.

This not only enabled programs to continue operations, but also revealed that in many situations meaningful data can be gathered more quickly and at lower cost, digitally. As a result, these new tools will hopefully continue to persist in large degree far beyond the pandemic, expanding the timeliness, frequency, and accuracy of feedback from communities.

Design for Scale

Many of the frontier technologies discussed in this book hold the potential to unleash massive scale by expanding reach, improving targeting, and minimizing incremental costs. For example, a remedial lesson effectively delivered by a teacher could be designed to be accessed by thousands through an app without incurring the additional cost and logistics of in-person lessons. Artificial intelligence could further identify and target students most in need of an additional boost based on their grades and attendance. Of course, we must be cognizant that any technology-based intervention runs the risk of further exacerbating inequity if it leaves out poorer and more rural populations by requiring a smartphone or internet access to participate.

At the same time, technology projects themselves must be designed for scale and sustainability from the start if they hope to have a breakthrough effect. A case study of AloWeather, a CARE Vietnam project to provide SMS-based weather forecasts to ethnic minority farmers, is emblematic of the common challenges that arise. While the team was able to demonstrate a significant increase in crop yields compared to the control site in the first year, bringing this promising service to scale was another matter. Many challenges stemmed from the structure of development projects that emphasize predictable delivery over rapid iteration and program management over business acumen. The model itself was also too complex, with costs far exceeding any willingness to pay. Thus, despite its promise, it was discontinued after the initial grant money was depleted.[14] This is an all-too-common scenario that plays out across the development sector.

The constraints imposed on typical grant-funded projects are fundamentally at odds with the flexibility, appetite for risk, and long-term horizon that frontier technology projects need to thrive. More often than not, they encourage short-term deliverables that result in projects like AloWeather and the dozens of mHealth pilots in Uganda that do not have a clear path forward. The cost is huge, in both opportunities lost and the disruption that comes from upending vulnerable people's lives with new tools constantly popping in and out of existence.

14. Phẫm.

The Power of Twentieth-Century Solutions

Over seven hundred years ago, a new technology was invented that has been proven to increase productivity, sustain earning potential, and enhance learning—corrective eyeglasses. Yet an estimated 2.7 billion people who need glasses still do not have them. VisionSpring, a nonprofit social enterprise, was founded with a mission to bridge this gap. To date, it has distributed almost 7 million pairs of eyeglasses and estimates that each US$1 invested can unlock US$43 in income earning potential.[15]

There's a tendency in the global development industry to rush toward the next shiny new thing, in search of a silver bullet that will be transformative. Yet, many game-changing advances have, in fact, already been identified, piloted, and shown to be effective. Nevertheless, they have not reached the vast majority of those who stand to benefit. The long, hard slog of scaling best practices for what may seem like last-generation technology is simply not sexy. But, in many cases, it can be the most prudent investment to drive progress.

While frontier technologies may capture the imagination, it is often seemingly prosaic technologies from the twentieth century that, in fact, hold the most potential for improving the lives of the poorest and most vulnerable. The first and overarching goal for the SDGs is to end poverty in all its forms everywhere. Yet, for the over 700 million people—or 10 percent of the world's population—living in extreme poverty on less than US$1.90 a day,[16] even the most basic technologies may be out of reach. In rich countries like the United States, a new app may be the best way to reach people and improve lives. But in places such as the remote areas of rural Africa, a technology that stretches as far back as the late nineteenth century may, in fact, hold more power.

Advantage: Low-Tech

When the COVID-19 outbreak began spreading across the world, UNESCO turned to community radio to provide lifesaving information to remote and marginalized communities in Ethiopia. Local journalists were kept informed about the latest updates and safety tips through the community radio network, and, in turn, educated their communities.[17] Community radio turned out to be the most effective means of educating the public and reaching millions who would not otherwise have been informed. With the adult literacy rate in Ethiopia estimated

15. VisionSpring.
16. World Bank Group (2020), figure 1.4.
17. UNESCO.

at just over 50 percent,[18] written messaging, whether traditional or digital, would have significantly limited reach and comprehension. The ability to broadcast in over thirty local languages through the voices of known and trusted community members made this channel particularly effective.

Despite the proliferation of digital technologies over the past decade, radio remains "by far the dominant mass medium in Africa."[19] Beyond moments of crisis, community radio has been successfully leveraged by numerous organizations as a channel to expand education, dispel dangerous rumors, empower women, discuss health issues, share farming techniques, and beyond—in a format that is broadly accessible to all.[20] Efforts to transform the lives of the most vulnerable must consider the real limitations and constraints of both individuals and infrastructure, which can often point toward low-tech options such as radio, TV, or voice calls.

Long-standing does not necessarily mean staid. Although radio broadcasting has been around for over a century, organizations like Farm Radio International are continuing to innovate with both new programming formats to better engage key audiences and multimodal services that leverage mobile phones to create a two-way communication channel. And traditional technologies can be combined with new advances to bring together the advantages of each. For example, to support households affected by COVID-19, GiveDirectly worked with the government of Togo to get the message out through radio broadcasts, enable signups via SMS, and target aid to the poorest recipients using machine learning analysis of satellite photos and cellphone data.[21]

The Explosion of Mobile Devices

Around the turn of the twenty-first century, mobile phones began to proliferate exponentially across developing countries. As of 2016, even among the poorest 20 percent of households, nearly 70 percent had a mobile phone—more than those who had toilets, clean water, or electricity.[22] This simple device continues to offer an unprecedented opportunity to directly reach the poorest and most disadvantaged with valuable information and services.

IVR, SMS, and Unstructured Supplementary Service Data (USSD) are available on even the most basic feature phones as channels for communications. While SMS campaigns may seem simpler and, in some cases, cheaper, IVR can

18. UNESCO Institute of Statistics.
19. Madomombe.
20. Ibid.
21. Simonite.
22. World Bank Group (2016), figure O.4.

hold substantial advantages when attempting to reach the most marginalized populations. To start, with literacy rates in the least developed countries estimated at under 70 percent,[23] text-based messages can leave out many of those in need, particularly women and girls. An audio format also allows for richer, more engaging messages, including music, intonation, and multiple voices. And, for two-way interactive services, studies have shown a higher overall response rate and lower cost per interaction for IVR compared to SMS.[24]

Numerous services have shown they can make a meaningful difference across most of the SDGs by leveraging basic feature phone technologies. Some examples include agriculture (SDG 2), where SMS and IVR have been shown to be effective as a more scalable way to improve fertilizer usage, relieving the pressure on overburdened agricultural extension workers.[25] In health (SDG 3), MomConnect has been integrated into South Africa's healthcare system and reaches over 3 million women, with participants more likely to participate in antenatal visits, postnatal visits, and recommended vaccinations.[26, 27] In education (SDG 4), Eneza Education supplements government curriculum with SMS-based access to tutorials, quizzes, and support from teachers—with students scoring 22 percent higher on national tests.[28] VIAMO's Calling All Women program is using IVR to improve digital and financial literacy for women (SDG 5) in Tanzania and Pakistan.[29] The list goes on. Yet, despite low costs, high accessibility, and evidence of impact, most reach only a small fraction of those who stand to benefit. Investments to scale such simple but effective solutions through broader government adoption or sustainable business models could likely make a bigger difference than launching yet another pilot based on cutting-edge technology that may be expensive, unproven, and difficult to access.

Expanding Internet Access

The COVID-19 pandemic shone a light on how crucial internet access has become in the digital age. During lockdowns, those who were not online were shut out from participation in online education, virtual work, telehealth, and the digital economy. The internet is no longer a luxury, and has become as essential to a thriving community as food, water, energy, healthcare, and education.

23. World Health Organization.
24. Hortinela.
25. Singh, Jalote, and Adlakha.
26. Coleman and others.
27. 1 World Connected.
28. Dalal.
29. USAID.

Expanding connectivity will not only help lift households out of poverty, but also drive economic growth. Progress toward nearly all of the SDGs could be significantly boosted by connecting far more of the global population.

Although the internet first came to life in 1983, it has yet to reach 40 percent of the world's population. This gap is by far the greatest in Africa, with an estimated 60 percent of the population still unconnected as of 2020.[30] A disproportionate number of the unconnected are poor, rural, women, or all of the above. The gender gap in mobile internet usage is 51 percent in South Asia and 37 percent in Sub-Saharan Africa.[31] For already marginalized populations, being cut off from the digital world only further exacerbates existing inequities.

While many of the most prominent initiatives to bridge the digital divide have focused on building new infrastructure to expand last-mile connectivity, the reality is that approximately 85 percent of the world's population is already covered by existing broadband networks.[32] Expanding coverage remains important, but the larger barrier is a "usage gap" driven by a lack of affordability, digital literacy, and relevant content. Addressing these gaps also happens to be far less expensive than digging trenches, laying cables, and erecting cellular towers.

Across Africa, 1 GB of data costs 7.12 percent of the average monthly salary.[33] While internet access has become increasingly affordable, in many low- and middle-income countries costs remain artificially inflated. This is often a result of poor policies and regulations that have allowed rent-seeking behavior due to weak market competition at various stages of service delivery. Other inefficiencies, such as limited sharing of infrastructure among telecom providers, result in higher than necessary operating costs. Encouraging host country governments to create a conducive enabling environment can make this foundational technology more accessible to all.

Beyond the supply side, weak demand is also a significant and underattended factor that limits connectivity. Those who are functionally illiterate or lack basic digital skills are unable to make effective use of many online resources, even where coverage exists. While numerous aid projects, including by tech corporations, have offered various training programs, they have generally amounted to subscale one-offs that are tackling an important need but reaching only a tiny fraction of the population. Digital literacy should be treated more holistically, in line with basic literacy, as part of the core education system. Finally, ability makes usage possible, but relevancy drives it. Content must be accessible and

---

30. Internet World Stats.
31. GSMA Connected Women.
32. International Telecommunications Union.
33. Alliance for Affordable Internet.

compelling, available in local languages, including local businesses and events, covering local news and interests. Despite well-meaning programs that aim to engage the unconnected with development-related content on health, education, or agriculture, it is social media platforms (such as WhatsApp, Facebook, and YouTube) that are by far the most powerful forces driving people online. No different from the historical trends for internet adoption in high-income countries, it is the core human desire to connect and be entertained that is, in fact, the most compelling "killer app."

Financing Breakthroughs

Funders—whether bilateral/multilateral aid agencies, foundations, impact investors, or governments themselves—play an outsized role in creating the incentives for what and how investments are made in global development. Their collective desire for immediate, tangible results can favor proven end-solutions over more ambitious innovations or invisible enabling infrastructure. Yet, given their potential to reward smart risk-taking as well as invest in public goods that can smooth the introduction of new technologies, donors are in a unique position to fuel breakthroughs.

Incentivize Smart Risks

To fully unleash the promise of frontier technologies for sustainable development, new funding mechanisms and modalities are needed. While the detailed designs, workplans, and budgets required by traditional grants are effective at ensuring predictability and compliance for well-understood interventions in a stable environment, they are simply not fit for purpose when seeking breakthroughs—which, by definition, requires stepping into the unknown. In fact, such funding encourages quick and shallow wins that are unlikely to meaningfully move the needle on the SDGs. The only way to potentially bridge the huge gaps that remain is with bolder, more ambitious efforts that will inherently entail some risk.

Effective funding for breakthroughs should do three things: encourage smart risk-taking, provide abundant flexibility to learn and adapt, and incentivize delivery of outsized results. At the USAID Global Development Lab, we piloted several grant mechanisms along these lines. Prize awards, such as the DESAL Prize and the Global LEAP Off-Grid Refrigerator Competition, specify predetermined performance criteria for a desired advancement. The incentive to explore beyond the limitations of existing solutions is a perfect opening to consider frontier technologies. Similarly, challenge competitions shine a light more broadly on one or more areas of need in search of better solutions. To date, USAID and its partners have launched ten Grand Challenges for Development on issues ranging from education and agriculture to combating Ebola and Zika. Another approach to manage risk and reward success is tiered, evidence-based funding. Modeled after venture capital, Development Innovation Ventures (DIV) was envisioned by Nobel laureate Michael Kremer as a way to test and scale breakthrough solutions for global poverty.

The first organization to receive all three award tiers from DIV was Off Grid Electric (now ZOLA Electric), a home solar company in Tanzania that was among the pioneers of a pay-as-you-go business model powered by mobile money. An initial US$100,000 grant fueled its early tests of this innovative, and as yet unproven approach and technology. After successfully validating their model, a second-tier grant of US$1 million helped Zola build the infrastructure required to become fully operational. Finally, a US$5 million grant enabled it to scale by catalyzing US$40 million in private debt to serve as working capital. Where a traditional development program might have simply distributed a limited number of solar panels to those in need, the innovation-oriented nature of the DIV awards resulted in a valuable technological advance along with a sustainable and scalable business model. A 2020 survey of the burgeoning off-grid energy sector found that 88 percent of customers reported a positive difference in their families' lives, 20 percent have been able to generate additional income, and the overall use of polluting and dangerous fuels such as kerosene has dropped.[34]

The Tragedy of the Commons

In order for technological advances to fully realize their potential to address development challenges, investments are needed not only in the solutions themselves, but also the underlying infrastructure and platforms that can accelerate their development and adoption. Witness the breathtaking pace of progress in Silicon Valley, which is built on the back of powerful platforms that make creating a new, innovative solution far, far easier. Android and iOS include rich toolkits upon which a mobile app can be easily built. Facebook's social graph allows a new offering to plug into a thriving community. Google Maps powers many location-based services. And, with Amazon Web Services, a startup no longer has to set up and manage their own server cluster. The presence of such robust building blocks has lowered the barrier to entry for innovation and unleashed creativity by empowering anyone with a promising idea to spend the vast majority of time creating their unique value add, and a relatively small amount building

34. Harrison and others.

the underlying scaffolding. On top of that, market forces in the ecosystem are aligned with these benefits, richly rewarding successful platform providers.

In contrast, the vast majority of investments in digital development have been focused on building end-to-end solutions rather than enabling platforms. Donors and developers alike are motivated to seek immediate and tangible benefit to real people that will result in compelling stories of lives changed. Abstract concepts like "enabling infrastructure" generate neither financial returns nor easily attributable impact. To make matters worse, there is little incentive to build on top of the platforms that do exist—less work means a smaller grant and less overhead to keep the doors open. The result is that many technology-based projects end up spending much of their effort reinventing the wheel and only a small amount on their unique value add. The duplication of effort is astounding. In one major funder's recent call for proposals related to digital inclusion, half of the applications suggested building a custom IVR system as part of their program. When so much of the investment in frontier technologies is duplicative, the overall pace of progress suffers.

Prioritizing public goods is a challenge across the development sector, but holds particularly powerful upsides when it comes to technology. For instance, in 2002, a U.K. Department for International Development (DFID) £1 million matching grant led to the creation of M-Pesa, a mobile money service that now reaches 96 percent of households in Kenya. M-Pesa also underpins numerous transformative services such as low-cost digital savings, loans, insurance, and pay-as-you-go solar. Another powerful example is India's Aadhaar program, the world's largest biometric digital identity system, which has enrolled over 99 percent of the adult population. The existence of a unique ID has enabled many participants to access basic banking for the first time, companies and nonprofit organizations to roll out a vast array of new innovations, and the government to save over US$10 billion through better targeting and reduced waste.[35] Alas, these frequently cited platforms are the exception, not the rule.

We will be better positioned to capitalize on breakthroughs if collaboration and the commons are prioritized—particularly by funders. In recognition of this need, a number of major institutional donors came together to launch the Digital Impact Alliance (DIAL) in 2015. It has gone on to invest in open-source platforms, disseminating best practices, and research into burgeoning fields such as data analytics, responsible data, and innovative finance. Far greater investments in both developing and utilizing common infrastructure, platforms, and toolkits will be needed to lay the groundwork to unleash the potential of technology for development.

35. Perrigo.

Conclusion

The enormous potential for technology to accelerate our progress toward achieving the Sustainable Development Goals is indisputable. Technology is a powerful amplifier that can unlock impact, insights, and far greater reach. However, to achieve more meaningful breakthroughs, we need to focus more on the "how" than the "what," and avoid deploying the latest technology for technology's sake. This requires a shift in approach by both solution providers and funders to utilize sound design methodologies, leverage appropriate technology whether old or new, and take smart risks to seek out the transformative breakthroughs that are needed while remaining humble to the inherent uncertainties. Given the significant gap that remains between our current trajectory and our goals for 2030, we must quickly move beyond both traditional interventions and the hype of frontier technologies if we are to succeed in delivering real change.

References

1 World Connected. 2020. "MomConnect," September 1, http://1worldconnected.org/project/africa_health_momconnectsouthafrica/.

Alliance for Affordable Internet. 2019. *2019 Affordability Report.* http://a4ai.org/affordability-report/report/2019/.

Burg, John, Christine Murphy, and Jean Paul Pétraud. 2018. "Blockchain for International Development: Using a Learning Agenda to Address Knowledge Gaps," MERL Tech, September 7, 2018, http://merltech.org/blockchain-for-international-development-using-a-learning-agenda-to-address-knowledge-gaps/.

Coleman, Jesse, and others. 2020. "Evaluating the Effect of Maternal mHealth Text Messages on Uptake of Maternal and Child Health Care Services in South Africa: A Multicentre Cohort Intervention Study." *Reproductive Health,* vol. 17, no. 1, 160.

Dalal, Ami. 2019. "Why We Invested: Eneza Education," FINCA Ventures, March 18, https://medium.com/finca-ventures/why-we-invested-eneza-education-2089a9db4d43.

Emeana, Ezinne M., Liz Trenchard, and Katharina Dehnen-Schmutz. 2020. "The Revolution of Mobile Phone-Enabled Services for Agricultural Development (m-Agri Services) in Africa: The Challenges for Sustainability." *Sustainability,* vol. 12, no. 2, 485.

GSMA Connected Women. 2020. *The Mobile Gender Gap Report 2020,* GSM Association.

Harrison, Kat and others. 2020. "Why Off-Grid Energy Matters," 60 Decibels, February, https://60decibels.com/user/pages/energy-report/60%20Decibels%20-%20Why%20Off-Grid%20Energy%20Matters.pdf.

Hortinela, Christine. 2017. "Comparing the Benefits of Automated Phone Calls (IVR) versus SMS Campaigns," engageSpark blog, May 22, www.engagespark.com/blog/blogcomparing-benefits-automated-phone-calls-ivr-versus-sms-campaigns/.

International Development Innovation Alliance (IDIA). 2019. *Development Innovation Principles in Practice.* Report.

International Telecommunications Union. 2020. "Connecting Humanity: Assessing Investment Needs of Connecting Humanity to the Internet by 2030." ITU Publications.

Internet World Stats. 2021. www.internetworldstats.com/stats1.htm.

Madomombe, Itai. 2005. "Community Radio: A Voice for the Poor," Africa Renewal, July, www.un.org/africarenewal/magazine/july-2005/community-radio-voice-poor.

McCann, David. 2012. "A Ugandan mHealth Moratorium Is a Good Thing," ICTworks, February 22, www.ictworks.org/ugandan-mhealth-moratorium-good -thing/.

Peixoto, Tiago, and Micha L. Sifry. 2017. *Civic Tech in the Global South.* Washington, D.C.: World Bank and Personal Democracy Press.

Perrigo, Billy. 2018. "India Has Been Collecting Eye Scans and Fingerprint Records from Every Citizen. Here's What to Know," *TIME*, September 28.

Phạm, Ấn. 2020. "Scale, Design, and Follow Through: Lessons on Moving from a Development Project to a Business in Vietnam's AloWeather Project," CARE International in Vietnam, www.care.org.vn/project/scale-design-and-follow -through-lessons-on-moving-from-a-development-project-to-a-business-in-vietnams -aloweather-project/.

Principles for Digital Development. 2017. http://digitalprinciples.org/.

Rehman, Hira Hafeez ur. 2020. "UNICEF's U-Report Reaches 10 Million Young People," UNICEF, March 27, www.unicef.org/innovation/stories/unicefs-u-report -reaches-10-million-young-people.

Simonite, Tom. 2020. "A Clever Strategy to Distribute COVID Aid—With Satellite Data," *Wired*, December 17.

Singh, Rupika, Sumedha Jalote, and Raghav Adlakha. 2019. "When Is the Best Time to Send IVR and SMS Messages to Farmers?" ICTworks, July 24, www.ictworks.org/ send-ivr-sms-messages-farmers/.

Starr, Michelle. 2014. "Power-Generating Soccer Ball Fails Dismally," CNet, April 22, www.cnet.com/news/power-generating-soccer-ball-fails-dismally/.

Stellar, Daniel. 2010. "The PlayPump: What Went Wrong?" State of the Planet (Earth Institute, Columbia University), July 1, https://blogs.ei.columbia.edu/2010/07/01/ the-playpump-what-went-wrong/.

Sterling, S. Revi. 2020. "Global Broadband and Innovations Alliance What's Next," NetHope, September, https://solutionscenter.nethope.org/assets/collaterals/Whats_ Next_-_Closing_the_Gender_Digital_Divide.pdf.

Toyama, Kentaro. 2015. *Geek Heresy: Rescuing Social Change from the Cult of Technology.* PublicAffairs.

UNESCO. 2020. "Fostering Access to Health Information on COVID 19 through Community Radio," September 21, https://en.unesco.org/news/fostering-access -health-information-covid-19-through-community-radio.

UNESCO Institute of Statistics. 2021. http://uis.unesco.org/en/country/et.

Unwin, Tim. 2017. *Reclaiming Information and Communication Technologies for Development.* Oxford University Press.

USAID. 2020. "Viamo," February 12, www.usaid.gov/wcc/round-1/viamo.

VisionSpring. 2021. http://visionspring.org/why-eyeglasses.

Wooster, Martin Morse. 2018. "The Spectacular Failure of One Laptop Per Child," *Philanthropy Daily*, May 24.

World Bank Group. 2020. *Reversals of Fortune*. Poverty and Shared Prosperity.

———. 2016. *Digital Dividends*. World Development Report.

World Health Organization. 2017. *Least Developed Countries Health and WHO: Country Presence Profile*.

CONTRIBUTORS

ZACHARY BOGUE is co-founder and managing partner of DCVC, a venture fund that backs entrepreneurs solving trillion-dollar problems using Deep Tech, which multiplies the benefits of capitalism for everyone while reducing its costs. He brings to bear two decades of experience in Silicon Valley as an entrepreneur, venture capitalist, attorney, and angel investor. At DCVC, he invests in companies that are transformative for the climate and for human health, having led investments in Recursion Pharmaceuticals, Planet, Twelve, Oklo, and Gro Intelligence. The World Economic Forum has named him a Young Global Leader in recognition of his leadership at the intersection of transformative technology and urgent global issues. He graduated from Harvard University with a degree in environmental science and public policy and earned his J.D. from Georgetown Law School.

YOLANDA BOTTI-LODOVICO is the current policy lead in the Sabeti Lab at the Broad Institute of MIT and Harvard. Working in close collaboration with Dr. Pardis Sabeti, she leads and advises on a range of policy and science communication projects dedicated to building pandemic preparedness on both the national and community levels. Prior to her role at the Broad Institute, she worked in immigration law and then consulted for the French national government and Save the Children Germany on EU refugee and migration policies. She holds a master of public policy from the Harvard Kennedy School and a bachelor of arts in international studies and art history from Boston College.

ANN MEI CHANG is a leading expert on social innovation and author of *Lean Impact: How to Innovate for Radically Greater Social Good* (2018). She served as the chief innovation officer at USAID and the first executive director of the

U.S. Global Development Lab, engaging the best practices for innovation from Silicon Valley to accelerate the impact and scale of solutions to the world's most intractable challenges. In addition, she was chief innovation officer for Pete for America, chief innovation officer at Mercy Corps, and senior advisor for Women and Technology at the U.S. Department of State. Prior to her pivot to the public and social sector, she was a seasoned technology executive, with more than twenty years' experience at such leading companies as Google, Apple, and Intuit, as well as at a range of start-ups.

LESLY GOH is a senior technology advisor and former chief technology officer at the World Bank Group. She is a fellow at the Cambridge Centre for Alternative Finance and senior fellow at the National University of Singapore Lee Kuan Yew School of Public Policy. She is a board member of Singapore GovTech and advisor for the Harvard Project for Asian and International Relations. At the nexus of technology and policy, she brings an extensive international experience advising policymakers on the regulatory impact from digital technologies, such as artificial intelligence, blockchain, the Internet of Things and 5G, and cloud and edge computing. From her experience in the public and private sectors, she develops strategic partnerships to support the Sustainable Development Goals, leveraging data and technology innovations in emerging markets.

TAREK GHANI is an assistant professor of strategy at Washington University in St. Louis and a nonresident fellow in the Global Economy and Development program at the Brookings Institution. His research on global economic, security, and strategy issues has appeared in the *American Economic Review: Microeconomics*, *Foreign Affairs*, and *Harvard Business Review*. He is a senior economic adviser at the International Crisis Group, where he previously served as chief economist and director of the Future of Conflict Program. He has also worked with the Center for Global Development, the Center for Strategic and International Studies, Humanity United, the United States Institute of Peace, and the World Bank. He holds a Ph.D. from the University of California, Berkeley, and a B.S. from Stanford University.

GRANT GORDON is the founder and CEO of Essential, a nonprofit that uses innovative technologies to create the next generation of cost-effective life-saving products for those affected by conflict and crisis. He is the former senior director of innovation strategy at the International Rescue Committee (IRC), where he oversaw the organization's R&D unit and innovation portfolio for humanitarian response and forced migration. Prior to joining the IRC, he worked in leadership positions at the UN Department of Peacekeeping Operations and the UN Office of Humanitarian Coordination, as well as for a set of humanitarian NGOs. He is currently a term member of the Council on Foreign Relations. He holds a Ph.D. from Columbia University and a B.A. from the University of Chicago.

HOMI KHARAS is a senior fellow in the Center for Sustainable Development at the Brookings Institution. In that capacity, he studies policies and trends influencing developing countries, including aid to poor countries, the emergence of the middle class, and global governance and the G-20. He previously served as interim vice president and director of the Global Economy and Development program. He has served as the lead author and executive secretary of the secretariat supporting the High-Level Panel advising the UN Secretary General on the post-2015 development agenda (2012–2013). His previous co-edited books include *Leave No One Behind: Time for Specifics on the Sustainable Development Goals* (Brookings Institution Press, 2019).

JONATHAN LEDGARD mobilizes large-scale AI and robotics investments in emerging economies. He leads the Multispecies Group, which seeks to build digital assets for other species. As a director at the Swiss Federal Institute of Technology he developed the first cargo drone routes and droneports in Africa. Previously, he was a long-time foreign and war correspondent for *The Economist*, including a decade as Africa correspondent. As J. M. Ledgard, he is an acclaimed novelist. His novel, *Submergence*, was a New York Times Book Review 100 Notable Books of 2013.

JOHN W. MCARTHUR is senior fellow and director of the Center for Sustainable Development at the Brookings Institution. He co-founded and co-chairs the 17-Rooms initiative, a new approach to spurring action, insight, and community for the Sustainable Development Goals. He is also a board governor with the International Development Research Centre and a senior adviser to the UN Foundation. He was previously the chief executive officer of Millennium Promise Alliance, the international nongovernmental organization, and served as manager and deputy director of the UN Millennium Project, Secretary-General Kofi Annan's independent advisory body on the Millennium Development Goals. His previous co-edited books include *From Summits to Solutions: Innovations in Implementing the Sustainable Development Goals* (Brookings Institution Press, 2018).

VIJAY MODI is a professor in Columbia University's Department of Mechanical Engineering, and a faculty member of the Earth Institute and Data Science Institute. He directs the Quadracci Sustainable Engineering Laboratory. His areas of expertise are energy resources and energy conversion technologies. He has more than thirty years of experience in energy resources/conversion applied research, including thermal power generation, gas turbines, and solar and wind technologies. In the last decade his laboratory has carried out pioneering work in digital mini-grids, which integrate electricity supply/demand monitoring, dynamic allocation of energy/power resources to individual customers, and the use of the Internet of Things for account management.

TAKAHIRO MORITA is the chief representative of the Japan International Cooperation Agency (JICA) Thailand office and former senior deputy director-general of the Global Environment Department at JICA, where he served as the group director for Forestry and Nature Conservation Group.

TOMOYUKI NAITO is a vice president and professor at the Graduate School of Information Technology, Kobe Institute of Computing, Japan. His professional interests include digital economy, smart city, distance learning, ICT innovation ecosystem, mobile big data solution, and other related areas. Prior to assuming his current position, he was a senior advisor for ICT and innovation at JICA, the program manager at the World Bank, and the director of transportation and ICT at JICA. He has been serving on public advisory committees as a designated member, including the Global Steering Committee of the "Internet for All" project at the World Economic Forum. He is also a registered first-class architect in Japan. He holds a master of arts in international relations from the Graduate School of Asia-Pacific, Waseda University, Japan.

IZUMI OHNO is a professor at the National Graduate Institute for Policy Studies (GRIPS) in Japan, and a senior research advisor to the Japan International Cooperation Agency (JICA) Ogata Sadako Research Institute for Peace and Development. She also served as director of the JICA Ogata Research Institute during 2018–2020. She specializes in international development policy, industrial development cooperation, and business and development. Prior to joining GRIPS, she worked at JICA, the World Bank, and the Japan Bank for International Cooperation. Her previous co-edited books include *Industrial Human Resource Development in Developing Countries: Knowledge and Skills in the Era of SDGs* (2021) and *Leave No One Behind: Time for Specifics on the Sustainable Development Goals* (Brookings Institution Press, 2019).

HIROAKI OKONOGI is a special advisor of the Forestry and Nature Conservation Group in the Global Environment Department at the Japan International Cooperation Agency (JICA). His areas of expertise are forest ecology, forest sociology, and remote sensing. He is also the JICA expert for the technical cooperation project with the Brazilian Institute of the Environment and Renewable Natural Resources for combating illegal deforestation in Brazil (entitled the "Project for improving control of illegal deforestation through advanced SAR and AI technologies in the Brazilian Amazon").

PARDIS SABETI is a professor at Harvard University and the Harvard T.H. Chan School of Public Health, an institute member of the Broad Institute of Harvard and MIT, and a Howard Hughes Investigator. Her lab has contributed to fields including human and microbial genomics, information theory, and infectious disease surveillance and education in West Africa. She has a B.S. from MIT, a M.Sc. and D.Phil from Oxford University, and an M.D. from Harvard Medical School. She is a National Academy of Medicine member, World Economic Forum Young Global Leader, National Geographic Emerging Explorer, National Academy of Sciences Richard Lounsbery Award recipient, Smithsonian American Ingenuity Award winner for natural science, a *TIME* magazine Person of the Year as an Ebola fighter for 2014, and a TIME 100 Most Influential honoree for 2015.

BRIGHT SIMONS is the President of mPedigree, a social enterprise working on three continents with governments, Fortune 500 companies, and activists to safeguard human health and food security using technology, mostly digital. A career inventor and innovator, he is also a board-level advisor, with current and previous appointments, including with the Sustainability Board of UCB, a European biopharma pioneer; the Salzburg Global Seminar; the Care International Supervisory Board; the Lancet Commission on the Future of Health in Africa; the World Economic Forum's Africa Strategy Group; APHRC as vice chair; and the inaugural Microsoft Africa Advisory Council. He holds TED and Tutu fellowships and was featured on the 2016 Fortune 50 World Greatest Leaders list.

TOMICAH TILLEMANN is the global head of policy at the venture capital firm Andreessen Horowitz. Before this, he served as the executive director of the Digital Impact and Governance Initiative (DIGI) at New America, where he collaborated with the Rockefeller Foundation, World Bank, Harvard, and governments around the world to develop open-source technology platforms to power the public sector. Prior to New America, he served as senior advisor to two secretaries of state, leading a team of experts that built twenty major initiatives in fifty-five countries. Previously, he spent four years on the staff of the Senate Foreign Relations Committee working with Joe Biden, John Kerry, and Barack Obama. He is a co-holder of four patents.

EIJI YAMADA is a research fellow at JICA Ogata Sadako Research Institute for Peace and Development and a representative of the JICA Bangladesh Office. His research fields are urban and spatial economics, migration and remittances, environmental economics, and impact evaluation of development programs. He earned Ph.D. in economics from l'Institut d'études politiques de Paris.

Milton Keynes UK
Ingram Content Group UK Ltd.
UKHW022143310324
440371UK00001B/221